REINVENTING PAULO FREIRE

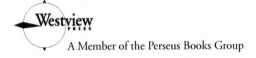

A PEDAGOGY OF LOVE

ANTONIA DARDER

Westview
PRESS
A Member of the Perseus Books Group

Copyright © 2002 by Westview Press, A Member of the Perseus Books Group

Westview Press books are available at special discounts for bulk purchases in the United States by corporations, institutions, and other organizations. For more information, please contact the Special Markets Department at The Perseus Books Group, 11 Cambridge Center, Cambridge MA 02142, or call (617) 252-5298.

Published in 2002 in the United States of America by Westview Press, 5500 Central Avenue, Boulder, Colorado 80301–2877, and in the United Kingdom by Westview Press, 12 Hid's Copse Road, Cumnor Hill, Oxford OX2 9JJ

Find us on the World Wide Web at www.westviewpress.com

Library of Congress Cataloging-in-Publication Data to come
Darder, Antonia.
    Reinventing Paulo Freire : a pedagogy of love / by Antonia Darder.
      p.   cm. — (The edge, critical studies in educational theory)
    Includes bibliographical references and indes.
    ISBN 0-8133-3968-5 (pbk.) ; ISBN 0-8133-9105-9
    1. Freire, Paulo, 1921–   2. Education—Philosophy.   3. Popular education—
Philosophy.   4. Critical pedagogy.   I. Title.   II. Series.

LB880.F732 D37   2001
370'.1—dc21
The paper used in this publication meets the requirements of the American National Standard for Permanence of Paper for Printed Library Materials Z39.48–1984.

10   9   8   7   6   5

REINVENTING PAULO FREIRE

The progressive educator must always be moving out on his or her own, continually reinventing me and reinventing what it means to be democratic in his or her own specific cultural and historical context.

PAULO FREIRE (1997)

CONTENTS

MAKING HISTORY: EDUCATION FOR THE FUTURE

PAULO FREIRE

The future is something that is constantly taking place, and this constant "taking place" means that the future only exists to the extent that we change the present. It is by changing the present that we build the future, therefore history is possibility, not determinism.

PAULO FREIRE,
Pedagogy of the City (1984)

For me, it is not easy to think of education or what kind of education we should develop without first asking myself a fundamental question about precisely what history means for me. How do I see history, while I am in history with others?

Note: This is a transcription of the speech given at the President's Forum at Claremont Graduate University on May 12, 1989, at the commencement activities in which Paulo Freire was awarded an honorary doctorate.

When I think of history I think about possibility—that history is the time and space of possibility. Because of that, I reject a view of history governed by determinism; as. I also reject a fatalistic or pessimistic understanding of history with a belief that what happens is what should happen. No! I don't accept that. What I do accept is that we all arrive in the world; that we arrive in the world as generations and we find a process, certain material conditions, certain events, problems, understandings, actions, reactions, and we start from what we find and we begin to make history. In making history we choose and realize possibilities. And in making history we begin to be made by history.

The moment I understand history as possibility, I must also understand education in a different way. But there is a further consequence of this understanding: once I understand history as possibility, I also understand the role of subjectivity in the historical process. Then the old question in philosophy about subjectivity and objectivity—whether it is possible to write history objectively—appears much easier to understand, even if it isn't completely solved. So if history is a possibility it means that I can make history consciously and am not obliged to solely participate passively in the historical process. It means that I recognize a very important role for human consciousness. Of course, I don't contend that human consciousness has fantastic, absolute power through which it can make reality. On the other hand, I don't accept that consciousness is completely formed by an external, "concrete" reality. Dialectically, human consciousness is to some extent established by concrete externalities, but it is not exclusively the result of the struggle with material conditions. Human consciousness also has the ability to think about the conditions that influence its construction.

This view of consciousness casts education in a different light. Education then is no longer the key for transformation of consciousness, but education is absolutely necessary for transformation. To understand the relationship of education and consciousness it is necessary to think dialectically, in terms of ongoing apparent contradictions. It cannot be understood if we just think linearly.

After that I would say, of course, this country as well as the world cannot stop the development of the technological innovations and the evolution of science. The Third World has a tremendous problem concerning this, because it is increasingly difficult for the Third World, in the necessary realm of development, to arrive near to the First World. So it is becoming more and more dependent on the First World; and this is very bad, even for the First World. Thus, one of the questions now, because of this understanding of history and education, is, for example: What kind of education could increase and improve our knowledge of science and technology and also meet the social needs of people? What kind of education could answer these needs and also think of freedom and creativity?

When I speak of freedom and creativity I am not just speaking about the right to vote—this is not enough. When I speak about democracy and freedom, about creativity, I am not speaking about just going to school. But I'm speaking about the role of subjectivity in the process of creating science, in the process of innovating technology. For example, it makes me frightened that, more and more, we have little groups of people, scientists, who produce new knowledge, but who are very far away from the large majority of people who don't understand anything about the knowledge that is being created. That is, we place an emphasis on the curiosity of small groups of people in the world and the passivity of curiosity for the majority. I'm sure that the kind of education we need for the end of the century and beginning of the next one is an education which is serious—very serious. When I say serious, I'm not saying that this kind of education should be "dressed with a black tie"—absolutely not! No, serious from the point of view of rigor, intellectual rigor, which this kind of education has to create and cultivate among us, among the teachers and among the students.

When I speak of serious education I am also speaking about happiness. I cannot understand how it is possible to have an education through which we believe that studying is something difficult, impossible to be done, and exclusively painful. Studying, knowing, really are processes that are very, very demanding. In our efforts to understand with greater depth, we get tired. For example, it is not easy to read, if we understand reading as rewriting what we read and not just memorizing what others wrote; if we understand reading as a very creative experience. It is difficult. But we need an education that does not make the students afraid of studying, but curious, full of desire to study; because every time we begin to study, we must have in ourselves the certainty that at some moment we will become full with pleasure. And this is the moment in which we arrive to knowledge.

We need an education that does not dichotomize the act of knowing the existing knowledge from the act of creating the knowledge not yet created. We are dichotomizing everything. It is the same dichotomy between research and teaching. It is such an absurdity that in major universities, teachers who exclusively teach are not considered to be doing something serious, as if it were possible for one to teach without doing research. It is necessary to rethink what research means and what teaching means. This dichotomy is an old dichotomy; it began precisely with the system of power created by the evolution of capitalism. Before, a physicist was also a teacher of physics. He taught what he researched. Afterward, we have the researchers and those who, unable to do research, become "experts" and teach what the others create.

We need an education in which teachers are no longer merely transmitters of knowledge that other people create and about whose origins the teachers know nothing—reinforcing a way of teaching where teachers transfer this knowledge, without any kind of historical curiosity, to the students, who also receive the knowledge in this manner. To change this, education needs to embrace philosophy; we need not only—exclusively—technology and science but also philosophy of science, philosophy of technology, philosophy of knowledge. We must seriously question how we think and how we know. In the last analysis, I am sure that here in the United States as in Brazil, we need an education which helps us to be not solely objects of history but also subjects of history.

◄ACKNOWLEDGEMENTS►

I want to express first of all my tremendous appreciation to my many students over the years, but particularly to those whose words give life to this volume. They have all truly provided me with rich moments of learning and teaching upon which to ground both my theory and my practice and are the true inspiration for this volume.

I also extend my great appreciation to my many colleagues and friends who over the years have lovingly provided me with support and, in solidarity, have challenged me to become more disciplined, coherent, and mature as a teacher, scholar, activist, comrade, and friend.

With enormous gratitude, I thank my children, Gabriel, Christy, and Kelly, for the consistent love and respect they have always showered upon me through the ups and downs of life; and to my two beautiful granddaughters, Jessica and Naomi, who keep me renewed, hopeful, and committed to the struggle for a new world.

I am most lovingly indebted to my mother for teaching me that it is never too late for us to transform our lives through love and courage—even when death is knocking on our door.

And lastly, I am forever indebted to Paulo Freire, always my "father in the struggle," for his love, influence, direction, and visionary spirit.

IN MEMORY OF PAULO FREIRE

May we stop long enough to hear love
echoed in the still voice of your memories,
the childlike laughter of your eyes and
the sweet intonations of your passion.

May we find ourselves each day walking in
step with that revolutionary vision that gave
richness to your life and brought courage
and hope to those who could no longer dream.
May our teaching never find itself too far
from the fountain of your joy and tenderness,
even when the words may sting or the
task of struggle appear insurmountable.
May we find the courage to embrace strong
the quiet wisdom of your sweet humility,
as we dance on in solidarity to songs that
will tear down the ancient walls of Jericho.

EDUCATION IN THE AGE OF "GLOBALIZATION" AND "DIFFERENCE"

What excellence is this that manages to coexist with more that a billion inhabitants of the developing world who live in poverty, not to say misery? Not to mention the all but indifference with which it coexists with "pockets of poverty" and misery in its own, developed body. What excellence is this that sleeps in peace while numberless men and women make their home in the street, and says it is their own fault that they are on the street? What excellence is this that struggles so little, if it struggles at all, with discrimination for reasons of sex, class, or race?

PAULO FREIRE,
Pedagogy of Hope (1994)

As these words illustrate, Paulo Freire was deeply conscious of the myriad of illusions that masquerade within modern society as justice, freedom, autonomy, and democracy. At a time when the United States touts its agenda of "excellence" for the democratization of the world, what we find is greater economic

inequality on the planet than ever in recorded history. As the major
world power, the United States has effectively extended its dominion through an ideology of modernization, technological domi-
nance, military superiority, and its stronghold on the world's political economy. There was a time when this would have been publicly
denounced as outright imperialism or capital monopoly, but now it
travels under the more palatable euphemism of "globalization."

The closing years of the twentieth century resulted in major
changes in the socioeconomic landscape of U.S. society—changes
that potentially could herald greater class conflict and social unrest
than U.S. modern history has ever known. Nowhere are these
changes more evident than in California, where large populations
have been directly affected by the impact of economic restructuring,
"postindustrial" conditions of urban life, and the "globalization" of
the economy. Moreover, these represent significant material changes
that must be considered within the context of educational reform
debates currently taking place. Yet despite a blatant concentration
of wealth and its harsh impact on subordinate populations, schools
continue to view contemporary social conflicts and conditions of inequality as if their primary causes were the intellectual deficiencies
or psychological problems of individual students or their parents. By
so doing, they ignore the structural conditions of social injustice and
economic inequality at work in the process of schooling.

Paulo Freire (1970, 1993) recognized very clearly how public
schooling is implicated in the perpetuation of cultural invasion and
economic domination. He understood that in order to comprehend
the pervasive nature of late capitalism and its rapidly changing cultural maps, class relations, gender patterns of discrimination, and
racialized exploitation, teachers must recognize how schools function undemocratically, in complicity with the political economy.
More specifically, schools play an important role in the process of
capital accumulation as they organize student populations in an economic hierarchy and officially carry out an unfair system of meritocracy that ultimately functions to legitimate the ideological formations necessary for the reproduction of inequality (Apple 1995).

Hence, schools are sites of ideological struggle and contesta-
tion, where the values of the marketplace are cultivated, nurtured,

and reinforced. There are ideological tensions clearly at work in the educational debates related to affirmative action, vouchers, charter schools, bilingual education, and student and teacher assessment. Generally speaking, however, these issues are hotly debated without serious attention given to their direct connection to economic restructuring, the dismantling of the middle class, the increasing polarization of wealth, and the subsequent racialization of populations.

For example, a key issue raised in many discussions related to the problems with public education today is the concern over increasing immigration and the subsequent changing demographics of many inner-city schools. Yet if we look at this issue with a more critical lens, we will discover that inner-city schools have consistently educated diverse populations of students. Thus, educating diverse student bodies or meeting the needs of diverse communities is not the central impetus for the concern. Rather, the true source of the concern is the growing realization that immigrant populations are not going away, they are not assimilating as predicted, and they can no longer be ignored. Moreover, the number of people seeking both documented and undocumented entry into the United States more than likely will increase in the coming years. In fact, these numbers have consistently remained high for a variety of reasons, not the least of which is the impact of the last fifty years of U.S. foreign policy in Southeast Asia and Latin America and the accelerated movement toward economic "globalization."

During the 1990s, economic policies such as the North American Free Trade Agreement (NAFTA) had a debilitating effect on the labor participation in the United States of Latinos, African Americans, and other workers through the swift transfer of factories to countries in Latin American and the Pacific Rim. Even more disconcerting is the ever-increasing rate of poverty in the United States and the failure of schools to contend with changing class formations and their impact on the academic needs of students in poor communities. Consequently, many teachers, content with trite, psychological notions of student failure, fail to engage with the fundamental historical practices of domination and exploitation that perpetuate social, political, and economic relationships of inequality.

It seems that few teachers are prepared to grapple with the impact of the widening gap between the rich and poor on the lives of the students who sit in their classrooms. Yet, according to the latest U.S. Census Bureau, 20.5 percent of the 70 million children in the United States live in poverty. And although there is an alarming disproportionate representation of children from subordinate cultural communities, 62.5 percent of all poor children are identified as "white." It is also significant to note that almost 70 percent of all poor children live in families in which one or both parents work. Yet public educational policy regarding poor students—often made by people who themselves have never seen a hungry day in their lives—continues to perpetuate false portrayals of the actual conditions that are responsible for poverty in the first place.

These false portrayals of poverty result from the particularly American predisposition to evade the question of class inequality. Rather than address the structural inequalities that underlie the plight of economically disenfranchised people, social commentators psychologize, pathologize, or demonize the poor, then systematically categorize them as criminals, drug addicts, homeless people, juvenile delinquents, or the chronically unemployed (Aronowitz 1992).

THE POLITICS OF RACISM AND ECONOMIC INEQUALITY

The politics of racism and economic inequality are at the heart of the social conditions that oppressed communities face. Since its inception, the United States has always been a multicultural and multilingual nation-state, yet a denial and negation of class inequalities and cultural differences has long been reflected in the alienating values and practices of most private and public institutions, including churches, schools, and social welfare organizations. For over two hundred years there has been a fierce assimilative drive at work in America. Under its influence the doctrine of Manifest Destiny was conceived and practiced to the detriment of colonized and enslaved populations who were socially and economically exploited as cheap labor and reserve armies. Simply stated, the worst consequence of such a practice is the shameful creation of economic dependency.

The forceful ideology of capitalism, justified by the politics of racism, has fueled widespread global economic conquest under the guise of "freedom and democracy" or the banner of "human rights" (Clairmont 1995). In concert with economic dependency, such rhetoric has instilled in both dominant and subordinate populations the socially destructive notion that there is only one legitimate way of being an acceptable and "free" human being. What has been ignored is the manner in which class formations and mainstream beliefs, attitudes, and values are deeply anchored within dominant cultural and class expectations—expectations defined by the interests of the economically and politically powerful and carried out by the country's most inconspicuous moral leaders—namely, teachers.

In the arena of social services, "healthy" is the ubiquitous euphemism for normalcy and its implicit expectations of cultural conformity and homogeneity. Hence, institutional expectations of conformity reinforce the notion that for a working-class family to be deemed "healthy," its members must fit within the prescribed roles that sustain both the labor force and the marketplace. "Good" families are expected to adhere to the norms of patriarchal structures and capitalist interests. Meanwhile, poor and working-class people, along with members of subordinate ethnic communities, are expected to passively follow the institutional rules established for them by the dominant society—even when these rules are blatantly unfair and unequal and perpetuate human suffering.

The history of the U.S. health, education, and welfare system is filled with heart-wrenching examples of the dominant society's class-based, ethnocentric responses to cultural differences and working-class sensibilities—responses that, subsequently, led to the imposition of practices of conformity on families from subordinate populations–practices that often reinforced the loss of cultural identity through subtle and not-so-subtle forms of assimilation. This is well illustrated by the experiences of Native American children who were taken from their families on the reservation and placed in boarding schools or foster homes, had their hair cut, and their language and cultural rituals prohibited by the interventions of well-meaning social service agencies–all done, of course, for the good of the children.

And although federal laws and policies supposedly outlawing discrimination based on "race" have been in place for over fifty years, similar interventions have been carried out in African American and Latino communities, grounded in dominant-class perceptions of the parents in these communities as dirty, immature, neglectful, aggressive, or feeble-minded—all deemed legitimate reasons for intervening. What is even more disconcerting is the manner in which these racialized perceptions continue to be reflected in the policies and practices of education, health, and welfare agencies across the country.

Such class-bound, racialized perceptions of "difference" were clearly at work in the drafting of the 1996 Welfare Law that virtually eliminated the economic safety net for millions of children. These perceptions also drive the unrelenting emphasis that public schools have placed on bilingual transition programs for language minority students, despite the wealth of data (including government studies) that document its detrimental impact on academic achievement. Even more recently, in California, these perceptions fueled the racialized public debates and the strong anti-immigrant climate that led to the passage of Proposition 187 to prohibit education, health, and social services to undocumented immigrant children and their families; the overreaction of the public to the Oakland School Board's effort to include Ebonics in the public school curriculum; and the rhetoric, including the bogus title "English for the Children," used in the campaign to pass Proposition 227 (the Unz Initiative), whose aim was to dismantle bilingual education.

In *Shifting Fortunes: The Perils of the Growing American Wealth Gap* (1999), Collins and his colleagues argue that while the government "generously subsidizes those who don't need any help with building assets," the poor are being stripped of their safety net. The authors report that "an estimated $125 billion in federal subsidies are directed to corporations in the form of loopholes, direct cash transfers and subsidized access to public resources" (62), even though corporate profits totaled 4.5 trillion last year. This amount is equivalent to the paychecks of over 50 million working Americans (Collins et al. 1998). Nor can we ignore a heavily funded scientific community that has no compunction about spending over $350 million on a single Mars project, while millions of people starve from famine and the consequences of war.

Given such examples of economic inequality and racialized injustice in contemporary society, teachers must become more cognizant of the alienating conditions faced by poor ethnic communities—conditions that are indelibly linked to historical events that position members of subordinate populations very differently from members of the ruling class. Consider just for a moment the manner in which the historical experience of slavery (forced unpaid labor) continues to impact the overall economic conditions of African Americans. Or how the betrayal of the 1848 Treaty of Guadalupe Hidalgo, which explicitly "respected and guaranteed the civil and property rights of Mexicans" remaining in the United States after the Mexican-American War (San Miguel and Valencia 1998, 354), continues to be at work in the inadequate education available for Chicanos in the Southwest today. Or the negative impact of "Operation Bootstrap" in Puerto Rico during the 1950s, which resulted in the sterilization of almost 35 percent of Puerto Rican women. Or how the political atrocities and economic expenditures of the Vietnam War continue to affect the lives of Vietnamese American families, or the families of soldiers seriously wounded or killed in the war, or Latino and African American working-class families, who suffered the greatest proportion of casualties.

Similarly, we need to recognize that events that are taking place today in Bosnia or Chiapas or Nigeria or the Middle East are not solely the result of regional struggles. Conflicts in these regions are closely tied to the manner in which industrial development and U.S. "postindustrial" interests have exercised global control of mass populations, influencing the economic and political climates in these parts of the world. These interests are the ones that are sustained by the values and practices that shape educational institutions. In other words, the traditional values and expectations of many health, education, and welfare agencies are inextricably tied to the same interests and values that on one hand support the "globalization" of U.S. corporate "common culture" and on the other sustain deepening economic inequalities here and abroad. Moreover, as an industry, the education, health and welfare system historically has functioned as a formidable buffer between the ruling elite and the disenfranchised.

"GLOBALIZATION" AND THE FREE MARKET

At this juncture, it is helpful to note that "globalization" has become the new buzz-word for economic imperialism and its ruthless mechanisms to maximize capital accumulation. It seems to have become the "dominant political, social, economic issue of our era" (McChesney 1998, 1). Consequently, everyone has begun to use this term, even when speaking about issues which were once domestic concerns. Everything is talked about as global–labor rights, housing issues, citizens' rights, and even education. Such ubiquitousness requires that we ask whether the global term functions primarily to obscure the problems of local politics and debilitate the value of local struggles or whether it can shed some light on the conditions we're facing in urban centers today. It seems it is wise here not to fall into dichotomized notions and recognize that both are inherently possible, given the nature of these times.

What is meant by "globalization"? The earth's diverse societies are being arranged and united in complicated ways by global capitalism through a politics of "global convergence." Robert W. McChesney (1998, 1) defines "globalization"[1] as

> The process whereby capitalism is increasingly constituted on a transnational basis, not only in the trade of goods and services but, even more important, in the flow of capital and the trade in currencies and financial instruments. The dominant players in the globalization are the world's few hundred largest private corporations, which have increasingly integrated production and marketing across national borders over the past decade.

McChesney (1998, 2) also points out that there has been considerable debate as to "just how advanced this globalization process is, or is likely to become, as well as its political implications."

In response, some might want to rally to the "postmodernized" notion that the current economy reflects a grand epochal shift. Ellen

Meiksins Wood, however, in "Modernity, Postmodernity or Capitalism" (1998, 47), argues that what we are seeing is not a major shift in the logic of capitalism, but rather "the consequences of capitalism as a comprehensive system . . . capitalism itself reaching maturity."

So, although there might be some new forms, new rhythms, new impetuses in the globalizing process of capital or "universalization of capitalism" (Wood 1998, 47), for the majority of populations around the world the so-called "global economy" began in 1492. "In their histories, the centuries of conquest and economic colonization were integral to the rise of industrial capitalism in Europe and North America, but the returns were never really shared with them. In fact, the global economy long ago consigned most regions of the world to lowly status as commodity producers" (Greider 1997, 19).

Some of the consequences of the last decade of global capitalist expansionism include high profit and sales with low human labor requirements. These consequences have resulted in much of the current labor needs being met by technology and a dramatic shift in the number of workers required; the downsizing or closure of companies in the United States with corporate transfers of historically well-paying manufacturing jobs to "cheap labor" manufacturing centers around the world; and the U.S. shift from an industrial to a postindustrial economy predicated on what many are calling the Information Age and the knowledge society, an age that is defined by a new international division of labor.

Workers are the biggest losers, having "lost substantial control over their labor markets and terms of employment" (Greider 1997, 24) and their purchasing power, while salaries and benefits of top executives, consultants, and advisors have soared. Decentralization of control has resulted in corporations becoming global webs, with stakeholders becoming a large diffused group, spread over the world—less visible, less accountable, and less noisy than national stakeholders. The modern welfare state with "the social protections that rich nations enacted to ameliorate the harsh inequalities of industrial capitalism, is now in peril. [Corporate emphasis is on] maximizing returns on capital without regard to national identity or political or social consequences" (ibid., 25), while the "Third World" grows more and more economically dependent as a consequence of imposed economic systems, industrial exploitation of natural resources, and obligatory participation in the global market.

What U.S. capitalism has effectively produced is what John Cavanaugh (1996) terms "global economic apartheid," for of the 100 largest economies in the world, 51 are now global corporations. The Ford Motor Company is bigger than the economy of South Africa, and Wal-Mart is bigger than the economies of 161 countries. The top 200 companies have been job destroyers, wielding enormous power but creating few jobs. The heads of these companies use the phrase "global village" and other such celebratory rhetoric of "difference" to impress on us how they're bringing people together as workers and consumers. But while the profits of "difference" are being happily celebrated, "the characteristics of the global cultural system . . . suggest that its massive inequities remain both potent and deeply rooted" (Golding 1998, 70).

Meanwhile, the United States remains the dominant force of culture production—homogenizing the experience of 90 to 95 percent of the world's people through music, movies, and other cultural outlets. Transnational corporations such as Nike use free-trade zones in Mexico, the Philippines, and the Caribbean Basin where workers are paid 5 to 10 percent of what people would be paid in the United States and child labor—common practices of these global factories—is rampant. There is no question but that "globalization" is about the power inherent in the "new" flexible capitalist modes of production and accumulation and the control of life—a control of life that has widened the gap between the rich and the poor. Xavier Gorostiaga wrote, in a 1993 United Nations report entitled "Is the Answer in the South?":

> Throughout the world the last decade has been characterized by the rise of inequality between the rich and the poor. . . . In 1989 the richest fifth controlled 82.7 percent of the revenue; 81.2 percent of the world trade; 94.6 percent of commercial loans, 80.6 percent of internal savings and 80.5 percent of all investments. If in terms of distribution the panorama is untenable, it is equally so regarding resources. The rich countries possess one fifth of the world's population but consume 70 percent of world energy, 75

percent of the metals, 85 percent of the timber, and 60 percent of the food. Such a pattern of development . . . is only viable in the degree to which the extreme inequality is maintained, as otherwise the world resources would be exhausted. Therefore, inequality is not a distortion of the system. It is a systematic prerequisite for growth and permanence of the present system (4).

Yet it is this tendency to overlook the "systemic prerequisite" of capitalism in discussions of "cultural difference" or cultural identity that permits the construction and imposition of deceptive myths related to notions of "difference"—myths that function to preserve and deepen the institutional structures of "cultural invasion" and the social processes of racialization (Darder and Torres, forthcoming).

Given, then, the disastrous implications of an intensifying "globalized" political economy, both locally and abroad, educators need to understand the impact of capitalism around the world and link it to the local conditions that exist in their schools and communities. There is no question but that capitalism is advanced upon contradictory terrain, and does not function as simple imposition. Instead, the notion of society as a collection of possessive individuals is reinforced and any serious sense of the common good is marginalized. This is advanced effectively through the dynamics of the "free market" ideology.

The forces of the marketplace and the interest of corporations also drive educational rhetoric and classroom curricula. This was apparent in corporate America's response to the 1983 *Nation at Risk* report, which alleged that public schooling was a fiasco. It was a response that overwhelmingly emphasized school improvement as a matter of the national economy—if schools failed the economy would crumble (Molner 1996). Consequently, in today's world, schools are often considered to be economic engines. Unfortunately, schools generally function in the interest of the marketplace rather than serving as a democratizing influence upon local economies. Take, for instance, language policies and their relationship to the economy. While Sacramento is busy setting up mandates for the implementation of a phonics curriculum in the schools, the marketing divisions of corporations that publish phonics texts and materials are revving their engines for multi-million-dollar sales.

Democracy too has become principally tied to the creation of conditions of "free consumer choice" in an unfettered market. Hence, democracy is no longer a political concept but an economic metaphor. In the same way, education and its democratizing purpose is lost to the wiles of market-driven educational solutions such as the privatization of education—one of the most dangerous threats facing public schools today. Through the rhetoric of "consumer choice" prevalent in the privatization debate, capitalism articulates a classless, homogenous society of consumers, all existing within a common, transcendent culture (Apple 1995). In a similar manner, the "pluralism" of the marketplace appropriates conflicting cultural forms, ideas, and images, in order to guarantee its own expansion.

Rupturing the ideological bubble that insulates this false notion that democracy equals capitalism seems to be one of the most difficult tasks that teachers face when working with students, colleagues, and parents. Exposing the hidden values, beliefs, and practices of a political economy that greedily seeks maximum returns on capital, with little concern for human life or the sustainability of the planet, is key to rethinking democratic schooling. Teachers cannot disregard the manner in which transnational capital whips around the world placing a neck hold on the economies of "developing" nations. Simultaneously, the market appropriates whatever shred of cultural capital as can be commodified to appease the cultural industry's fabricated hunger for chic ethnic paraphernalia—whether clothing, food, music, art, or spiritual artifacts. In the process, the consumptive wiles of one third of the world's population reign over the subsistence of the other two thirds, condemning millions to conditions of subhuman material existence.

THE DISPOSABLE AND EXPENDABLE

Although it may seem very unfamiliar or terribly uncomfortable at moments, teachers who say they are committed to antiracist struggle and social justice must become fully conscious to what is perhaps America's most concealed truth—an all-consuming capitalist system that is everywhere at work in sustaining, perpetuating, and exacerbating all forms of social discrimination, economic exploitation, cultural invasion, and systematic violence against women, gays and lesbians, working-class people, and racialized populations. Freire often argued that "racism and sexism [are] very much linked to capitalist production. . . . I don't see the possibility of overcoming racism and sexism in a capitalist mode of production" (Shor and Freire 1987, 167). What exists in the United States is a political economy nourished and bolstered by an ideology of power relations and a class structure that render members of disenfranchised groups virtually disposable and expendable.

This ideology of disposability is at work in a variety of contemporary examples of urban life. For instance, when a Euro-American professional woman was raped and killed in Cambridge, Massachusetts, there was a public outcry by the Boston community in response to this crime. The police and community had to do something! This seemed like a logical response. However, this was a sharp contrast to the Boston community's lack of concern for the three poor African American women who had been raped and killed the week before in Roxbury, a predominantly low-income African American neighborhood. The latter can only be considered a logical response within a context in which poor African American women are considered expendable.

In public schools the ideology of disposability is evident in the mania of high-stakes standardized testing, where tests acknowledged to be flawed are used to make inaccurate and inappropriate decisions about the fate of millions of students across the nation. The results of these tests are linked to the practice of student retention and nonpromotion—a practice that has consistently been shown to result in long-term negative effects to student achievement and loss of educational resources and opportunities. Retention rates are higher for African American, Latino, and other children from poor families. And of all students who are retained, 50 percent are more likely to not graduate from high school. Hence, early in their lives these children are officially classified and tracked, rendering them members of a disposable and expendable class. What is completely unconscionable from a social and economic-justice perspective is not

only the perpetuation but overwhelming revival that standardized
testing has been undergoing during the last decade.[2] Hence, early in
their lives, these children are officially classified and tracked, which
renders them members of the disposable and expendable class.

It is impossible to consider the issue of populations deemed
disposable and expendable without discussing the prison industrial complex. The U.S. prison population is now over 2 million—
the largest incarceration rate in the world. This constitutes 25
percent of the entire world's prison population, although the
United States has less than 5 percent of the world's population.
During the 1990s the prison population grew at a greater rate than
in any earlier decade in recorded history (see Justice Policy Institute 2000). In California, in particular, greater and greater numbers of Latinos, African Americans, and working-class men and
women are being incarcerated by a society that has systematically
rendered them disposable—disposable because they are problematic
to capital accumulation.

An attempt to make sense of this growing phenomenon from a
perspective that focuses only on the deviant psychological health or
immorality of particular individuals or, worse, on racialized cultural
explanations of criminal behavior is sheer fallacy. Instead, teachers
must make the connection between the increasing imprisonment of
working-class men and women and the control by transnational corporations of everyday life. Never in the history of the United States
have workers been subjected to more corporate mergers and movements of companies to foreign countries. These moves resulted in an
overwhelming number of layoffs and terminations during one of the
most profitable economic eras of all time—an era of enormous profits for the 10 percent of the population who reaped almost 90 percent of the benefit, while real wages for the majority of U.S. workers
declined (Collins et. al. 1999).

Often, educators are incredulous or find it distasteful and disturbing to be confronted with these issues head-on, given the sense of pow-
erlessness that difficult social and economic issues elicit in most people.
However, we must fully recognize that as long as any group of people is
deemed disposable or expendable, any popularized American notion of
"liberty and justice for all" will remain nothing but a myth—or, in the

words of Donaldo Macedo, a "big lie" (1994, 9). It is, in fact, he argues, a "pedagogy of big lies" that perpetuates a process of schooling in which the majority of students are so domesticated with fragmented and disconnected knowledge that they are left virtually uneducated and with little access to the political and economic spheres of society.

In light of traditional educational policies concerning testing, assessment, curriculum, second-language acquisition, and promotion that blatantly perpetuate the systemic marginalization of subordinate groups, it seems nearly impossible to envision how teachers might begin to break through the hegemonic forces at work. This is particularly difficult when teachers fail to embrace a revolutionary ethic of civic responsibility and social value for all people, irrespective of culture, gender, economic status, sexual orientation, physical ability, or age. Such forms of social consciousness must be actively cultivated and nourished within classrooms through critical dialogues and social relationships that reshape our perceptions and interactions with one another and the world in which we must survive as teachers and students. Through an educational practice that encourages ongoing questioning and the development of critical social thought, teachers and their students can engage critically the profound social, political, and economic issues at work in their lives.

It is through such a process of critical inquiry that links can also be made between the increasing profit and wealth of transnational corporations and the growing numbers of economically disenfranchised people here and around the globe. Through such inquiry, teachers can come to understand the cause of poverty as structural, rather than accepting simplistic and fallacious interpretations of poverty to explain why students from particular communities are more likely to do poorly in school, drop out, be incarcerated, or end up pregnant and on welfare. This shift in consciousness represents a fundamental step in redefining our politics and constructing a new vision of schools and the society.

RACISM AND THE IMAGINARY MIDDLE

The relationship that exists between racism, class conflict, and the construction of the mythical "normal" or "healthy" child, adolescent, or adult should be of grave concern to teachers of all educational levels. Paulo Freire referred to this phenomenon as the necessity to "mythicize the world" in fixed categories that serve to perpetuate the subjugation and cultural invasion of oppressed populations. He saw this as an extension of the "banking" concept of education, which, in conjunction with paternalism, considers marginal those

> ... who deviate from the general configuration of a "good organized and just society." The oppressed are regarded as the pathology of the healthy society, which must therefore adjust these "incompetent and lazy" folk to its own patterns by changing mentality. These marginals need to be "integrated," "incorporated" into the healthy society that they have "forsaken" (1970, 60–61).

Hence, a critical view of schooling must unveil and openly challenge the manner in which ideologies of racism and class conflict function to distort the realities and conditions of working-class students, particularly those who come from subordinate cultural communities. It is important to note how differing forms of racism are often produced through the perpetuation of racialized language in the conceptual development of public policies and practices within both public and private institutions. Essentialized language is produced through false dichotomous notions of black/white existence that fail to engage substantively with the diversity of social, political, and economic realities that make up racialized populations. Further, such language is given meaning within the dominant belief system that shapes the practices of public and private institutions—a belief system that for centuries has functioned to effectively exclude the democratic participation of subordinate populations through the process of racialization (Darder and Torres 1999).

More specifically, "racialization" refers to those instances where social relations between people are structured by the significance that is given to specific human biological characteristics, particularly when such significance is used to define, categorize, and construct meaning about different social groups (Miles 1993)—for example, when skin color is perceived to signify a whole array of psychological, cultural, and social information. This information is then utilized to construct reified interpretations of the character of individuals from different cultural communities. Yet those who are from subordinate cultural communities know that our communities are never monolithic. Moreover, the color of one's skin does not guarantee one's intelligence, skill, competency, personality, or, for that matter, politics. Along the same lines, Paulo Freire (1997) argued against the notion that racism is

> . . . inherent to the nature of human beings. . . . We "are" not racist; we "become" racist, and we can also stop being that way. The problem I have with racist people is not the color of their skin, but rather the color of their ideology. Likewise, my difficulty with the "macho" does not rest in their sex, but in their discriminatory ideology. Being racist or macho, progressive or reactionary, is not an integral part of human nature (85–86).

Unfortunately, even today with the abundance of information available, most teachers working within oppressed communities still lack substantive knowledge related to the manner in which discriminatory ideologies related to political, economic, and cultural policies and practices influence the lives of students in their classrooms. This is particularly disturbing when teachers must confront daily the negative impact of social and economic injustice on the lives of students who have been historically marginalized, solely because of their skin color, the material conditions of their parents, or the communities in which they reside.

This is particularly the case for teachers who practice in large urban centers. Despite the great War on Poverty of the sixties, segregation and distress rates in urban centers such as New York, Chicago, Detroit, Cleveland, Los Angeles, and Philadelphia continue to increase, as residents must grapple with stagnant wages, the loss of jobs, the elimination of welfare benefits, and fewer vocational training opportunities (Wilson 1997). And despite a significant improvement in the educational attainment across all communities—including students from extreme poverty areas—during the last thirty years, there is more poverty today in many of these cities than there was in 1968 (Cisneros 1993).

THE IMPACT OF THE MEDIA

Over the course of the twentieth century the media have come to occupy an increasingly central role in the formation of individual and collective identities and in shaping the aesthetics and politics of a generation. In today's world, it is impossible for teachers to fully grasp the insidious process of racialization, sexism, and other forms of ideological distortions without noting the overwhelming impact of the media on the manner in which students come to make sense of their world. Through its captivating influence and fictitious representations of "difference," the media function effectively to sustain through commonsense approval the ideology of social and economic domination. "In a society such as [that of] the United States where most of the people do not have any direct access to nor power over the bulk of decisions that affect their lives, the media plays a powerful legitimating role in the production of social consensus" (Darder 1995, 10).

Hence, the role of the media in the perpetuation of class-bound and racialized attitudes cannot be overlooked in our understanding of schooling or how students perceive their world and the relationships they forge in the classroom and the larger community. This reality has reached such blatant proportions that even a simple analysis of Disney[3] movies, teen flicks, or music industry products easily reveals the insidious market values and interests of capitalist America. These are the values and interests that actively shape and influence the attitudes and behaviors of young consumers and give meaning to fabricated ideals that are deceptively proselytized by the monopoly of the mass media.

From popularized cartoon images to the values of family sitcoms to the "cool" representations of athletes and movie stars, students are barraged daily with conflicting notions of who they should strive to be. Simultaneously, the hidden culture of the "imaginary ideal" powerfully influences the way teachers think and talk about "smart students," "caring parents," or "loving homes." Unfortunately, the problematic nature of such homogenizing discourse generally goes unquestioned within public schools, despite its influence on how teachers view students and how schools assess and evaluate the legitimacy of student knowledge, skills, worth, and potential.

Inherent in the mainstream popular gaze is a class-based and racialized view of "difference." When mainstream references to "man" or "woman" are made, the reference is always to a "white man" or "white woman" who are further ascribed with a "natural" set of acceptable, and often superior, traits. On the other hand, those who are considered "the other" are distinguished by the use of specific class-based or racialized categories. Obvious examples of this aspect of racialization are found in mainstream newspapers where reporters must identify people who are not "white" by using some sort of ethnic label (*black* mothers, *Korean* parents, *Hispanic* children, *Filipino* workers, etc.). A very similar dynamic is at work concerning class assumptions. Categories that immediately suggest class difference generally include "high-risk children" "latch-key kids," "illegal aliens," or "underclass populations." The racialized and class-bound images perpetuated by such language, and the values that inform its use, give students some very clear messages about their particular place in the socially constructed hierarchy of American life.

It is vitally important that teachers recognize how the media function as a subtle and not-so-subtle means of defining and shaping our innermost desires and dreams—which, more often than not, are linked directly to the interests of the marketplace. As we embark on the twenty-first century, corporate interests of greed and consumption are enjoying a field day even with what at one time were considered counterhegemonic or revolutionary images, artifacts, and symbols. This is exemplified by the worldwide marketing of, for instance, rap music, which as marketed only faintly mimics the political, cultural, and class origins of resistance of African American street youth. This is true also of the polished and packaged images of civil rights leaders, Third World revolutionaries, cultural celebrations and rituals, or exotic vacations in Third World "island paradises." These lucrative "multicultural" products serve to create the illusion that there truly exists greater acceptance of diversity and difference and increasing social freedom and equality—all because a small percentage of the privileged world population can freely sell and consume multiculturalism, to their little heart's content.

What teachers cannot ignore is that a people's culture is not a fashion statement. It embodies meaningful collective knowledge about how communities have struggled to survive, work, love, and dream. It often contains significant historical remnants of cultural capital that potentially can inspire and motivate students toward greater social agency, political resistance, and community self-determination. But not surprisingly, it is precisely this revolutionary dimension that is stripped away from the fashionable products and images that are peddled on the big screen, on MTV, in popular magazines, and in slick educational materials—all sold under the rubric "celebrating diversity."

PRIVILEGE AND ENTITLEMENT

Americans are subject to political manipulation, exploitation, and complicity with an oppressive system of privilege and entitlement based on gender, skin color, sexual orientation, and other discriminatory signifiers (Macedo 1993). Implicated in this process are public schools that function to reproduce, as well as maintain, privilege by taking dominant-culture knowledge forms and content and defining it as legitimate knowledge to be preserved and transmitted. In this way, schools play a fundamental role in assisting in the accumulation of cultural capital and serving as one of the primary modes of production for the cultural commodities required by U.S. corporate society. Moreover, through the creation of jobs and the implementation of market-driven curricula, schools perpetuate commodity knowledge as economically essential products. Hence, the school's role in the accumulation process allows for the creation of reserve workers and cultural capital required to sustain the U.S. global economy.

The construction and institutionalization of racialized stereotypes in both the academic and popular imagination protect the established privilege and entitlement of those who hold political and economic power. These stereotypes are generally built and perpetuated against the backdrop of a mainstream belief in an "ideal." From the vantage point of privilege, racialized stereotypes are conceived according to the level of phenotypic and behavioral differences that supposedly exist between those who are considered outside the norms of appropriate behavior. As inferred earlier, those who deviate are deemed genetically inferior or culturally defective—judgments inherent in perceptions of the disenfranchised as too loud, hyperactive, oversexed, weak, passive, too emotional, hysterical, too intense, or just plain lazy.

The failure of teachers to acknowledge entitlements and privileges that come from the color of one's skin or one's class, gender, or sexual orientation powerfully obstructs their capacity to break through mythicized illusions of diversity and forge a critically democratic vision of schooling and American life. Such denial of entitlement and privilege also perpetuates alienating beliefs within the educational system of what is legitimate knowledge, classroom practice, and teacher-student relationships. To be considered a legitimate or valuable educator or student requires the willingness to conform to a standard and protocol rooted in the dominant cultural and class values of the educational system. It is this set of values which also then determines whether a student or teacher will be considered a "good fit" within most institutions.

Furthermore, the perpetuation of universal psychological norms by which all students are evaluated is generally coupled with an expectation that those who are culturally different, rather than the schools, should change. Hence, persistent deficit notions of those perceived to be outside the mainstream abound, with often rigid and alienating expectations of what teachers, students, or parents must do, or how they must change, to "merit" additional educational resources or opportunities. In his writings on cultural identity and education, Freire exposes the ideological roots of such expectations.

> The dominant class, then, because it has the power to distinguish itself from the dominated class, first rejects the differences between them but, second, does not pretend to be equal to those who are different; third it does not intend those who are different shall be equal. What it wants is to maintain the differences and keep distance and to recognize and emphasize in practice the inferiority of those who are dominated (1998b, 71).

Consequently, assimilative expectations of conformity often veil a virulent discourse of what Freire called "false generosity" (1970), a feigned benevolent concern for the well being of culturally diverse or poor students that works to strip away their sense of identity and social power, often interfering with their very ability to act on their own behalf. The loss of self-determination and academic motivation that can result from difficult experiences with educational institutions constitutes one of major causes for students' dropping out of high school or withdrawing from colleges and universities. Unfortunately, this is a social phenomenon that is linked to their further disempowerment, particularly when their failure to "become educated" seriously impedes their full participation in the labor force and community life.

Again, there is no question but that the media are major culprits in perpetuating debilitating notions and false racialized images of class entitlement and privilege. Examples of this are highly prevalent in the media's portrayal of poor ethnic communities. Although the majority of people on welfare are Euro-American, a favorite portrayal of recipients is the large African American women with many children, living in poor conditions. Along the same line, African American and Chicano youth are often portrayed as violent "gang-bangers," notwithstanding the fact that less than 10 percent of these youths are actually involved in gangs (Vigil 1997). Hence it is not surprising to learn that an African American youth is six times more likely to be incarcerated than a white peer, even when the latter has had similar charges brought against him and neither youth a prior record; nor that minority youths are more likely than white youths who commit comparable crimes to be referred to juvenile court, be detained, face trial as adults, and be jailed with adults (National Council on Crime and Delinquency 2000).

A BRIEF COMMENT ON POLITICAL BACKLASH

As teachers become more conscious of social and economic injustice and move to engage critically with the inequalities so prevalent within public schools, they must not naïvely overlook the politics of political backlash. The response to losing power as a consequence of shifting entitlement and privilege within schools can elicit a feeling of threat or displacement among teachers, administrators, parents, and even students who identify principally with mainstream ideology and traditional institutional values. This can result in further political backlash that expresses itself as fear that the "other" is "taking over," irrespective to how the "other" is identified. Paulo Freire addressed this concern as he sought to consider critically the impact of shattering the oppressor/oppressed contradictions that result when traditional hierarchical relations of power become more equalized.

> But even when the contradiction is resolved authentically by a new situation established by the liberated laborers, the former oppressors do not feel liberated. On the contrary, they genuinely consider themselves to be oppressed. Conditioned by the experience of oppressing others, any situation other than their former seems to them like oppression. Any restriction on this way of life, in the name of the rights of the community, appears to the former oppressors as a profound violation of their individual rights (Freire 1970, 43).

Unfortunately, such responses are not rare whenever women, working-class people, or communities of color are perceived as making too many gains or in-roads into the decision-making process and the control of resources.

Given the nature of backlash politics, one common tactic in schools is to make exaggerated requests for justification or proof that one's teaching practice or academic knowledge is legitimate—that one is truly worthy of equal standing. The institutional expectation of exaggerated proofs of legitimacy is a prevalent theme that is often privately discussed by both teachers and students from subordinate class and ethnic communities. The alienation so often experienced by teachers who are perceived as "other" is well illustrated when they find themselves in schools where they are a lone voice among their coworkers, administrators, or parents who adhere to the prescribed values of the dominant culture. Often in such a context, teachers are questioned incessantly about every aspect of their practice or details of their decisions that do not comply with what are considered acceptable mainstream methods, even when a teacher has been hired specifically to function as an "ethnic representative" of a particular community.

In such school settings, it seems beyond the capacity of many administrators, coworkers, or parents to believe that these teachers who seem so "different" are adequately competent to determine alternative practices on the basis of their cultural and class understanding of their students—knowledge that others in the institution may not possess. This generates further hiring debates, for example, as to whether minority teachers are actually required to serve students who come from diverse communities. These highly biased and uncritical responses are often rooted in hidden racialized notions of intelligence and aptitude, as well as fears of job displacement. Most disconcerting is how these responses can serve to obstruct the ability of teachers from subordinate communities to carry out appropriate educational strategies and alternatives, based on an understanding of particular cultural histories as well as of the conditions of economic marginalization that their students face daily.

This example also illustrates the manner in which backlash politics is driven not only by an ideology of racism but by the potential class or economic impact of expanding institutional opportunities to diverse populations. Hence, teachers cannot neglect the fact that if a revolutionary practice is to be central to our vision of schooling, it can only be actualized in conjunction with a struggle for a radical shift in the current distribution of power and wealth. In the absence of such a redistribution of power and resources, the politics of pluralism, diversity, or antiracism constitutes only an illusion, an empty rhetoric, a mystified politics of deception.

THE NEED FOR A CRITIQUE OF CAPITALISM

Given the changing dimensions of the political economy and its impact on schooling, Paulo Freire recognized the tremendous need for educators to infuse their teaching with a critique of capitalism. He argued that "criticism of the injustice within the capitalistic system must be strong" (1997b, 77–78). To launch such a critique, capitalism must be exposed as the most totalizing system of social relations the world has ever known. For it is precisely this totalizing dimension that renders capitalism unique and so difficult to challenge (Wood 1996, 1998). As a consequence, most teachers find it very difficult to even comprehend, let alone effectively critique, the way capitalism shapes and controls their teaching, as well as the educational experiences of students in this country.

Forging a substantive critique requires that teachers unveil class-bound values inherent in education materials, classroom practices, and public policy, through dialogue and study. This is to say that teachers must come to comprehend with greater clarity and specificity how the dynamics of class formation function to structure the social conditions of all institutions, including schools. Through developing this knowledge, teachers can begin to infuse their work in schools, cities, and communities with a more substantive critique of capitalism and develop democratic strategies for intervention that will challenge the structural conditions of class and racialized inequalities. More important, educators together can rethink their current understanding of public policies directed toward the erosion of linguistic democracy, immigration rights, the dismantling of affirmative action, and the revival of standardized testing and high school exit examinations within the context of a class analysis of schooling. By so doing, they will not only develop the language and strategies to effectively counter the tirades of the political right, but effectively construct and articulate new possibilities for democratic schooling. This task is best accomplished when teachers understand patterns of distribution and redistribution that produce relations of exploitation within schools (McLaren, 2000).

A well-formulated critique of capitalism is also essential to understanding the complex relationship between schools and community development. Through the lens of such a critique, teachers can challenge more skillfully policies and practices that impact their students, parents, and community in oppressive ways. Here it is useful to note that cultural forms within social organizations are never simply mysterious unexplained creations, but are always linked to particular relations of *power*. This is why the question of power is essential to our understanding of schooling: its patterns of distribution seriously impact all aspects of our personal and social lives (Naiman 1996). In engaging the question of power, Paulo Freire seldom minced words when it came to defining the institutional objective of his pedagogy. "This struggle is a fight for power. Perhaps to be more exact, it is a fight for the reinvention of power" (1993, 124). His vision entailed the reconstruction of power relationships that could break through those reified processes of alienation and allow us to recognize ourselves as full human beings.

Associated then with this view of power is a basic premise of the classroom as a workplace, teachers as workers who are integrated into the local economy, and parents as workers immersed in the context of "globalization." From this radical perspective, teachers can perceive more readily that the material conditions in which parents live and work frequently provoke particular responses to their environment. The choices parents make are influenced by their class position. Yet teachers seldom seem to note that working-class parents often see the relationship between schools and work more narrowly, given class constraints. There are material forces at work that shape parents' sense of opportunities and limitations for themselves and their children within the larger social structure. Consequently, more times than not, the expectations parents have of schools and their children's academic future are also linked to their class position.

In light of all this, teachers must work collectively to enter into relationships of solidarity and struggle with parents, teachers, and students. Through the formation of such relationships, collective efforts can be made toward changing material conditions within communities. This is a significant contrast to the fact that one good teacher in a school cannot eliminate plant closures, loss of economic benefits, or change oppressive public policies or practices alone. The transformation of schools—a critical process that must be aimed at overcoming the social and economic injustices of society—requires a collective political struggle that can only be waged successfully through our collective efforts.

BUILDING SOCIAL MOVEMENTS

Paulo Freire believed till his death that "to change what we presently are, it is necessary to change the structures of power radically" (1997b, 80). Yet this did not "presuppose an inversion of the oppressed-oppressor poles; rather it intends to reinvent, in communion, a society where exploitation and the verticalization of power do not exist, where the disenfranchised segments of society are not excluded or interdicted from reading the world" (Freire and Macedo 1998, 9). To accomplish such a "communion," Freire encouraged progressive educators to forge groups of struggle founded on his critical utopian notion of "unity within diversity." For Freire, the inability to establish alliances across the "reconcilable" differences only serves to preserve the structures of domination and exploitation. Hence, he urged in *Pedagogy of the Heart* (85):

> The "different" who accept unity cannot forgo unity in their fight; they must have objectives beyond those specific ones of each group. There has to be a greater dream, a utopia the different aspire to and for which they are able to make concessions. Unity within diversity is possible, for example, between antiracist groups, regardless of the group's skin color. In order for that to happen, it is necessary for the anti-racist groups to overcome the limits of their core racial group and fight for radical transformation of the socioeconomic system that intensifies racism.

In the spirit of Freire's dream, teachers need to create alliances across cultural communities and class positions that are firmly grounded in a process that can help us overcome our lack of democratic experience through participation, while superseding the irrational and dehumanizing hegemonic forces that prevail. Such a process requires that we remain ever cognizant of the increasing significance of class and the specificity of capitalism as a system of social and political relations of power; one where all forms of social injustice exist within particular social formations, where power is not equitably distributed, and where the struggle for power is in constant flux and change. Hence, part of the task is to rescue the concept of power from its diffused and immeasurable position "where power is everywhere and no where, back to where the possibility of collective political action remains possible" (Naiman 1999, 16). In so doing, we become better prepared to contend with such issues as livable wages, adequate health care, welfare reform, affordable housing, and equal education—all issues that are acutely influenced by the political economy.

Moreover, through the creation of alliances, progressive teachers can participate in counterhegemonic political projects that do not dichotomize their work as cultural workers and social activists. Instead, such participation supports their work within schools while simultaneously providing the opportunity to collectively take positions on current educational issues that directly impact their teaching practice, such as school vouchers, charter schools, teacher certification, high school graduation exams, literacy, and bilingual education. In addition, through alliances where a solidarity of differences is cultivated, teachers from diverse communities and class positions can work together to create unifying, albeit heterogeneous and multifaceted, anticapitalist political strategies to counter conservative efforts to destroy public schooling. Most important, such community relationships of struggle can support teachers as they fight together to break out of the paralysis that has been plaguing the left for years. Through social-movement organizations, teachers can boldly move together to build an alternative vision of schooling in this county—a vision that must be connected to a larger political project of liberation.

History has repeatedly shown that significant institutional change can truly take place only as a result of collective work within social-movement organizations. True, legal and policy strategies have had some impact, but ultimately the collective pressure of the masses has had the greatest impact in quickly mobilizing these forces. Despite political and economic efforts to render the masses voiceless through the fabricated confusion of false cultural representations and the imposition of crippling myths, teachers working together can restore and empower the public will to take back our lives and our communities. Within such a context of solidarity, we can powerfully reanimate political self-determination and with courage speak out boldly in defiance of social and economic injustice. Through our collective participation, teachers can discover the means to channel the fears, guilt, rage, and despair into productive action. Through the building of ethical communities for struggle and change, we can develop the critical strength, reflective ability, political knowledge, social commitment, personal maturity, and sol-idarity across our differences necessary to reinvent our world. But most important, as Freire consistently stressed, we must restore the inalienable rights of what it means to have full citizenship.

> Yes, citizenship—above all in a society like ours, of such authori-tarian and racially, sexually, and class-based discriminatory tradi-tions—is really an invention, a political production. In this sense, one who suffers any of these discriminations, or all of them at once, does not enjoy the full exercise of citizenship as a peaceful and recognized right. On the contrary, it is a right to be reached and whose conquest makes democracy grow substantially. Citizen-ship implies freedom—to work, to eat, to dress, to wear shoes, to sleep in a house, to support oneself and one's family, to love, to be angry, to cry, to protest, to support, to move, to participate in this or that religion, this or that party, to educate oneself and one's family, to swim regardless in what ocean of one's country. Citizen-ship is not obtained by chance: It is a construction that, never fin-ished, demands we fight for it. It demands commitment, political clarity, coherence, decision. For this reason a democratic educa-tion cannot be realized apart from an education of and for citizen-ship (1998b, 90).

The strength of such communities, as Freire imagined them in *Pedagogy of the Heart*, is their fundamental capacity to establish, cul-tivate, and support humanizing relationships, while teachers collec-tively struggle for social and economic justice. Through their partic-ipation in such relationships, teachers can break down the debilitating alienation and isolation they often experience within public schools. In the process, they begin to find the freedom to em-brace all aspects of their humanity more fully and openly—the pain, the suffering, the fear, the disappointments, the uncertainties, the pleasures, the joy, and the dreams—and by so doing, to discover the political power generated by our collective humanity.

Paulo Freire held that a critical vision for the future is impossi-ble without a sense of hope, firmly anchored in the knowledge that there exists "no historical reality which is not human" (1970,

125). Only through a praxis of hope can alliances across differences be forged—alliances sufficiently strong for teachers and students to "learn together, teach together, be curiously impatient together, produce something together and resist the obstacles" (1998a, 69) that prevent the full expression of our humanity and steal our place as subjects of history. In *Pedagogy of Freedom*, Freire again connected the relationship of hope to the possibility of historical transformation.

> Hope is a natural, possible and necessary impetus in the context of our unfinishness. Hope is an indispensable seasoning in our human, historical experience. Without it, instead of history we would have pure determinism. History exists only where time is problematized and not simply a given. A future that is inexorable is a denial of history (69).

There is no question that in today's world, no authentic form of democratic life is possible for the future without a revolutionary praxis of hope that works both for the transformation of social consciousness on one hand and the reconstruction of social structures on the other. Freire urged us "to think of political strategies and state policies that will humanize the culture of global capital as it lands in our locality. But the struggle is not only ideological. Social policy has real economic and social consequences for the poor and marginalized, *and* for the rich and middle class. The consequences are not just symbolic. They shape people's lives and their place in the material world" (Carnoy 1997, 16). For Freire, our true vocation never entailed that we should live as agents of capital or "detachable appendages of other people's dreams and desires" (McLaren 1997b, 153). Rather, he embraced and cherished the hope and possibility that we could exist as full human beings, with the freedom to live passionately with an "increasing solidarity between the mind and hands" (1997b, 33).

Living a pedagogy of love in our classroom and our communities defies the prescriptive formulas and models of the past, calling for the "reinvention" of our radical vision not only of schooling but of American society—a vision of a society that is unquestionably shaped by a democratic commitment to human rights, social justice, and a radical redistribution of wealth and power. It is a revolutionary vision of society that calls for the eradication of all forms of human suffering and oppression; and inspired by radical hope, openly challenges and rejects the cruel fatalism of poverty arguments among the elite that echo the familiar biblical adage "The poor will always be amongst us." Instead, it courageously declares that the poor are necessary and inevitable in the context of economic domination and human exploitation. Paulo Freire argued forcefully that poverty, racism, sexism, heterosexism, and other forms of discrimination are not natural traits of our humanity. Instead, these conditions exist as "naturalized" aberrations, invented within history by human beings. And because this is so, oppression in all its faces can be "reinvented" out of existence (1997, 308).

Most important, Freire was convinced that schools are significant sites of struggle and that teachers, who embrace an ethical responsibility as citizens and subjects of history, are in an ideal position to collectively fight for the reinvention of the world.

> Within an understanding of history as possibility, tomorrow is problematic. In order for it to come, it is necessary that we build it through transforming today. Different tomorrows are possible. . . .
> It is necessary to reinvent the future. Education is indispensable for this reinvention. By accepting ourselves as active subjects and objects of history, we become beings who make division. It makes us ethical beings (1997b, 55).

Although the task before us may often seem insurmountable, we are fortunate to find in Paulo Freire's life and work precious words that breathe life into our revolutionary visions of teaching and learning—a revolutionary vision that is uncompromisingly grounded in an *armed love*. He firmly held, as did Che Guevara before him, that it is this revolutionary love which fuels our political commitment to liberation and ultimately must embody our work in schools and society. For through this love, we not only prevent "nihilism and despair from imposing their own life-denying inevitability in times of social strife and cultural turmoil (McLaren 2000,

171), we incarnate the history we are now making together with the passion, beauty and joy of liberation.

NOTES

1. See also the debate that has transpired in issues of *Monthly Review* over the last several years.

2. For more information regarding the issue of testing in public schools, contact the National Center for Fair and Open Testing in Cambridge, Massachusetts, at www.fairtest.org@aol.com or (617) 864–4810.

3. For an incisive and revealing critique of Disney's impact as popular culture, see the writings of Henry Giroux, in particular *The Mouse That Roared: Disney and the End of Innocence* (Lanham, Md.: Roman & Littlefield), 1999. Also excellent is the Media Education Foundations' video *Mickey Mouse Monopoly: Disney, Childhood, and Corporate Power* (Chyng Sun 2001), which provides a critical look at the world Disney films create in terms of race, gender, and class.

CHAPTER 1

THE PASSION OF PAULO FREIRE: REFLECTIONS AND REMEMBRANCES

What inheritance can I leave? Exactly one. I think that it could be said when I am no longer in this world: "Paulo Freire was a man who lived. He could not understand life and human existence without love and without the search for knowledge. Paulo Freire lived, loved and attempted to know. For this very reason, he was a human being who was constantly curious."

PAULO FREIRE,
Pedagogy and the City (1993)

I live my life intensely. I am the type of person who loves his life passionately. Of course, someday, I will die, but I have the impression that when I die, I will die intensely as well . . . with an immense longing for life, since this is the way I have been living.

PAULO FREIRE,
Learning to Question (1989)

Note: This article originally appeared as "Teaching As an Act of Love," in A. Darder, ed., *Reclaiming Our Voices* (Los Angeles: California Association of Bilingual Education, 1998), pp. 25–44.

For Paulo Freire, life was unquestionably his most enduring passion. As I reflect on his life and his great passion, with every turn of ideas, I'm brought back to the intensity of his love and its manifestation in our work and our lives. Here, let me say quickly that I am speaking neither of a liberal, romanticized, or merely feel-good notion of love that so often is mistakenly attributed to this term, nor the long-suffering and self-effacing variety associated with traditional religious formation. Nothing could be further from the truth. If there was anything that Freire consistently sought to defend, it was the freshness, spontaneity, and presence embodied in what he called an "armed loved—the fighting love of those convinced of the right and the duty to fight, to denounce, and to announce" (1998b, 41); a love that could be lively, forceful, and inspiring, while at the same time critical, challenging, and insistent. Thus, Freire's brand of love stood in direct opposition to the insipid "generosity" of teachers or administrators who would blindly adhere to a system of schooling that fundamentally transgresses every principle of cultural and economic democracy.

Rather, I want to speak to the passion of his love as I came to understand it through my work and friendship with Freire. I want to write about a political and radicalized form of love that is never about absolute consensus, or unconditional acceptance, or unceasing words of sweetness, or endless streams of hugs and kisses. Instead, it is a love that I experienced as unconstricted, rooted in a committed willingness to struggle persistently with purpose in our life and to intimately connect that purpose with what he called our "true vocation"—to be human. In Freire's world, to be passionate and to love in the midst of all our fears, anxieties, and imperfections truly constituted powerful expressions of our humanity—the humanity we had to courageously embrace as educators committed to the practice of freedom.

A COMMITMENT TO OUR HUMANITY

A humanizing education is the path through which men and women can become conscious about their presence in the world. The way they act and think when they develop all of their capacities, taking into consideration their needs, but also the needs and aspirations of others (Freire and Betto 1985, 14–15).

For Freire, a liberatory education could never be conceived without a profound commitment to our humanity. Once again, I must point out that his notion of humanity was not merely a simplistic or psychologized notion of "having positive self-esteem," but rather a deeply reflective interpretation of the dialectical relationship between our cultural existence as individuals and our political and economic existence as social beings. From Freire's perspective, if we were to solve the educational difficulties of students from oppressed communities, then educators had to look beyond the personal. We had to look for answers within the historical realm of economic, social, and political forms, so that we might better understand the forces that give rise to our humanity as it currently exists. In so many ways his work pointed to how economic inequality and social injustice dehumanizes us, distorting our capacity to love each other, the world, and ourselves. In the tradition of Antonio Gramsci before him, Freire exposed how even well-meaning teachers, through their lack of critical moral leadership, actually participate in disabling the heart, minds, and bodies of their students— an act that disconnects these students from the personal and social motivation required to transform their world and themselves.

There is no question that Freire's greatest contribution to the world was his capacity to be a loving human being. His regard for children, his concern for teachers, his work among the poor, his willingness to share openly his moments of grief, disappointment, frustration, and new love, all stand out in my mind as examples of his courage and unrelenting pursuit of a coherent and honest life. I recall our meeting in 1987, six months after the death of his first wife, Elza. Freire was in deep grief. During one of his presentations, he literally had to stop so that he could weep the tears that he had been trying to hold back all morning. For a moment, all of us present were enveloped by his grief and probably experienced one of the greatest pedagogical lessons of our life. I don't believe anyone left the conference hall that day as they had arrived. Through the courageous vulnerability of his humanity—with all its complexities and contradictions—Freire illuminated our understanding of not only what it means to be a critical educator, but what it means to live a critical life.

In the following year, I experienced another aspect of Freire's living praxis. To everyone's surprise, Freire remarried a few months later. Many were stunned by the news and it was interesting to listen to and observe the responses of his followers in the States. Some of the same radical educators who had embraced him in his grief now questioned his personal decision to remarry so quickly after the death of Elza. Much to my surprise, the news of his marriage and his public gestures of affection and celebration of his new wife, Nita, were met with a strange sort of suspicion and fear. Despite these reverberations, Freire spoke freely of his new love and the sensations that now stirred in him. He shared his struggle with loneliness and grief and challenged us to *live and love* in the present—as much personally as politically.

FEAR AND REVOLUTIONARY DREAMS

The more you recognize your fear as a consequence of your attempt to practice your dream, the more you learn how to put into practice your dream! I never had interviews with the great revolutionaries of this century about their fears! But all of them felt fear, to the extent that all of them were very faithful to their dreams (Shor and Freire 1987, 57).

Challenging the conditioned fears with which our dreams of freedom are controlled and the "false consciousness" that diminishes our social agency are common themes in Freire's work. In *Pedagogy of the Oppressed* (1970), he wrote of the *fear of freedom* that afflicts us, a fear predicated on prescriptive relationships between those who rule and those who are expected to follow. As critical educators, he urged us to question carefully our ideological beliefs and pedagogical intentions and to take note of our own adherence to the status quo. He wanted us to recognize that every *prescribed behavior* represents the imposition of one human being upon another—an imposition that moves our consciousness away from what we experience in the flesh to an abstracted reality and false understanding of our ourselves and our world. If we were to embrace a pedagogy of liberation, we had to prepare ourselves to replace this conditioned fear of freedom with sufficient autonomy and responsibility to struggle for an educational praxis and a way of life that could support democratic forms of economic and cultural existence.

Freire often addressed the notion of fear in his speeches and in his writings. In his eyes, fear and revolutionary dreams were unquestionably linked. The more we were willing to struggle for an emancipatory dream, the more apt we were to know intimately the experience of fear, how to control and educate our fear, and, finally, how to transform that fear into courage. Moreover, we could come to recognize our fear as a signal that we are engaged in critical opposition to the status quo and in transformative work toward the manifestation of our revolutionary dreams.

In many ways, Freire attempted to show us through his own life that facing our fears and contending with our suffering are inevitable and necessary human dimensions of our quest to make and remake history, of our quest to make a new world from our dreams. Often, he likened our movement toward greater humanity as a form of *childbirth, and a painful one.* This *labor of love* constitutes a critical process in our struggle to break the *oppressor-oppressed* contradiction and the conflicting beliefs that incarcerate our humanity. Freire's description of this duality is both forthright and sobering.

> The oppressed suffer from the duality which has established itself in their innermost being. They discover that without freedom they cannot exist authentically. Yet, although they desire authentic existence, they fear it. They are at one and the same time themselves and the oppressor whose consciousness they have internalized. The conflict lies in the choice between being wholly themselves or being divided; between ejecting the oppressor within or not ejecting him; between human solidarity or alienation; between following prescriptions or having choices; between being spectators or actors, between acting or having the illusion of acting through the action of the oppressors; between speaking out or being silent, castrated in their power to create and re-create, in their power to transform the world (1970, 32–33).

Freire firmly believed that if we were to embrace a pedagogy of freedom, we had to break out of this duality. We had to come to see how the domesticating power of the dominant ideology causes teachers to become ambiguous and indecisive, even in the face of blatant injustice. Critical educators had to struggle together against a variety of punitive and threatening methods used by many administrators to instill a fear of freedom. Because if this domesticating role were not rejected, even progressive teachers could fall prey to *fatalism*—a condition that negates passion and destroys the capacity to dream—making them each day more politically vulnerable and less able to face the challenges before them.

Fatalism is a notion that Freire refused ever to accept. At every turn, he emphatically rejected the idea that nothing could be done about the educational consequences of economic inequalities and social injustice. "If the economic and political power of the ruling class denied subordinate populations the space to survive, it was not because it should be that way" (Freire 1997b, 36). Instead, the asymmetrical relations of power that perpetuate fatalism among those with little power had to be challenged. This required teachers to problematize the conditions of schooling with their colleagues and students, and with parents, and through a critical praxis of reflection, dialogue, and action become capable of *announcing justice*. But such an announcement required a total *denouncement of fatalism*, which would unleash our power to push against the limits, create new spaces, and begin redefining our vision of education and society.

CAPTITALISM AS THE ROOT OF DOMINATION

Brutalizing the work force by subjecting them to routine procedures is part of the nature of the capitalist mode of production. And what is taking place in the reproduction of knowledge in the schools is in large part a reproduction of that mechanism (Freire and Faundez 1989, 42).

The question of power is ever present in Freire's work, as is his intimacy with the struggle for democracy. At this juncture, it is vitally important that we turn to Freire's ideological beginnings—a dimension of his work that often has been negated or simply ignored by many liberals and progressives who embraced his pedagogical ideas. A quick scan of the writings cited in *Pedagogy of the Oppressed* clearly illustrates that Freire's work was unabashedly grounded in Marxist-socialist thought. Without question, when Freire spoke of the "ruling class" or the "oppressors," he was referring to historical class distinctions and class conflict within the structure of capitalist society—capitalism was the root of domination. His theoretical analysis was fundamentally rooted in notions of class formation, particularly with respect to how the national political economy relegated the greater majority of its workers to an exploited and marginalized class. However, for Freire the struggle against economic domination could not be waged effectively without a humanizing praxis that could both engage the complex phenomenon of class struggle and effectively foster the conditions for critical social agency among the masses.

Although heavily criticized on the left for his failure to provide a more systematic theoretical argument against capitalism, Freire's work never retreated from a critique of capitalism and a recognition of capitalist logic as the primary totalizing force in the world. This is to say that he firmly believed that the phenomenon of cultural invasion worldwide was fundamentally driven by the profit motives of capitalists.

During my early years as a critical educator, I, like so many, failed to adequately comprehend and incorporate this essential dimension of Freire's work. Critical educators of color in the United States saw racism as the major culprit of our oppression and insisted that Freire engage this issue more substantively. Although he openly acknowledged the existence of racism, he was reticent to abandon the notion of class struggle and often warned us against losing sight of the manner in "which the class factor is hidden within both sexual and racial discrimination" (Freire 1997b, 86).

Our dialogues with him on this issue often were lively and intense because in many ways, Freire questioned the limits of cultural nationalism and our blind faith in a politics of identity. At several different conferences, where educators of color called for separate dialogues with him, he told us that he could not understand why we insisted in dividing ourselves. With true angst, Freire explained to us: "I cannot perceive in my mind how blacks in America can be liberated without Chicanos being liberated, or how Chicanos can be liberated without Native Americans being liberated, or Native Americans liberated without whites being liberated." He insisted that the struggle against oppression was a human struggle in which we had to build solidarity across our differences if we were to change a world engulfed by capitalism. "The lack of unity among the reconcilable 'different' helps the hegemony of the antagonistic 'different,' " he said. "The most important fight is against the main enemy" (Freire 1997b 85). As might be expected, many of us walked away frustrated. Only recently have I come to understand the political limitations of our parochial discourse.

The world economy has changed profoundly since the release of *Pedagogy of the Oppressed*, yet Freire's message remains more relevant than ever. As capital, labor, and knowledge increasingly are conceived of in global terms, the influential role of capital is expanded exponentially, and the "globalization" of national and local economies is changing the underlying basis of the nation-state (Carnoy 1997). These structural changes are reflected in the theories and practices of public schooling. As a consequence, "There is now a radical separation in the curriculum between the programs that do the most concrete training for jobs and the programs that do the most critical reflection. Such job separation reduces the capacity of workers to challenge the system" (Shor and Freire 1987, 47).

Moreover, as Ladislau Dowbor (1997) eloquently argues in his preface to *Pedagogy of the Heart*, we must remove the blinders and see capitalism as the generator of scarcity. We cannot afford to ignore the growing gap between the rich and the poor caused by an increasing economic polarization that belies neoliberal theories of the trickle-down effect. And despite an abundance of technological devices flooding the marketplace, clean rivers, clean air, clean drinking water, chemical-free food, free time, and the space for adult and children to socialize freely has diminished. "Capitalism requires that free-of-charge happiness be [replaced with] what can be bought and sold" (26). Yet seldom do we find, along with the resounding praises paid to technology, a discussion of how technological revolutions have exposed the wretchedness of capitalism—millions of people dying from starvation alongside unprecedented wealth. And even more disconcerting is the deleterious impact of globalized capitalism upon the social and environmental interests of humanity—interests that seem to receive little concern next to the profit motives of transnational corporations.

CHALLENGING OUR LIMITATIONS

In order to achieve humanization, which presupposes the elimination of dehumanizing oppression, it is absolutely necessary to surmount the limit-situations in which men [and women] are reduced to things (Freire 1970, 93).

Although Freire's historical, regional, and class experiences were different from many of ours, his political purpose was clear and consistent. To achieve a liberatory practice, we had to challenge the conditions that limit our social agency and our capacity to intervene and transform our world. Freire's frequent response to questions about factors that perpetuate educational injustice was to challenge us to consider the nature of the limits we were confronting. He urged us to consider how we might transcend these limitations in order to discover that beyond these situations, and in contradiction to them, lie *untested feasibilities* for personal, institutional, and socio-economic restructuring. For example, in thinking back to how many educators of color responded to Freire's insistence that we create alliances to struggle against capitalism, many of us could not break loose from our deep-rooted (and objectified) distrust of "whites," nor could we move beyond our self-righteous justification of our sectarianism. These represented two of the limit-situations that prevented us from establishing the kind of democratic solidarity or *unity within diversity* that potentially could generate profound shifts in the political and economic systems that intensify racism. Freire knew this and yet listened attentively to our concerns and frustrations within the context of our dialogues, always with respect and a deep faith in the power of our political commitment and perseverance.

Freire deeply believed that the rebuilding of solidarity among educators was a vital and necessary radical objective because solidarity moved against the grain of "capitalism's intrinsic perversity, its anti-solidarity nature" (Freire 1997b, 88). Throughout his writings, Freire warned us repeatedly against sectarianism. "Sectarianism in any quarter is an obstacle to the emancipation of [human]kind" (Freire 1970, 22). "While fighting for my dream, I must not become passionately closed within myself" (Freire 1997b, 50). In many instances, he linked our ability to create solidarity with our capacity for *tolerance*.

At a critical scholars' conference in Boston during the summer of 1991, I came face to face with Freire's notion of tolerance. The meetings had been quite intense, particularly with respect to the concerns of feminist scholars within the field. Rather than exemplifying dialogue, I felt the exchanges began to take on a rather virulent tone. In my frustration, I stood up and fired away at one of the presenters. Freire seemed upset with my response. The following day during my presentation, I again proceeded to critique passionately the lack of substantive commitment to the principles of dialogue and solidarity among the group, focusing my critique on issues of cultural and class differences among many of us. Freire's response to my comments that afternoon remains with me to this day. He was particularly concerned with what he judged as my lack of tolerance and beseeched me to behave with greater tolerance in the future, if I was to continue this work effectively. With great political fervor, I rejected Freire's position, making the case that what we needed was to be more *intolerant*—of oppression and social injustice! For years, I licked my wounds over being *scolded* in public by Freire. But eight years later, I must confess that I recognize great wisdom in Freire's advice. Despite my undeniable political commitment, I was lacking tolerance as "revolutionary virtue—the wisdom of being able to live with what is different, so as to be able to fight the common enemy" (Freire and Faundez 1989, 18).

Let us stop for a moment and recognize that just as we all face limit-situations in our world and within ourselves, Freire, too, faced such issues in his private and public life. In 1964, after launching the most successful national literacy campaign Brazil had ever known, he was imprisoned and exiled by the right-wing military dictatorship that had overthrown the democratically elected government of João

Goulart. Freire remained in exile for almost sixteen years. But despite the pain and hardships he and his family experienced, Freire's work as an educator and cultural worker continued unabated. In reminiscences of those years, I recall most the sense that Freire clearly understood domination and exploitation as a worldwide phenomenon. He recognized that within the political struggle for a socialist democracy, a myriad of legitimate political projects existed that, regardless of location, were unequivocally linked by their purpose and commitment to economic and cultural democracy. On a more personal level, he spoke of enduring the pain and suffering of exile, while at the same time not reducing his life to grieving alone. "I do not live only in the past. Rather, I exist in the present, where I prepare myself for the possible" (Freire 1997b, 67). Hence, Freire's experience of exile was as much a time of facing a multitude of fears, sorrows, and doubts within unfamiliar contexts as it was a time for remaking himself anew and restoring the dreams that had been shattered.

As Freire's work became more prominent within the United States, he also grappled with a variety of issues that both challenged and concerned him. For almost three decades, feminists across the country fiercely critiqued the sexism of his language. In some arenas, Marxist scholars criticized him brutally for his failure to provide a systematic analysis of class, capitalism, and schooling. To the dismay of many scholars, educators, and organizers of color, Freire seemed at times unwilling (or unable) to engage, with greater depth and specificity, the perverse nature of racism and its particular historical formations within the United States. Neither could he easily accept, from a historical materialist perspective, the legitimacy of the Chicano movement and its emphasis on a mythological homeland, Atzlan. Along the same lines, Freire also questioned the uncompromising resistance or refusal of many radical educators of color to assume the national identity of "American"—an act that he believed fundamentally weakened our position and limited our material struggle for social and economic justice. Beyond these issues, he also harbored serious concerns over what he perceived as the splintered nature of the critical pedagogy movement in the United States. Yet most of these issues were seldom engaged substantively in public, but rather were the fodder of private dialogues and solitary reflections.

Given this history, it is a real tribute to Freire that in *Pedagogy of the Heart* (its original title was *Under the Shade of the Mango Tree*), written shortly before his death, Freire demonstrated signs of change and deepening in his thinking about many of these issues. For example, the language in the book finally reflected an inclusiveness of women when making general references, which had been missing in his earlier writings. He spoke to the issue of capitalism more boldly than ever before and considered the nature of "globalization" and its meaning for radical educators. He also addressed issues of diversity and racism, acknowledging openly that "we cannot reduce all prejudice to a classist explanation, but we may not overlook it in understanding the different kinds of discrimination" (86). And more forcefully than ever, he spoke to the necessity of moving beyond our reconcilable differences so that we might forge an effective attack against the wiles of advanced capitalism in the world.

THE CAPACITY TO ALWAYS BEGIN ANEW

This capacity to always begin anew, to make, to reconstruct, and to not spoil, to refuse to bureaucratize the mind, to understand and to live [life] as a process—live to become—is something that always accompanied me throughout life. This is an indispensable quality of a good teacher (Freire 1993, 98).

The examples above are not intended to diminish in any way Freire's contribution or the memory of his work, but rather to remember him within his totality as a human being with many of the conflicts and contradictions that confront us all and yet with an expansive ability for sustained reflection, inquiry, and dialogue. But most important, he had an incredible capacity to reconstruct and *begin always anew*. For Freire, there was no question but that he, others, and the world were always in a state of becoming, of transforming, and reinventing ourselves as part of our human historical process. This belief served as the foundation for his unrelenting search for freedom and his unwavering hope in the future. In the tradition of Marx, he believed that we both make and are made by our world, and thus all human beings are the makers of history. In Freire's view, knowledge could not be divorced from historical continuity. Like us, "History is a process of being limited and conditioned by the knowledge that we produce. Nothing that we engender, live, think, and make explicit takes place outside of time and history" (Freire 1997b, 32). More important, educators had to recognize that "it was when the majorities are denied their right to participate in history as Subjects that they become dominated and alienated" (Freire 1970, 125).

Freire was convinced that this historical process needed to take place within schools and communities, anchored in relationships of solidarity. He urged critical educators to build communities of solidarity as a form of *networking*, to help us in problematizing the debilitating conditions of globalized economic inequality and in confronting the devastating impact of neoliberal economic and social policies on the world's population. Freire believed that teachers, students, parents, and others could reproduce skills and knowledge through networks formed around schools and adult education, youth organizations, and religious organizations that have a common democratic interest to enhance individual and collective life. More important, through *praxis*—the authentic union of action and reflection—these education networks could enter into the remaking of a new culture of capital, both as sites for the integration of dissociated workers and for the development of critical consciousness (*conscientização*), ultimately shaping the future of local and national politics and hence altering the nature of the global economy. Freire's notion of establishing critical networks is a particularly compelling thought considering the current political struggles in California for the protection of immigrant rights, affirmative action, and bilingual education.

In many ways, the idea of critical networks is linked directly with the struggle for democracy and an expanded notion of citizenship. Freire urged us to strive for *intimacy with democracy*, to live actively with democratic principles and deepen them so that they could come to have real meaning in our everyday life. Inherent in this relationship with democracy was a form of citizenship that could not be obtained by chance. It represented a construction that

was always in a state of becoming and required that we fight to obtain it. Further, it demanded *commitment, political clarity, coherence,*
and *decision* on our part. Moreover, Freire insisted that

> . . . no one constructs a serious democracy, which implies radically
> changing the societal structures, reorienting the politics of pro-
> duction and development, reinventing power, doing justice to
> everyone, and abolishing the unjust and immoral gains of the all-
> powerful, without previously and simultaneously working for these
> democratic preferences and these ethical demands (1998b,
> 66–67).

Freire also repeatedly associated the work of educators with an
unwavering *faith in the oppressed,* who, too, were always in a state of
becoming. "Never has there been a deeper need for progressive men
and women—serious, radical, engaged in the struggle for transforming society, to give testimony of their respect for the people" (Freire
1997b, 84). Freire consistently identified this respect for and commitment to marginalized people as an integral ingredient to the cul-
tivation of dialogue in the classroom. "Dialogue requires an intense
faith in [others], faith in their power to make and remake, to create
and re-create, faith in [their] vocation to be more fully human
(which is not the privilege of an elite but the birthright of all)"
(Freire 1970, 79). Moreover, he insisted that true dialogue could
not exist in the absence of love and humility. But for Freire, dialogue also implied a critical posture as well as a preoccupation with
the meanings that students used to mediate their world. He believed it was impossible to teach without educators' knowing what
took place in their students' world. "They need to know the universe of their dreams, the language with which they skillfully defend themselves from the aggressiveness of their world, what they
know independently of the school, and how they know it" (Freire
1998, 73). Through such knowledge, teachers could support students in reflecting on their lives and making individual and collective decisions for transforming their world. Through reflection and
action, dialogue could never be reduced to blind action, deprived of
intention and purpose.

INDISPENSABLE QUALITIES
OF PROGRESSIVE TEACHERS

In *Teachers as Cultural Workers*, Freire wrote what he called "letters to those who dare to teach." Again, his passion brings us back to an ethics of love and challenges us to reconsider our practice in new ways and to rethink our pedagogical commitment. Freire argued that the task of a teacher, who is always learning, must be both joyful and rigorous. He firmly believed that teaching for liberation required seriousness and discipline as well as scientific, physical, and emotional preparation. Freire stressed often that teaching was a task that required a love for the very act of teaching. For only through such love could the political project of teaching possibly become transformative and liberating. For Freire it could never be enough to teach only with critical reason. He fervently argued that we must dare to do all things with feeling, dreams, wishes, fear, doubts, and passion.

> We must dare so as never to dichotomize cognition and emotion. We must dare so that we can continue to teach for a long time under conditions that we know well: low salaries, lack of respect, and the ever-present risk of becoming prey to cynicism. We must dare to learn how to dare in order to say no to the bureaucratization of the mind to which we are exposed every day. We must dare so that we can continue to do so even when it is so much more materially advantageous to stop daring (1998b, 3).

To be a progressive teacher who dares to teach requires, in Freire's eyes, a set of very particular and indispensable qualities. He believed these qualities could protect radical teachers from falling into the trappings of *avant-gardism*, by helping them becoming more conscious of their language, their use of authority in the classroom, and their teaching strategies. Through striving to develop these qualities, teachers could also come to understand that they cannot liberate anyone, but rather that they were in a strategic position to invite their students to liberate themselves, as they learned to read their world and transform their present realities.

Unlike the traditional pedagogical emphasis on specific teaching methodologies, particular classroom curricula, and the use of standardized texts and materials, Freire's indispensable qualities reflect human values that expand a teacher's critical and emotional capacity to enter into effective learning-teaching relationships with their students. Freire begins with a *humility* grounded in courage, self-confidence, self-respect, and respect for others. In many ways, he believed that humility is the quality that allows us to listen beyond our differences, and thus represents a cornerstone in developing our intimacy with democracy. Freire associated humility with the *dialectical* ability to live an *insecure security*, which means a human existence that did not require absolute answers or solutions to a problem but rather that, even in the certainty of the moment, could remain open to new ways, new ideas, and new dreams. This anti-authoritarian position works to prevent teachers from squelching expressions of resistance in their students—resistance that, in fact, is not only meaningful, but also necessary to their process of empowerment. Inherent in this quality of humility also is the ability of teachers to build their capacity to express a *lovingness* rooted in their commitment to consistently reflect on their practice and to consider the consequences of their thoughts, words, and actions within the classroom and beyond.

In keeping with his consistent emphasis on the necessity of confronting our fears, Freire identified *courage* as another indispensable quality of educators. Courage here implies a virtue that is born and nourished by our consistent willingness to challenge and overcome our fears in the interest of democratic action—an action that holds both personal and social consequences. Freire believed that as teachers become clearer about their choices and political dreams, courage sustains our struggle to confront those myths, fueled by the dominant ideology that fragments and distorts our practice. Key to this process is our critical ability to both accept and control our fear.

> When we are faced with concrete fears, such as that of losing our jobs or of not being promoted, we feel the need to set certain limits to our fear. Before anything else, we begin to recognize that fear is a manifestation of our being alive. I do not hide my fears. But I

must not allow my fears to immobilize me. Instead, I must control them, for it is in the very exercise of this control that my necessary courage is shared (1998b, 41).

Tolerance is another of the indispensable qualities on Freire's list. Without this virtue, he contends, no authentic democratic experience can be actualized in the classroom or our own lives. But it is important to note that tolerance "does not mean acquiescing to the intolerable; it does not mean covering up disrespect; it does not mean coddling the aggressor or disguising aggression" (43). Freire adamantly stressed that neither is tolerance about *playing the game*, nor is it a civilized gesture of hypocrisy, nor a coexistence with the unbearable. Instead, the critical expression of tolerance is founded on the basic human principles of respect, discipline, dignity, and ethical responsibility.

Finally, Freire included *decisiveness, security*, the *tension between patience and impatience*, and the *joy of living* in his set of indispensable qualities. He wholeheartedly believed that the ability to make decisions, despite the possibility of rupture, is an essential strength of our work as progressive educators. He argued that teachers who lack this quality often resort to irresponsible practices of permissiveness in their teaching, a condition that is as damaging to students as the abuse of teacher authority. Further, a lack of confidence was often linked to indecision, whereas security (or confidence) stems from a sense of competence, political clarity, and ethical integrity.

The ability of teachers to practice their pedagogy within the *dialectical tension between patience and impatience* represented for Freire a significant leap in an educator's development. This virtue allows teachers to both feel the urgency of the difficult conditions they are facing within schools and at the same time respond with thoughtful and reflective tactics and strategies, rather than *blind activism*. Key to understanding this concept is recognizing the problematics of those who espouse an ethic of *absolute patience* on one hand, and those who manifest an *uncontainable impatience* on the other. Both can impair our ability to participate pedagogically in effective ways.

At no time is the ability to cultivate a *dialectical* understanding of the world more necessary than when we as educators are asked to live within the tension of two seemingly contradictory concepts of responses. Thus, living an *impatient patience* or *insecure security* is predicated on our willingness and ability to grapple with the complexity and ambiguity of the present, despite the heightened level of tension we may experience. We are called on to respond in *coherence* with our democratic dream, rather than to seek prescribed formulas or quick-fix recipes to alleviate the tension, which potentially is a creative and liberating force in our lives. This dialectical competence also implies a *verbal parsimony*, which helps us to rarely lose control over our words or exceed the limits of considered, yet energetic, discourse—a quality that Freire consistently demonstrated over the years during his participation in difficult dialogues.

Freire placed great significance on our ability to live joyfully despite the multitude of external forces that constantly challenge our humanity. The indispensable quality of *teaching with a joy of living* personifies most the ultimate purpose in both Freire's work and life. In retrospect, I am filled with wonderful memories of Freire— the beauty of his language, the twinkle in his eyes, his thoughtful and respectful manner, the movement of his hands when he spoke, his lively enthusiasm when contemplating new ideas, and his candid expressions of love and gratitude. In his words and his deeds, Freire persistently invited teachers to fully embrace life, rather than to surrender our existence to the stifling forces of economic and social injustice.

> By completely giving myself to life rather than to death—without meaning either to deny death or to mythicize life—I can free myself to surrender to the joy of living, without having to hide the reasons for sadness in life, which prepares me to stimulate and champion joy in the school (1998b, 45).

Although Freire does not explicitly speak of activism in *Teachers as Cultural Workers: Letters to Those Who Dare to Teach*, his theoretical work was never dissociated from his activism. Moreover, he argued tirelessly for the inseparability of political consciousness and political action in our teaching and in our lives. Hence, teachers as intellectuals, cultural workers, and community activists must "aspire to become an association of truly serious and coherent people, those who work to shorten more and more the distance between what they say and what they do" (Freire 1997b, 83). The transformation of schools can only take place when teachers, working in solidarity, take ownership and struggle to radically change the political and economic structures of power that defile our revolutionary dreams.

CHAPTER 2

RESTORING OUR HUMANITY: THE DIALECTICS OF REVOLUTIONARY PRACTICE

As individuals or as peoples, by fighting for the restoration of our humanity we will be attempting the restoration of true generosity. And this fight, because of the purpose given it, will actually constitute an act of love.

PAULO FREIRE,
Pedagogy of the Oppressed (1970)

Let me say, with the risk of appearing ridiculous, that the true revolutionary is guided by strong feelings of love. It is impossible to think of an authentic revolution without this quality.

CHE GUEVARA,
quoted in J. Anderson,
Che Guevara: A Revolutionary Life (1997)

Love and the dialectics of revolutionary practice provided Paulo Freire with the foundation for his pedagogy of liberation—a pedagogy committed to the collective struggle to restore our humanity. Starting from the realization that we live in an "unfree" and unequal world, this struggle involves "our struggle for our humanization, for the emancipation of labor, and for the overcoming of our alienation" (Freire 1970, 28), so that we might affirm ourselves as full subjects of our own lives and of history. But this struggle for the pursuit of our "full humanity could not be carried out in isolation or individualism, but only in fellowship and solidarity" (73).

In *Pedagogy of the Oppressed* (1970), Paulo Freire began to articulate his vision of freedom, one that he believed was "an indispensable condition for the quest for human completion" (31)—a completion that, although it could never be achieved, nevertheless could enliven our hope and commitment to resist the forces of exploitation and domination in our daily lives. In his view, freedom encompassed our capacity "to be," to "exist authentically" (33). Despite whatever ambivalence some might experience with these terms, for Freire our capacity to live free required a fundamental shift in how teachers and students define themselves and the conditions in which we exist. More specifically, this entailed our rejection of the oppressive conditions of domination, the establishment of solidarity with others, the existence of meaningful choices in our lives, the recognition of ourselves as historical beings, a developed capacity to speak out when necessary, and a well-developed sense of empowerment to create, recreate, and transform our world in the interest of social justice, human rights, and economic democracy.

In waging the struggle to restore our humanity, it was absolutely imperative to Freire that we recognize that oppression does not exist within a closed world from which there is no exit. Instead, he argued that it was precisely because oppression is an impermanent and changing historical reality constructed by human beings, that we as free subjects of history possessed the possibility of transforming its configuration. Our task then as teachers and students is to embrace fully this dialectical understanding of our relationship with the world and transform our teaching and learning into revolutionary praxis—a pedagogy of "reflection and action upon the world to transform it" (ibid., 36).

To accomplish this feat requires an incessant commitment to move beyond "pious, sentimental, and individualistic gestures and risk an act of love" (ibid., 35), in order to enter sustaining relationships of dialogue and solidarity—relationships grounded in our unwavering fidelity to break out of the domesticating conditions that trick us into complicity with "an economy that is incapable of developing programs according to human needs and that coexists indifferently to the hunger of millions to whom everything is denied (Freire 1997b, 36). And beyond this, Freire urged us to construct in schools and communities "advanced forms of social organizations, ones capable of surpassing this articulated chaos of corporate interests that we have called Neoliberalism" (36).

Freire recognized that the struggle of teachers to exercise our political will and capacity to decide within schools could be severely curtailed by the tendency to become "hardened" by the dominant bureaucracy's dehumanizing posture toward teachers who seek school change. Yet he recognized that there are legitimate reasons why this phenomenon is so prevalent among teachers. More often than not, teachers who are committed to such restoration of humanity within schools and communities are perceived as subversive, while our efforts to achieve greater freedom and autonomy are discouraged. In efforts to control and "inanimate" teachers and students, school districts, said Freire, "deter the drive to search, the restlessness and creativity which characterizes life" (1970, 46). Nevertheless, he argued, it is imperative that teachers and students strive to unveil and challenge the contradictions of educational policies and practices that objectify and dehumanize us, preventing our political expression as full subjects of history.

There is no question that Paulo Freire always recognized the enormity and difficulty of the pedagogical vision that he proposed. But through the years, he could see no other alternative to the restoration of our humanity than to "supersede" the debilitating fatalism and imposing myths that function to secure our consensus and participation in the political domination and economic exploitation of two-thirds of the world's population. Indeed such a vision entails an ongoing political process, one that can only be accomplished by our sustained collective labor—a labor born of love, but deeply anchored in an unceasing commitment to know through both theory and practice the nature of the beast that preys on our humanity, and with this knowledge, to fight with unwavering hope and solidarity for the inevitable birthing of a new world.

EDUCATION AS A POLITICAL ACT

One of the most significant issues for teachers within a revolutionary teaching practice is our understanding of education as a political act. "The politics of education is part and parcel of the very nature of education" (Freire 1993, 126–127). Teaching and learning within schools constitutes a political act tied to the ideological forces of the dominant class. Education never is, has been, or will be a neutral enterprise. Paulo Freire was adamant on this point: "It does not matter where or when it has taken place, whether it is more or less complex, education has always been a political act" (127).

Furthermore, he believed that teachers' political definition of their orientation in the classroom has to be understood explicitly with respect to their pedagogical responsibility to their students: "It doesn't hurt to repeat here the statement, still rejected by many people in spite of its obviousness, that education is a political act. Its non-neutrality demands from educators that they take it on as a political act . . . defining themselves . . . either in favor of freedom, living it authentically, or against it" (ibid., 63–64). He also said: "In the name of the respect I should have for my students, I do not see why I should omit or hide my political stance by proclaiming a neutral position that does not exist. On the contrary, my role as teacher is to assent the student's right to compare, to choose, to rupture, to decide" (Freire 1997b, 75).

Thus, whether we are conscious of it or not, teachers perpetuate values, beliefs, myths, and meanings about the world. Thus, education must be understood as a politicizing (or depoliticizing) institutional process that conditions students to subscribe to the dominant ideological norms and political assumptions of the prevailing social order. In addition, it socializes students to accept their particular role or place within that order—a role or place that historically has been determined for particular groups in society on the basis of the political economy and its sorted structures of oppression. Hence, schools are enmeshed in the political economy of the society and are at its service. In this role they are political sites involved in the construction and control of discourse, meaning, and subjectivity (Giroux 1983). "The more you deny the political dimension of education, the more you assume the moral potential to blame the victims (Freire and Macedo 1987, 123).

Given this reality, a revolutionary pedagogy discards the uncritical acceptance of the prevailing social order and its structures of capitalist exploitation, and embraces the empowerment of dispossessed populations as the primary purpose of schooling. In essence, a revolutionary praxis turns the traditional purpose of public education on its proverbial head, unveiling its contradictions and "false generosity." Instead of educating our students to become simply reliable workers, complacent citizens, and avid consumers, progressive teachers engage students in a critical understanding of the world, so they can consider innovative emancipatory directions for integrating this knowledge into their daily lives. I would like to highlight here that when Paulo Freire spoke of understanding "the world," his meaning was both material and ideological, not merely poetic:

> When I speak of the world, I am not speaking exclusively about the trees and the animals that I love very much, and the mountains and rivers. I am not speaking exclusively of nature [of] which I am a part, but I am speaking also of the social structures, politics, culture, history, of which I am also a part (1993, 103).

To bring such a perspective to the classroom requires that teachers understand how as a consequence of cultural, linguistic, and economic subjugation, subordinate populations in this country and abroad have historically been systematically disenfranchised. This knowledge impels teachers to unveil the hidden ideological values and beliefs that inform the development and establishment of standardized curricula, materials, textbooks, testing and assessment, promotion criteria, and institutional relationships, in an effort to support and better infuse our teaching with an emancipatory vision of school and community life. By so doing, teachers recognize that the task at hand is not to reproduce the traditional social arrangements that support and perpetuate inequality and injustice, but rather to

work toward the transformation of these social arrangements, within
the context of our vocation and daily lives as teachers.

Schools are inextricably linked to a large set of political and cultural processes that reinforce and give legitimacy to the reproduction of a "banking" system of education, in which the teachers see
themselves as the owners of knowledge and the students as empty
vessels into which teachers deposit their knowledge. The reflection
of the dominant class is inscribed in the educational policies and
practices that shape public schooling. One of the most pervasive of
these, which is currently gaining more and more attention around
the country, is teaching-to-the-test. This sterile and enfeebling pedagogical approach functions to "minimize or annul the students' creative power and stimulate their credulity" (Freire 1970, 60) so as to
reinforce their intellectual submissiveness and conformity to the
state's prescribed ideological definition of legitimate knowledge and
academic measures of achievement.

Moreover, teaching-to-the-test perpetuates the cultural values
of domination through teaching students that they exist "abstract,
isolated, independent and unattached to the world, that the world
exists as a reality apart" (ibid., 69). It deceptively structures the silences of students from subordinate groups by objectifying them,
even within their own learning process. The bankrupt logic of standardization, inherent in the current teaching-to-the-test madness,
adheres to a political "message of conformity . . . and proudly packages itself as an escape from the necessity of critical thought"
(Giroux 1983, 15).

Unfortunately, most teachers seem unable to effectively critique
the destructive impact of this disabling practice. More often than
not, they feel alienated and powerless to challenge the oppressive
apparatus of school districts that mythologize the authoritarianism
of standardized testing and its accompanying curricula so as to effectively conceal its domesticating role—not only on students, but also
on teachers. The "scientific" myths buttressing standardized testing
and meritocracy are further intensified in the popular imagination
by the seasonal publication of test scores in local newspapers. These
scores are then used to rank the achievement status of schools. This
public exposition places enormous public and state pressure on

school districts; pressure that school district officials displace upon principals; which principals, in turn, displace on teachers; and teachers on students and their parents.

To make matters worse, in some states, like California, teachers are promised additional merit pay if their students' scores improve. What goes unseen or unacknowledged is the way school administrators use such oppressive policies to further domesticate and instill in teachers a "fear of freedom" (Freire 1998b). Hence, it is not unusual for the majority of teachers to uncritically defend the contradiction of teaching-to-the-test in the name of helping their students to succeed academically. This takes place despite overwhelming research that challenges the validity of this approach. Moreover, the class-biased nature of this pedagogy of domination is seldom discussed. In reality, elite schools would never teach their students under such oppressive conditions. On the contrary, wealthy schools pride themselves in providing a multitude of resources and classroom experiences that promote freedom, creativity, and intellectual autonomy, in the interest of retaining the ruling classes' "inalienable" right to entitlement and privilege for their children, who are intended to become the future leaders.

Another politically motivated policy of public schooling that stagnates and hinders the development and improvement of teaching practice is the organization of a teacher's workday. What is most disconcerting, at almost every level of education, is the alienating and isolating characteristic of teacher work. The antidialogical arrangements of their labor prevents teachers from establishing deeper trust and knowledge about one another's practice, in terms of both strengths and limitations. Seldom are their contributions recognized or validated, and even less often do they receive the necessary support when they are struggling with tough pedagogical issues. Unfortunately, the authoritarian and antidialogical nature of the politics that govern teacher work makes most teachers reticent to ask for help for fear they will be judged incompetent.

In many ways, teachers replicate the same fears, frustrations, and insecurities as their students when they hit unfamiliar territory and receive no substantive support in developing their teaching abilities within the context of their everyday practice. Moreover, teachers experience enormous constraints as a result of the politics of the punishment and reward system used by administrators to control teacher labor. This is reflected in the authoritarian manner in which many school administrators seek to limit the decision-making role of teachers through prescribing rules for dress, conduct, curricula, textbooks, lesson plans, classroom activities, student assessment, and the nature of parent participation. Freire spoke to the political impact of such prescribed behavior on teaching practice. "Teachers become fearful, they begin to internalize the dominator's shadow and authoritarian ideology of the administration. These teachers are no longer with their students because the force of the punishment and threatening dominant ideology comes between them. . . . In other words, they are forbidden to be" (1998b, 9).

Freire also linked the destructive impact of the traditional punishment and rewards system to the politics of teacher evaluation. He highlighted the unfortunate manner in which traditional teacher evaluation methods tend to focus less on the teacher's practice and far more on evaluating the teacher's "personality"—namely, the teacher's willingness to conform and comply to traditional roles and expectations. As a consequence, "We evaluate to punish and almost never to improve teacher's practice. In other words, we evaluate to punish [and control] and not educate" (ibid., 7). This is not to imply that Paulo Freire was against teacher evaluation. On the contrary, he firmly argued that "the evaluation of practice represents an important and indispensable factor" (7) in the development of teaching practice. But his greatest concern was that teacher evaluation function dialogically, that is, with the participation of teachers and as a useful tool to support teachers in both the enhancement of their teaching and their theoretical understanding of why and how they carry out their practice as they do. Anything short of this simply functions as a powerful domesticating tool in the hands of a system that annuls teachers' efforts to take full responsibility for their practice, while rendering them "ambiguous and indecisive" (6). Freire asserted that it was this ambiguity and indecisiveness that generally leads teachers to grasp at "a false sense of security . . . informed by the paternalistic nurturing" (6) with which teachers are rewarded for their conformity.

In order to break out of the contradiction of this false sense of security, teachers must establish relationships with peers that are founded in critical dialogue. Through such ongoing relationships, teachers can openly interrogate the practices in schools and consider effective interventions for disrupting the politics and practices of domestication that inanimate their life and work, as well as the intellectual development of their students. Just as critical dialogue is a means in the classroom for the development of student empowerment, ongoing teacher dialogues focused on their practice and the conditions they face in schools can support "real teacher empowerment" (ibid., 8). Such collective empowerment reinforces the need for teachers to struggle together in identifying the tactical paths that competent and politically clear teachers must follow

> . . . to critically reject their domesticating role; in so doing they affirm themselves as teachers by demythologizing the authoritarianism of teaching packages and their administration in the intimacy of their world, which is also the world of their students. In their classroom, with the doors closed, it is difficult to have their world unveiled (Freire 1998, 9).

The significance of empowerment to a revolutionary practice of teaching is deeply rooted in a political understanding of schooling as a permanent terrain of struggle, resistance, and transformation. Hence, Freire categorically dismisses the common perception of public schooling as solely an innocent and benevolent educational enterprise. However, given a long history of conflicts and contradictions at work in the ideological formation of institutions, seldom is domination deterministically reproduced. In other words, domination does not arise as a matter of predestination or as a fixed or immutable set of conditions. Wherever oppression exists are also to be found the seeds of resistance at different stages of expression. Hence, Freire firmly believed that the political empowerment of teachers functions to nourish and cultivate the seeds of political resistance—a resistance historically linked to a multitude of personal and collective struggles waged around the world in efforts to democratize education. But most important, he asserted that "the question of . . . empowerment involves how [teachers] through [their] own experiences, own construction of culture, engage [themselves] in getting political power. This makes 'empowerment' much more than an individual or psychological event. It points to a political process by the dominated classes who seek their own freedom from domination, a long historical process where education is one front" (Shor and Freire 1987, 70).

HISTORY AND THE PRODUCTION OF KNOWLEDGE

More than almost any other educational philosopher before him, Paulo Freire asserted that our critical understanding of history and human beings as historical beings is fundamental to any revolutionary teaching practice. Yet teachers have traditionally been educated to think of history in a frozen and fixed manner. For most teachers, history is a subject taught from a book about things that happened in the past—it is a passive and objectified notion of history that strips most of those living in the present of being active participants in the making of history. This issue is of importance not only to teachers of history but to all teachers who are involved in the process of constructing knowledge with their students. Knowledge is always constructed within a historical context. Who we are and how we come to know the world is profoundly influenced by the particular events that shape our understanding of the world at any given moment in time. By the same token, our responses to these events can alter the course of history as well. Moreover, our concept of history must be understood as a plural phenomenon, for a myriad of histories constructed from a variety of subject positions and geographical locations are in the making all at the same time. Seldom unveiled in the teaching of history are the power relations at work that determine which particular intersections of history will be privileged and remain as the official record for all time.

Historical themes must, then, be understood as contextual. They don't just miraculously appear within a vacuum. All readings of history are constructed within a set of values and beliefs that shape the ideological interpretations given to particular collective moments of a group. "Historical themes are never isolated, inde-

pendent, disconnected or static; they are always interacting dialectically with their opposites" (Freire 1970, 91–92). Understanding history from this standpoint helps teachers recognize that official
recorded accounts of history are partial and limited and, thus, that
much of human history actually lies exiled in the undocumented an-
nals of time. Moreover, an important challenge that critical educators must undertake with their students is the process of uncovering,
wherever possible, the recorded and unrecorded histories that have
been marginalized and excluded from the official discourse of public-
school textbooks.

One important place for teachers to begin to explore a fresh
approach to history is with the life stories of our students. Through
the retelling of their stories, students begin to understand history
as a living process rather than a reified set of facts or dates. Paulo
Freire insisted that to discover themselves was one of the most important events in the life of students. As they come to see themselves as capable of affecting the course of their own lives through
their decisions and relationships, they also begin to experience this
process within the collective experience of classroom life. Teachers and students working together can develop greater consciousness of the historical process through their efforts to name and
change their world together. In naming the world and constructing
meaning, students begin to experience what it means to be subjects of their own lives; and through acting upon their world and
changing its configuration in some meaningful manner, they become familiar with the experience of social agency. Discovering
one's sense of being a subject of history and becoming comfortable
in exercising one's social agency constituted for Paulo Freire significant liberatory moments in the development of self-determination and collective empowerment—both essential to a student's
ability to establish solidarity and participate effectively in community struggles for liberation.

As they engage with diverse readings of historical accounts, students also discover that there is never one absolute truth about any
event. Instead, there are multiple truths linked to the different ideological perceptions of those who actually live through historical
events and those who later interpret those events at any particular

moment in time. Truths come into being within the contextual historical realities in which they are constructed. Given this principle, it is pedagogically significant to create consistent opportunities for students to reflect and connect the events that occur within their daily lives to events that take place within the larger world. It is tremendously valuable for students to consider the current events that are transpiring in their lives and the public arena in the light of past historical moments. In this way they can begin to recognize how events in the present are intimately connected to the decisions and events that came before them.

Here I would encourage teachers to consider their teaching in the same light. From time to time, deeply committed teachers can experience moments of despair as they struggle to challenge and oppose traditional methods, relationships, and structures within schools that oppress students, parents, and teachers alike. During these moments it is helpful for teachers to stop and consciously reconnect with the historical nature of their work and the larger social struggle for economic democracy and social justice around the world. Often, we must remind ourselves that "revolutionary practice" is not an end place but rather an ongoing process and life-long commitment to work toward overturning structures of the state that disable our collective capacity to exist in the world as fully integrated and coherent human beings. Moreover, this perspectives reminds us that we are not alone but are part of a long historical lineage of radical activists and cultural workers who have dedicated their lives to education as their primary political project. This perspective can help us not to fall into a debilitating "savior" complex, which ultimately objectifies teachers and students and can further alienate us all from potential allies necessary to fulfill our political dreams.

At issue, then, within a revolutionary practice is that teachers develop the wherewithal to establish relationships and construct conditions within public schools and communities that support personal and collective empowerment—actions that often go against the grain. Such critical relationships must be understood as both a personal and political process for developing the critical consciousness that will move us toward transformative social action. It must be noted that this notion of empowerment is often appropriated by liberal and conservative educators. As a consequence, this revolutionary principle becomes encased in an individualistic interpretation of empowerment that is concerned primarily with the individual's ability "to succeed" within the context of institutional structures relationships that support the status quo. It is thereby stripped of its critical link to the fundamental commitment to social justice, human rights, and economic democracy.

An understanding of the historical nature of our work in education must also be linked to the recognition that there are different historical moments to every struggle. Each epoch is defined by new circumstances and accompanying events that may require very different political strategies or tactics than those used in the past. Thus, our work must draw on the events and lessons of the past but must also consistently work to "reinvent" itself in order to meet current educational needs. This approach can only exist when teachers hold a dialectical view of knowledge, history, and the world. It is our capacity to observe and interpret the power relationships at work at any given moment within a school or district that provides us with the necessary information to move fluidly and contextually. Through experience, self-reflection, and dialogues with one another, teachers build their ability to respond critically to the actual conditions at work in their schools, rather than according to some prescription of action that is totally irrelevant to the moment. In order to accomplish this, we must understand the world in relational terms—even across opposing notions—rather than in dichotomous and fragmented ways. The world exists as it does because of the myriad of relationships and structures constructed by human beings, to which we all contribute. If this is so, then the dream of transforming this society is not only plausible, but also totally possible. To instill such hope in our students requires that we as teachers be convinced of the possibility of fulfilling this dream.

Incorporating this dialectical view of the world in the classroom is a necessary component of any revolutionary educational practice. It is vital to creating those conditions that can break down the alienating relationships that students are constantly navigating in the course of their lives. In the process, teachers must recognize that human beings are not entities separate from nature but are part of nature; that human beings and nature are intimately and intricately connected and cannot be separated. In fact, it is when we seek to artificially separate ourselves from nature that we construct relationships of alienation that result in all forms of domination and exploitation. As teachers, we must comprehend that our subjectivity and objectivity are dialectical and in constant flux. Dichotomizing these dimensions of our humanity only serves to produce fragmented knowledge that is divorced of the very tension that gives vitality to our teaching practice. Along the same lines, establishing hierarchical relationships that objectify students and exclusively privilege the teacher as subject ultimately stymies critical intellectual development.

Knowledge is dynamically produced and emerges out of our relationships with one another and the world. Knowledge is a living process—a living historical process that grows and transforms most freely and openly within an environment that is informed by dialogue. This is in direct opposition to "banking" educational processes, which are predominantly anchored in fragmented and static notions of teaching and learning. It is precisely for this reason that Freire placed such great emphasis on dialogue in his writings. He believed that only through the love and trust that generates and is generated by dialogue could students recover for themselves "the power to create and transform" (Freire 1970, 79) from which they could become "critical thinkers." But Freire's conceptualization of critical thinking is a far cry from the prepackaged sterile and instrumentalized seminars and curricula parading under the "critical thinking" banners in schools today. For Freire, thinking critically meant

> ... thinking which discerns an indivisible solidarity between the world and [humans] and admits of no dichotomy between them—thinking which perceives reality as process, as transformation, rather than static entity—thinking which does not separate itself from action, but constantly immerses itself in temporality without fear of the risk involved. ... The important thing is the continuing transformation of reality ... [rather than] to hold fast to this guaranteed space and adjust to it (ibid., 81).

Another important dialectical dimension of our teaching practice is tied to Antonio Gramsci's notion of the organic intellectual as he expressed it in *Selections from the Prison Notebooks*. Teachers as organic intellectuals strive to make meaning by grounding their knowledge construction upon the ongoing social interactions and political events that transpire in their world. This dialectical view of knowledge recognizes ongoing relationships and human activity in the context of ongoing competing tensions, which emerge from the differences in ideological values and beliefs. But it must be noted here that such tensions are actually a necessary and creative factor, for it is through the open and honest expression and engagement of existing tensions that critical knowledge is constructed within the context of dialogue. New knowledge results from forms of tension that create new possibilities for interaction between human beings and the world.

In light of the myriad of tensions that are ever at work when human beings are gathered, teachers can begin to see how an artificial emphasis on harmonious (tension-free) relationships actually functions to obstruct the critical development of students and thwart the construction of knowledge. This is particularly so when students who experience tremendous tensions owing to conflicting values and beliefs between the classroom curriculum and their daily lives are silenced by the traditional values and expectations of public schooling.

As a consequence, a revolutionary practice requires that teachers strive to stretch the limited boundaries of what is generally considered permissible discourse within the classroom, in order to provide the pedagogical space for students to engage more freely in their process of learning and knowledge construction. By stretching the boundaries of what is deemed acceptable discourse and legitimate knowledge, teachers can construct new spaces for learning and intellectual growth among their students and for themselves. This is, without question, one of the most important examples of the teacher's critical use of power within the classroom. Teachers are often in a position to decide what is considered legitimate knowledge, what topics, themes, and experiences will be privileged within classroom dialogues and student investigations, and how much time and attention will be given to these. On the basis of the decisions teach-ers make about these issues students construct their opinions about what is considered worthy fodder for classroom discussions and what will be promptly dismissed, negated, or forgotten.

The issue of knowledge construction is always linked to ques-tions of ideology, for how we construct knowledge is directly con-nected to the particular frameworks or set of values and beliefs we use to make sense of the world. Yet our ideological belief systems generally exist most steadfastly within the realm of unexamined as-sumptions. These hidden assumptions generally impact, for ex-ample, our notions about why we believe people are poor; what we think it means to be a person of color in U.S. society; the attitudes we hold about children and their rights; how we articulate the dif-ferences between men and woman; our views about God and spiritu-ality; and what we perceive to be legitimate power relations within schools. And on the basis of these assumptions we make pedagogical decisions about how we determine student expectations, select text-books and classroom materials, interact with parents and colleagues, and view our role within the classroom.

Given the uncanny way unexamined assumptions and beliefs about the world unexpectedly creep into our practice as teachers, it is imperative that critical educators consistently reflect on their practices and educational decisions. Doing so helps teachers to un-cover contradictions that may inadvertently interfere in their efforts to construct a revolutionary practice and thus, to make different choices. Paulo Freire saw this process as an ongoing and necessary one for progressive teachers who were striving toward greater coher-ence in their practice:

> In the struggle between saying and doing in which we must engage to diminish the distance between them, it is just as possible to change what is said to make it fit the doing as it is to change the doing to make it fit what is said. This is why consistency ends up forcing a new choice. In the moment that I discover the inconsis-tency between what I say and what I do—progressive discourse, authoritarian practice—if, reflecting, at times painfully, I learn the ambiguity in which I find myself, I feel I am not able to continue

like this and I look for a way out. In this way, a new choice is imposed on me. Either I change the progressive discourse for a discourse consistent with my reactionary practice, or I change my
practice for a democratic one, adapting it to the progressivist discourse (1998b, 67–68).

In many ways, this also points to the importance of creating opportunities to dialogue with students about their classroom experiences and with colleagues who are also engaged in similar efforts.
No individual has the capacity to identify or recognize all the ideological contradictions that impact on his or her own life. We all
have blind spots. Many of the ideological beliefs held within exist
solely as a consequence of early perceptions of the world internalized
before an individual could resist, question, or critique their meaning
or impact—perceptions that we nevertheless often spend much time
and energy defending. For this reason, a community of progressive
teachers who together consistently reflect critically about their
teaching is a vital source of necessary support and eases the path toward a more conscientious revolutionary practice.

This bring us back once again to the importance of building
communities of individuals who share a collective vision and recognize the importance of critical relationships of solidarity. They are
comrades, *compañeros* and *compañeras* who share a revolutionary
love for one another as brothers and sisters in struggle. This entails a
willingness to stretch out to one another through both acts of ac-
knowledgement and critique, in order to enhance in our practice
and develop our ability to contribute more effectively in the larger
struggle for economic democracy, social justice, and human rights.
Along the same lines, teachers can help cultivate relationships of
solidarity among their students that are fundamentally grounded in
a similar critical dialogical process by providing opportunities for
ongoing dialogue within their classroom community.

There is no question but that the effectiveness of such communities is directly linked to our capacity to uncover the hidden values
and beliefs that inform textbooks, curricula, instruments for testing
and assessment, teaching methods, classroom practices, and the
power relations that give rise to the governance of schools. Through

their capacity to critique, teachers also provide their students with alternative readings of the world whereby they can consider long and hard the hidden values and beliefs that shape their schooling experiences and ponder the larger consequences these may have on their lives and communities. Through the process of critique, teachers and students identify together the limitations and contradictions inherent in the practices and structures of the classroom, school, and society.

Teachers and their students also enter actively into posing problems in order to consider possible strategies for intervening within their world. Freire firmly believed that this problem-posing educational approach could support students to become active, critical subjects who could work collaboratively to produce knowledge historically, through their critique of existing conditions and the actions they took to transform them (McLaren 2000).

An understanding of hegemony is essential to a revolutionary practice of teaching and the power of critique. Hegemony encompasses the arrangement of social and political ideological forces that not only preserve the status quo but tenaciously resist transformation. The concept of hegemony applies to all the established institutional structures and belief systems that perpetuate asymmetrical relations of power; the cultural, political, and economic machinery that conserves the control of society as it is carried out by means of moral and intellectual leadership systems. For example, when teachers carry out educational practices that sustain structures and relationships of economic inequality, they are acting as agents of the state in carrying out the hegemonic political project of capitalism— whether they are aware of their function or not.

Teachers carry out their role as moral and intellectual leaders through the power and control or authority they are allotted within their classrooms. This is so even when teachers refuse to acknowledge the power and authority they hold or make the common proclamation that in their classrooms it is their students who hold all the power. The unwillingness or inability of teachers to recognize and engage forthrightly with the manner in which they themselves hold privileged positions in terms of their students and parents, particularly within public schools, constitutes one of the greatest stumbling blocks to transforming the current state of affairs. Irrespective of how powerless teachers may feel or perceive themselves to be, it cannot be denied that they are in a position to ultimately make decisions about what takes place within their classrooms. Daily, teachers make decisions about what will be taught, how texts will be discussed, what materials will be used, what type and quantity of homework will be required of students, and how student interactions will be structured, just to name a few examples.

Coming to terms with this essential issue of acknowledging teachers' power is central to a revolutionary vision of schooling. Teachers must not only accept responsibility for the power they hold within their classrooms, schools, and communities but also make wise decisions about how they will use their power in the interest of constructing a revolutionary practice. Teachers who are unaware of the political nature of their power and authority will find themselves constantly falling into contradictions and unable to develop well-conceived alternative pedagogical approaches. This generally occurs when teachers possess little or no coherent theoretical position by which to assess their teaching practice other than the fragmented hegemonic frameworks and rationales established by state and district officials.

Finding such a position becomes all the more critical given the mainstream curricula's drive to appropriate liberatory knowledge and strip it of its transformative potential—an inherent hidden function of hegemony. Understanding this process we will, for example, ask: How can teachers accept teaching a curriculum that presents Native Americans as if they were all part of one homogeneous nation, when in fact there are thousands of nations and tribes in the United States, all with differing historical, cultural, political, and economic realities. How can teachers not examine the different responses to the genocidal process of colonization undertaken by the U. S. government over the last 200 years—a destructive process that continues to impact Native American populations to this day? How can they teach a curriculum that presents the life of Martin Luther King disembodied from his leadership of an economically focused civil rights struggle intimately linked to the movement against racism, and fails to mention that King was murdered just prior to a massive multi-ethnic political march that was to take place in Washington, D.C., calling for the end of poverty and the creation of jobs and a fair living wage for all working people? How can they teach a "multicultural" curriculum that makes "heroes" of King and Cesar Chavez—i.e., idolatry of the individual—while ignoring the fact that little could have been accomplished if not for the political efforts of diverse civil rights groups within communities and universities across the country. Freire was an acerbic critic of the underlying individualism that informs such a curriculum.

> The notion of empowerment in U.S. society has been captured by individualism, by private notions of getting ahead . . . a utopian devotion to "making it on your own" . . . pulling yourself up by the bootstraps, striking it rich by ingenious personal efforts. This is a culture in love with self-made men. Here, a lot of rich land and no backward aristocracy made the economy very dynamic. . . . The exploitation of Black slaves helped build up the country's wealth, and the liquidation of Native Americans opened up the huge interior to pioneers, thieves, and adventurers. The very economic dynamism of this society has had an impact on pedagogy, putting a lot of force behind individual empowerment, self-help, self-reliance. . . . This emphasis on "self" is the equivalent of the capitalist infatuation with the lone entrepreneur, that romantic and fading factor in an economy now monopolized by giant corporations (Shor and Freire 1987, 110).

Given the covert and commonsensical manner in which the forces of the political economy impact our understanding of history and the production of knowledge within schools, progressive teachers must be willing to engage forces within schools that perpetuate a system of grossly unequal wealth distribution at the expense of the many. Through the courage to pose difficult questions and our refusal to fall into the complacency afforded to us by our privilege, teachers can support new readings of history and participate in unveiling the hidden faces of inequality within public schools. In this way, we can move to construct effective alternative practices and relationships of struggle that can enliven our dreams of justice.

SCHOOLING AND THE POLITICAL ECONOMY

A revolutionary practice of education is fundamentally grounded upon the notion that politics and the economy are inextricably linked. The ideological formations that preserve capitalist structures of domination and exploitation also function to preserve the political structures of inequality within the United States and abroad. Steeped in the logic of capitalism, schools function "as a part of an ideological state apparatus designed to secure the ideological and social reproduction of capital and its institutions, whose interests are rooted in the dynamics of capital accumulation and the reproduction of the labor force (Giroux 1983, 87). Moreover, the politics of public schooling, informed by the economic interests of the dominant class, support the reproduction of educational inequality by replicating "the authoritarianism of the capitalist mode of production" (Freire and Faundez 1989, 42). The impact of the political economy on the educational conditions of students from subordinate cultures is clearly visible in a variety of ways. For example, the intellectual expectations, the types of resources, and the educational opportunities for academic success available to students from economically oppressed communities are in extreme contrast to those found in private schools that educate the wealthy.

Unfortunately for the majority of people, this distinction has little significance beyond the widely accepted belief that if you can pay for an excellent education for your children, then you deserve the privilege. It is precisely through the commonsense acceptance of such naïve notions that conditions of economic apartheid are sustained within U.S. public schools. Hence, it should be no surprise to learn that the majority of students from economically disenfranchised communities are positioned within schools according to the manner in which their communities are positioned within the greater social and economic order. Meanwhile, blatant structural inequalities are successfully camouflaged in the popular imagination through the construction of individual myths that place exaggerated weight on "exceptional" success stories, despite the fact that a relatively small percentage of individuals from poor communities manage to improve their economic status. Such contradictory myths are then used to effectively conceal "the class war raging throughout the country . . . a class war that hides and makes confusing a frustrated class struggle" (Freire 1997, 50).

As a consequence, the class structure of America has remained virtually unchanged during the last fifty years. Teachers blinded by the myth that the United States is a classless society blindly perpetuate contradictory teaching practices that deepen the structures of class inequality. In an effort to challenge glaring economic contradictions and the myths that sustain them, a revolutionary practice makes visible and explicit historical issues of class and their impact on schooling. For example, the class-bound arrangement of public schools has existed since their inception. Public schools were designed to function as factories of learning for the future workers of the nation so as to ensure their consensual and efficient participation in the process of capital accumulation. The majority of public-school students were expected to simply move into the rank-and-file structure of industry.

However, things have gone amuck because of the changing nature of work and an emphasis on a globalized workforce. Rather than keep jobs within the United States—where union workers, after years of struggle, obtained improved "benefits" and worker rights such as the minimum wage, a forty-hour workweek, overtime pay, environmental safety, vacation time, abolition of child labor, and health benefits—corporations have relocated their factories to "undeveloped" countries, where massive worker exploitation can be carried out far more cheaply with greater ease and environmental regulations are few.

Meanwhile, the United States, in keeping with its privileged status as economic leader of the world, now has set itself up as the great information science society. The consequence of this shift in the nature of work is the virtual disappearance of thousands of well-paying jobs through rampant technological development and computerization—factors that, although they might increase the efficiency of capitalist interests, also function to increase the level of alienation in U.S. society. Workers are increasingly functioning within virtual contexts that have become so commonplace, that few even notice their disconnection from the product of their labor.

Moreover, the force of alienation provoked by this intense separation of workers and the natural world has reached such proportions that few seem to have the wherewithal to halt its movement or to challenge its impact. Teachers, too, are implicated in this process as they are systematically stripped of freedom to make decisions regarding curriculum and ushered into the nowhere-land of prepackaged materials, teaching-to-the-test, distance learning, and other technological devices to control their labor. For many, it just feels like an unstoppable "train of progress" that one must board or be forever left to the obscurity of the past.

Even more disconcerting is the destructive impact that such alienation, fueled by unbridled consumerism, has had on students and their educational process. All people, places, and things are potentially converted to commodities, whose value is determined by the whims of the marketplace. "Money is the measure of all things and profit the primary goal" (Freire 1970, 44). The marketplace then successfully "transforms everything surrounding it into an object of its domination. The earth, property, production, the creations of men [and women], [human beings] themselves, time—everything is reduced to the status of objects" (44). In the process objects are stripped of their cultural or class meanings and the relationships that inform their construction.

The impact of this process is often the blind acceptance and incorporation of, for example, multicultural curriculums or methods in the classroom with the intention of "fixing" students from subordinate cultural populations. Here a commodified content or method of instruction is packaged and sold as the "solution"—something it is not. Lilia Bartolomé, in her essay "Beyond the Methods Fetish: Toward a Humanizing Pedagogy" (1994, 173), speaks to this issue:

> The solution to the problem of academic underachievement tends to be constructed in primarily methodological and mechanistic terms dislodged from the sociocultural reality that shapes it. That is, the solution to the current underachievement of students from subordinate cultures is often reduced to finding the "right" teaching methods, strategies, or prepackaged curricula that will

work with students who do not respond to so-called "regular" or "normal" instruction.

Thus, the process of fetishization is as much at work within schools as in the society at large. Schools are constantly courted by large publishing companies hawking the latest educational textbooks and curricular materials that are deceptively "divorced from the leading ideas that shape and maintain them" (Macedo 1994, 182). Companies seeking to establish name recognition with young consumers are eager to generously provide teachers with prizes for school contests or curricular materials that just happen to be inscribed with their logo on every page. Meanwhile, many public-school teachers who are forced by a lack of resources to spend hundreds of dollars of their own money during the year purchasing materials for their classroom, without compensation, are generally very happy to receive any kind of classroom resources for their students.

It must be borne in mind that educational policies and practices have real economic consequences for students from all communities. Even more important for teachers to recognize is that these consequences "are not just symbolic . . . they shape people's lives and their places in the material world" (Carnoy 1997, 16). Nowhere is this more evident than in schools. Schools are the place where students are sorted, selected, and certified. Educational policies that govern student testing, assessment, and promotion ultimately determine which students are going to receive the privileges to be called teachers, doctors, lawyers, artist, etc. and, hence, receive the privileges that are afforded members of that particular profession.

Just as there is nothing free about the way the political economy is fueled and sustained, there is nothing neutral about the way testing, assessment, and credential requirements sustain the class-bound assumptions of each occupation. Through the process of legitimation, schools exercise their power freely to ordain fragmented and partial notions of the world as legitimate knowledge. Working hand in hand with this privileging of particular knowledge forms is the practice of meritocracy. The politics of meritocracy within schools determines which students will receive benefits, opportunities, and resources and which students are deemed undeserving. In this way it legitimates particular values, beliefs, relationships, and practices that are absolutely necessary to ensure that inequality in society is maintained and capitalism preserved.

For example, early in the public-school experience of young children the belief is conditioned and reinforced that the most significant aspect of schooling is scoring well on exams, so they will receive the extrinsic reward of a good grade. If students do poorly, they are socialized to believe that this directly correlates with their intellectual deficiency; hence, their value as a person is diminished. Many administrators and teachers adhere to this belief through their acceptance of the ultimate authority of standardized tests to determine whether students are academically succeeding or not. District officials and principals cling to test scores as trustworthy "scientific" measures of a teacher's competence, insisting that teachers teach-to-the-test and rewarding with merit pay those who successfully increase their students' scores. Yet, as Donaldo Macedo asserts in *Literacies of Power: What Americans Are Not Allowed to Know* (104):

> By giving token salary increases, one is paternalistically placating the majority of teachers, who find themselves in an increasingly powerless position as they confront a reductionist system that aims to further de-skill them. These approaches and their related proposals tend to overlook the material conditions with which teachers struggle in their attempts to survive [the] overwhelming task of teaching material that is politically and ideologically at odds with the subordinate students' reality.

Hidden in the rhetoric of standardized knowledge is its direct link to the market economy and the profit of corporations who are in the business of supplying educational equipment, textbooks, and curricular materials. An example in point is the field of technology. The sale of technology, "a main bastion of capitalism" (Freire 1997b, 56), has becoming one of the booming industries around the world. It has moved like hellfire because of the enormously profitable link it enjoys with the burgeoning so-called "information society" of the twenty-first century. Yet as schools get on the bandwagon of computerizing classrooms, curriculum, and so forth, the question is never asked: In whose interest and to what purpose is this technology functioning? When teachers introduce it into the classroom, what is the impact that technology has upon students and in what ways are students initiated into an uncritical acceptance of its glorified role? Do teachers recognize the privilege of access afforded by computers? A privilege that is certainly camouflaged by terms like the "World Wide Web" and "global communication," while obscuring the reality that "technological advances enhance with greater efficiency the ideological support for material power" (36).

In fact, participation in the age of the computer is only possible for less than 20 percent of the world's population, and even when access to computer technology is available to schools, distribution is not necessarily equitable. Thus, it should be no surprise to learn that even students in the United States do not have equal access to computers. In wealthier schools, state-of-the-art computers with access to the Internet and a multitude of programming options are commonplace, while most low-income schools offer access only to a few outdated computers, limited software, and little or no access to the Internet. In essence, the computer as an educational resource is distributed in pretty much the same fashion as other educational resources such as textbooks, library books, audiovisual equipment, musical instruments, uniforms, art supplies, and curricular materials. The children who already have the most at home continue to receive the most at school. Yet students are expected to compete academically as if they lived and learned on an equal playing field.

As teachers critically consider these issues within education, we are once again confronted with the destructive impact of U.S.-style capitalism on the world's population. What teachers must see is the manner in which we are unwittingly recruited as agents of the state to initiate students into an uncritical consensus and toleration of a political economy that immorally and greedily supports the gross accumulation of capital for a few, at the expense of the many. Along the same lines, teachers must critically consider what the future holds for poor and working-class students as the needs of the U.S. labor market continue to decrease. This is a major concern particularly within poor communities where the population rates are more rapidly increasing, while opportunities for economic development—the primary factor in reducing birth rates—continue to decline. What future will there be for youth workers whose schools failed to prepare them for material survival within the changing economy? And even more disconcerting, how will business and political leaders keep people at peace when they are forced to deal with the unrelenting consequences of unbridled capitalism? And how can teachers today continue to embrace the myths of neoliberal capitalism, when growing numbers of students are steadily losing all hope of ever achieving economic stability in their lifetimes? All this is happening at a time when the safety net of the welfare system is being effectively eroded by the latest wave of welfare reforms. While the mainstream media tout economic prosperity, the poorest people in the wealthiest country in the world are being stripped of the limited state resources available for them to sustain their already meager economic existence.

In the midst of this increasing economic polarization, the meaning of democracy in this country has become synonymous with the freedom to be a good consumer and an agent of capital. As a consequence, seldom are students encouraged to unveil exactly what it means to be a free-market consumer, nor to consider the consequences of overconsumption on the ecology of the earth or the relationship of oversupply and overconsumption to the tenuous stability of labor market conditions. Capitalism has rapidly become the transcendent culture—a phenomenon that is successfully being achieved through the market's grip on popular culture and its representation in the media. The market functions systematically to homogenize the dreams and desires of current and potential consumers, globally. This is poignantly self-evident in Third World countries where many exclusively prefer the rock music, films, clothing, and literature imported from "developed" countries, while rejecting their native folk traditions and customs as old-fashioned and obsolete. Meanwhile, within U.S. schools, very young students already measure their relationships according to the brand of tennis shoe or style of clothing worn or the number of Pokeman cards or computer games owned. The rapidity with which new fads move in and out is also linked to the way the marketplace instills very early in children the notion that the power to consume to their hearts' content is the epitome of justice and freedom for all.

Deeply concerned with the contradictions inherent in the politics of the marketplace, Freire urged teachers to "detach ourselves from the idea that we [and our students] are agents of capital" (McLaren 2000, 191). Further, he argued that teachers struggle "to retain a concept of the political beyond a reified consumer identity constructed from the panoply of market logic" (152). Freire believed that by so doing, teachers could engage students dominated and exploited by the capitalist system in

> . . . the process of forming intellectual discipline—to create a social, civic and political discipline which is absolutely essential to the democracy that goes beyond bourgeois and liberal democracy and that finally seeks to conquer the injustice and the irresponsibility of capitalism (Freire 1998b, 89).

Two serious issues for teachers are the "bad rap" given to public schools in general, and also the way the discourse of "failing schools" is used to justify reform efforts anchored in the language and logic of market solutions to resolve educational problems. These corporate-inspired reform efforts, couched in the "language of management that celebrates testing, privatization, and competition," are primarily concerned with how schools can help U.S. economic interests "compete in the world economy" (Macedo 1994, 165). It's like going from the frying pan into the fire! The consequences are readily evident in the corporatization of school districts, complete with institutional reorganizations. So now, instead of schools being public service "factories," public schools are business enterprises and the ideal superintendent is no longer the person who can lead the rank and file but one who can function effectively as a chief executive officer.

Another disheartening example of the market solution is the rapidly increasing political movement to institute school vouchers (an explicitly business term) in an effort to privatize education. The rhetoric here is tied to the belief that competition will improve educational efforts, irrespective of the conditions under which private schools will educate students. Furthermore, there is no serious willingness to contend with the fact that ultimately, inequality is bound to become more pronounced. Instead, in the name of stimulating competition to improve educational quality, "The hidden curriculum of school choice . . . [takes] precious resources from poor schools that are on the verge of bankruptcy to support private or well to do public schools" (Macedo 1994, 166). The result is that students whose parents can already afford private schools will now legally dip into the well of public-school funding to finance their already superior educational opportunities. Students of lesser means whose parents elect this option are now "free to chose" schools that are poorly funded. And the poorest of children will still be forced to remain within public schools that will now be left even poorer than before. Such a solution produces exactly the outcome that market solutions have always intended: increasing the profits for the wealthiest while leaving the most needy further disenfranchised. Given the deceptive quality of such neoliberal school reform efforts, very little can actually be achieved to transform the hegemonic structures of inequality without major shifts in the economic and political distribution of power. "The hierarchical system of capitalist production will not be altered . . . unless concurrent efforts are made to democratize the economy and state bureaucracy" (Carnoy 1983, 402). Exactly such efforts are prohibited by the interests of neoliberal "reformism"—the implementation of reforms in order to avoid deeper transformation.

Paulo Freire, rooted in a deeper "historic possibility," argued that "in a progressive practice, possible and necessary reforms [can be] viable" (1997b, 74). Nevertheless, he adamantly refused to accept reformism, urging instead that "fighting against reformism is a duty of the progressive, who must use the contradictions of reformist practice to defeat it" (74). Only through such historical social struggle can progressive teachers hope to challenge and transform those educational practices of domination and exploitation steeped in the demonic logic of the marketplace.

REVOLUTIONARY PRAXIS:
THE ALLIANCE OF THEORY AND PRACTICE

Paulo Freire taught that a revolutionary praxis was possible only when we, as subjects of history, retained the dialectical relationship between our objective and subjective worlds. Through this critical perspective, teachers could reflect on their pedagogy in ways that would permit them to unveil the social contradictions that serve to betray their vision of social justice, human rights and economic democracy. But to enter into such a process of critique effectively requires that teachers integrate the alliance of theory and practice in their work. Freire considered this alliance as the very foundation of his practice that could only be explained "in the actual process, not as a *fait accompli,* but as a dynamic movement in both theory and practice which make and remake themselves" (1985, 11).

Theory, then, as a product of a historical process of knowledge construction is ongoing and regenerative. It is never complete but always exists within a particular set of conditions shaped by particular relations of power. In the process of teaching, dialogue is considered the self-generating praxis that emerges from the relational interaction between reflection, naming of the world, action, and the return to reflection once more. It is a continuous, purposefully motivated, and open exchange that provides participants the space in which, together, to reflect, critique, affirm, challenge, act, and ultimately transform our collective understanding of the world.

Hence, teachers who embrace a revolutionary practice of teaching come to realize that this is best carried out through their commitment to praxis—a commitment to engage the dialectical connection that exists between theory and practice. This assumes an understanding that all human beings are intellectual. An automobile mechanic, a seamstress, a person who repairs appliances, an office secretary, or a hospital cook—all people who labor are involved in an intellectual process. However, our society arbitrarily privileges particular forms of thinking in social, educational, and economic terms. For Freire, this issue represented more than just a pedagogical concern. He argued that "the intellectual activity of those without power is always characterized as nonintellectual. I think this issue should be underscored, not just as a dimension of pedagogy, but a dimension of politics, as well" (1998c, 122). Access to "formalized" or "educated" intellectual formation is severely limited and curtailed for the majority of the population. This is not because people are incapable of such development, but rather because the wiles of capitalism with its extreme polarization of the economy require the control and dependency of the masses.

It is significant to note that Paulo Freire moved from speaking of the relationship between theory and practice as a "union" in *Pedagogy of the Oppressed* (1970) to an "alliance" in *The Politics of Education* (1985). This shift marked more than simply a semantic distinction. His concern was the manner in which the concept of "union" could cause teachers to artificially collapse or dissolve the two distinct, although connected, moments of knowing into one another and lose the significance of each dialectical contribution to the ongoing construction and remaking of knowledge in our lives. Freire expressed this concern when he wrote, in *Pedagogy of the City* (101):

> There is no way to reduce one to the other, in a necessary dialectical or contradictory relationship. In itself, inverse in its refusal of theoretical reflection, practice, in spite of its importance, is not sufficient to offer me a knowledge that explains the *raison d'être* of relations among objects. Practice does not by itself represent a theory of itself. But, without practice, theory runs the risk of wasting time, of diminishing its own validity as well as the possibility of remaking itself. In the final analysis, theory and practice, in their relationship, become necessary as they complement each other.

It is true that the concrete execution of teaching practice takes place within the localized boundaries of the classroom. But to remain solely within the confines of those four walls in one's analysis or interpretation of what constitutes the lives of students and teachers is naïvely to refuse to acknowledge the interdependent nature of all existence. For instance, efforts to understand why so many students from subordinate populations drop out of high school without engaging a theoretical analysis of the impact of racism and class inequality (as so often happens) produces fragmented and decontextualized "truths" or interpretations about the phenomenon. From this limited standpoint, "the problem" must be either students or teachers; meanwhile the structures, relationships, and practices of alienation produced by the politics of schooling remain concealed and hidden. Any solution that would be derived from such an analysis would require changing the teachers or the students.

When, on the other hand, teachers have access to theoretical principles, they are able to engage critically both their practices in the classroom and the societal forces at work in the reproduction and resistance of domination. Through this process of praxis, we can formulate well thought out critiques and design alternative strategies for changing the nature of our labor and transforming the pedagogical conditions of our students. Without theory, teachers are limited in their capacity substantively to influence life in schools. Freire believed it was a great disservice

> . . . to separate mechanically the world of practice and the world of theory. . . . Theory cannot be separated from practice. Theory is indispensable to the transformation of the world . . . without theory we lose ourselves in the middle of the road. But, on the other hand, without practice, we lose ourselves in the air. It is only through the . . . dialectical relationship of practice and theory that we can find ourselves and, if sometimes we lose ourselves, we will find ourselves again in the end (1993; 102, 132).

It is ironic that so many traditional educators malign critical forms of education that are based on Freire's work as impractical or lacking rigor. Nothing could be further from the truth. Within a revolutionary teaching practice, theory has as its central goal emancipatory practice. This is a living practice that is composed of relevant pedagogical actions within schools and communities that stimulate students' critical intellectual engagement with their world, support the development of compassionate relationships that reanimate sentient qualities, and fuel a shared sense of citizenship aimed at the well-being of our collective existence. In contrast, educational practices devoid of praxis quickly degenerate into senseless activities that objectify and dehumanize both teachers and students.

In *Teachers as Cultural Workers* (1998b), Freire spoke of revolutionary praxis as a means by which the "minds and hands" of both teachers and students could enter into coherent relationship in their efforts to construct knowledge together. But in addition, this knowledge could serve to rupture and disrupt the traditional structures and practices of domination and exploitation within schools and society that inanimate our pursuits of freedom and justice. To this end, Freire also urged teachers to grapple together with their own limitations and to recognize limited and partial characteristic of their knowledge. It is certainly humbling to confront our limitations, but to do this effectively we need others in our world with whom to learn, to grow, and to struggle. If I seriously want to engage the political conflicts and contradictions that sabotage my efforts to be an effective liberatory teacher, I need colleagues and students who can lovingly, but very honestly, critique my practice—herein lies one of the most important functions of solidarity. Freire considered this a "loving" act, for in his eyes "true solidarity is founded only in the plenitude of this act of love, in it existentially, in its praxis" (1970, 34–35). The important issue here is that one of the limitations we have as human beings is our inability to critique fully our practice solely in self-reflection. Such self-reflection is important and necessary, but lacks the dialogical reflection that provides different ways of thinking about our practice in relationship to our students, communities, and the world and from which transformative action can emerge.

Again, it is this very practical intent that is central to a revolutionary educational practice. It is not a pedagogy that exists only in the world of the mind. Rather, it supports the development of our critical faculties in conjunction with our bodies, hearts, and spirits in the interest of our collective struggle to learn and protect our democratic rights. This is not an educational politics of individualism and abstraction, but rather a living politics anchored in a personal and collective practice that is fueled by our revolutionary dreams of justice and liberation. Revolutionary praxis is rooted in our capacity to take action. Although we need and enjoy talk among ourselves, talk is not enough. Our talk and our reflections must be accompanied by actions—actions that further inform the continued development of our theoretical understanding. Freire considered this a rigorous yet rewarding process in the transformation of our teaching, stating in *Pedagogy of the City,* "The more critically and rigorously I think about the practice with which I participate and the practice of others, the more possibility I have, first, to comprehend . . . [my] practice; and second for the same reason, to expand the capacity to make better practice" (102). Earlier he had said, "Education is thus constantly remade in praxis" (1970, 72).

Moreover, as teachers lose their fear of theory and gain a deeper understanding of its significant role in their work, they develop a greater ability to assess and critique more lucidly the consequences of their teaching practice. By the same token, these teachers also gain a better understanding of the nature of resistance and how it operates within the classroom. In so doing, teachers are able to utilize their theoretical understanding of power to identify the limitations and possibilities within schools for the creation of counter-hegemonic spaces. These are alternative public spaces shaped by emancipatory interests, where students can experience, through a free and open process of reflection, dialogue and action, real opportunities for personal and collective empowerment that are linked to social change. It is "through such revolutionary praxis that [students] . . . learn to proclaim their world, thus discovering the real reasons for their past silence" (Freire 1985, 146).

FREIRE'S UTOPIA OF HOPE

In spite of the overwhelming nature of the political project that informed his dreams, Paulo Freire remained till his death an emissary of hope for teachers around the world. It was his deep belief that hope represented an "ontological requirement for human beings" (1997b, 44). In his view, hope was fundamentally rooted in the "inconclusion" of our being. Without hope, he surmised, only cynicism and fatalism remained, and they were forces of political strangulation, indispensable to the preservation of the status quo. In *Pedagogy of Hope* (1996, 44), Freire stated:

> Hope of liberation does not mean liberation already. It is necessary to fight for it, within historically favorable conditions. If they do not exist, we must hopefully labor to create them. Liberation is possibility, not fate nor destiny nor burden. [For] the more subjected and less able to dream of freedom [we] are, the less able will human beings be to face the challenges. The more of a somber present there is, one in which future is drowned, the less hope

there will be for the oppressed and the more peace there will be for the oppressors.

Freire's utopia of hope is anchored in his lifelong held revolutionary commitment to struggle against all forms of poverty, to contest the arbitrary power of the society's ruling class, to overcome the dehumanizing forces of violence within schools and society, and to confront the destructive consequences of capitalist dominion over the earth. In *The Politics of Education* (1985), Freire began to articulate his vision of a revolutionary utopia, using the metaphors that were so common to his critical pedagogical thesis.

> Revolutionary utopia tends to be dynamic rather than static; tends to life rather than death; to the future as a challenge to man's creativity rather than as a repetition of the present; to love as liberation of subjects rather than as possessiveness; to the emotion of life rather than cold abstractions; to living together in harmony rather than gregariousness; to men [and women] who organize themselves reflectively for actions rather than order; to creative and communicative language rather than prescriptive signals; to reflective challenges rather than domesticating slogans; and to values that are lived rather than myths that are imposed (82).

Paulo Freire deeply believed that one of the principal tasks of liberation was "to affirm our humanity in solidarity" (McLaren 1989, 196). This in no way implied that we should "aspire to create a frictionless world that exists outside of human engagement and struggle" (196). Rather, he urged teachers to embrace the concrete purpose of transforming the structures, relationships, and practices within schools and society that produce human suffering, through our pedagogical efforts to democratize democracy. "I do not have any doubt about the need we have . . . to create a practice of a democratic nature—a practice in which we learn how to deal with the tension between authority and freedom, a tension that cannot be avoided unless through the sacrifice of democracy" (130).

Paulo Freire, the man who so completely embraced hope and possibility, just as completely rejected any notions of guarantees or entitlements to freedom. "No one receives democracy as a gift. One fights for democracy" (1998b, 89), he often said. Change had to emerge from our serious, disciplined, and committed experiences of struggle within a praxis of liberation—an outcome that could never be foretold, prophesied, or assured. Change and its consequences could only ultimately be known in the living moment where we collectively produce our historical existence.

Over the years, Freire received criticism for not being sufficiently rigorous in the language of his analysis and for being an idealist. Some were disturbed by his unwillingness to abandon poetic metaphors, which, incidentally, is very reminiscent of the linguistic style of many Latin American writers. Freire reminded critics that if "you read some of my texts . . . you will find easily in them the influence of the Brazilian culture on me (Shor and Freire 1987, 153). Moreover, Freire was anything but an idealist. From the standpoint of a critical utopianism, his political vision was more akin to that of "utopian realism" (Gidden 1994). He furiously rejected "capricious notions of consciousness" extricated from reality and the "absurdity" of "the transformation of an imaginary reality" (69). Instead his revolutionary utopian vision was grounded in the concrete of lived experience and its dialectical impermanence. He rejected the myth that once transformation of society was achieved a "new world" would automatically be created. Instead, Freire argued in *The Politics of Education* (106) that

> . . . the new world does not surface this way. It comes from the revolutionary process which is permanent and does not diminish when . . . power [is achieved]. The creation of this new world should never be made "sacred"; it requires the conscious participation of all people, the transcendence of the dichotomy between manual and intellectual labor, and a form of education that does not reproduce [inhumanity].

In Paulo Freire's vision, this participatory and transcendent education could result only through our permanent commitment and fidelity to a global project of emancipation, a commitment and fidelity born of a profound love for the world and for people—the love from which a revolutionary praxis of dialogue and solidarity emerges. From such love, Freire insisted, we could develop humility and patience to honor the capacity of our students, even when it is not readily evident; to not write off parents who resist our efforts; and to not give up on our colleagues who oppose our political dreams. In fact, "I have always seen, in the depth of courage of the renegade, even if it was not always transparent, his ability to love, indispensable to the reinstatement of justice" (1997b, 65).

In the spirit of Freire's utopia of hope, we must not only uphold our faith in others but also truly come to learn with them through our practice. We come to recognize more concretely that living a pedagogy of love is intimately linked to our deep personal commitments to enter into relationships of solidarity with our students, parents, and colleagues that support our humanity—namely our existence as full subjects within our world. But it cannot stop there! A pedagogy of love must encompass a deep political commitment to social justice and economic democracy—a revolutionary commitment to release our humanity from the powerful death grip of capitalist dominion.

CHAPTER 3

TEACHING AS AN ACT OF LOVE: THE CLASSROOM AND CRITICAL PRAXIS

It is impossible to teach without the courage to love, without the courage to try a thousand times before giving in. In short it is impossible to teach without a forged, invented, and well-thought-out capacity to love.

> PAULO FREIRE,
> *Teachers as Cultural Workers:*
> *Letters to Those Who Dare to Teach* (1998)

Throughout his life, Paulo Freire affirmed the revolutionary power of *teaching as an act of love*. In *Pedagogy of the Oppressed* he wrote, "Love is an act of courage, not fear . . . a commitment to others . . . [and] to the cause of liberation" (1970, 78). Freire was thoroughly convinced that the process of dialogue, central to his pedagogical project, could not exist "in the absence of a profound love for the world and for people" (1993a, 70). It was through such love, he surmised, that teachers could find the strength, faith, and humility to establish solidarity and struggle together to transform the oppressive ideologies and practices of public education. In an interview with Pepi Leistyna, Freire expressed his view of love within the educational process was, first and foremost, tied to our passion for teaching.

> I understand the process of teaching as an act of love. I mean, it is not an act of love in the formal sense, and never in the bureaucratic sense. It is an act of love as an expression of good care, a need to love, first of all, what you do. Can you imagine how painful it is to do anything without passion, to do everything mechanically (Leistyna 1999, 57)?

Freire's words are truly consistent with what I have personally experienced and observed in the course of my work. Teachers who have answered the call to a liberatory practice of education are, in fact, truly motivated by their passion for learning and teaching and their love for others. There is an enthusiasm and awakened commitment to the possibilities of education as an emancipatory force. They seem to sense, even if they cannot readily articulate it, the manner in which the very act of learning and making knowledge stimulates our human capacity to experience ourselves as subjects in our world. For many progressive teachers, particularly working-class teachers of color, education has served a vital role in our personal and political development.

Often, teachers arrive to their first classroom experience after years of quietly dreaming and envisioning the day when they would stand before their students. For some, their vision of themselves as teacher began when they were children, when they played with their small friends or siblings at being "the teacher." For others it was awakened as they helped a sister or brother do their homework, struggling to learn how to read or write or prepare for a test. As they witnessed themselves as participants in another's intellectual growth—in another's process of coming to know—the dream of becoming a teacher began to form and, like a small seed, take root within. It was a very similar experience for Freire. In reminiscing with Carlos Alberto Torres about his childhood, in *Pedagogy of the City*, he recalled,

When I was a child, as far as I can remember, I had certain tastes, some inclinations, some desires that announced my predisposition to becoming the teacher I am today. . . . In adolescence, I remember many times. . . . I would dream, seeing myself in the classroom teaching. Awake, I would dream of being a teacher. . . . I would play with the idea of being a teacher. . . . The more I experimented by teaching youth like me, the more I was becoming a teacher, something I always wanted to be (1983, 95–96).

It is then no wonder that Paulo Freire believed so strongly that liberatory teaching and our capacity to dream are intimately linked. I recall one day when Freire was talking to us about Amilcar Cabral, whom he deeply respected and considered a "pedagogue of the revolution" for "he put his thinking into practice" (Freire and Macedo 1987, 103). Cabral was in a meeting with his comrades to discuss the revolutionary process that was taking place in Guinea-Bissau. He closed his eyes and said, "Now let me dream." Then he began to talk about what he was dreaming. When someone said it was "just a dream," he said, "Yes, it is a dream; a possible dream." For Cabral, such a process was vital to the political reinvention of a society, where for so long people had been denied the right to dream their destinies awake. He ended the meeting by exclaiming, "How poor is a revolution that doesn't dream!" (See Shor and Freire 1987, 186–187, for a version of this story.)

In a similar sense, many teachers are familiar with this process, as they have struggled to reinvent conditions within their classrooms. They have arrived to new activities or developed new projects or designed new learning opportunities for their students, through their critical capacity to listen to the innovative ideas that emerge from their dreams. This creative intuitive process often helps teachers discover new ways of being with their students in the classroom and new ways of introducing experiences that can effectively assist students to connect more deeply with their own critical capacities, in order to explore the world and understand themselves more fully. This is particularly true for progressive teachers who seek new ways to make a difference, not only in the lives of their

students, but also their communities. However, it is important to
note that Freire's openness to the intuitive "stirrings of the soul" did
not mean that we did not need to reflect critically before moving to
put our dreams into action. For he was always quick to remind us
that it was essential to submit our intuition to "the rigorous test it
requires" in solidarity with others, while "never depreciating its role
in coming to knowledge" (1993, 106). Moreover, he believed that
intuition and dreaming were necessary human elements of a revolutionary process and a pedagogy committed to the critical development of students as full integral human beings.

Students As Integral Human Beings

The concern with engaging our students as integral human beings
has not often received significant attention in critical discussions of
Freire's writings in the United States. Perhaps this has resulted from
the need to theoretically overcompensate for the misdirected tendency in this society to overemphasize the role of subjectivity or
overpsychologize the self in liberal alternative educational programs,
at the expense of critical development and collective consciousness.

On the other hand, reticence about focusing on this issue may
also be linked with historical tendencies on the left to place far
greater importance on the political analysis of societal structures and
the political apparatus of the state than on the concerns of individuals who struggle. Though I agree with the fundamental political
concerns of both arguments, as a teacher I cannot pretend that individual needs and concerns within the classroom beyond the intellectual domain are not significant to the development of students'
critical capacities. Nor can we ignore that Paulo Freire attempted, in
a variety of ways, to present a more integral understanding of our humanity and students' critical formation. Although he never provided a systematic theory related to this issue, he often made references when speaking and writing that reflected the need to
overcome the false separation between learning and the expression
of feeling.. In *Pedagogy of Hope* he wrote, "I know with my entire
body, with feelings, with passion and also with reason" (1997b, 30);
and in *Pedagogy of the City* he wrote, "It is my entire body that so-

cially knows. I cannot, in the name of exactness and rigor, negate my body, my emotions and my feelings" (1993, 105).

Moreover, anyone who ever had the opportunity to spend time with him could not deny that what was particularly extraordinary about Paulo Freire was his enormous capacity to love and to extend himself as a full human being, in both public and personal settings. From his example, we can assert that to become "full subjects of history" requires the recognition that our intellect is but one dimension of our humanity. This view also requires our willingness to engage our students more substantively in our efforts to forge a revolutionary practice of education. It is not enough to teach and learn solely through cognitive processes—in our minds or from books (although Freire often expressed how very important and pleasurable this was for him). Teachers and students also have to also immerse themselves "materially" within the practice of education and the struggle for a new world. Freire firmly believed that

> . . . we learn things about the world by acting and changing the world around us. It is to this process of change, of transforming the material world from which we emerged, of which creation of the cultural and historical world takes place. This transformation of the world was done by us while it makes and remakes us, which I have been calling "writing" the world even before we say the word and long before we write it (1993, 108).

Furthermore, Freire argued that in our efforts to understand the process of teaching, learning has to be acknowledged as an experience that takes place within the totality of our being, as we strive to make sense of lived experiences within the larger social contexts of our lived histories. Only through such an approach can teachers begin to build a revolutionary practice of education that is truly resonant with the actual lives of teachers and students and the conditions in which we must teach and learn. In *Pedagogy of the Heart*, Freire expounded on this issue with respect to himself.

> I refuse to accept a certain type of scientistic criticism that insinuates that I lack rigor in the way I deal with these issues or the

over-affective language I use in this process. The passion with which I know, I speak, or I write does not, in any way, diminish the commitment with which I announce or denounce. I am a totality and not a dichotomy. I do not have a side of me that is schematic, meticulous, and other side that is disarticulated or imprecise which simply likes the world. I know with my entire body, with feelings, with passion and also with reason (1997b, 30).

In a dialogue with Moacir Gadotti in *Pedagogy of the City*, Gadotti questions Freire regarding his view of the body and its relationship to pedagogy. Both Gadotti and Freire make several references to the fact that the experience of the body is integral to the development of consciousness and the construction of knowledge. For Freire, the body is important not only in the process of "coming to know," but also in the struggle for liberation.

The importance of the body is indisputable; the body moves, acts, rememorizes the struggle for its liberation; the body, in sum, desires, points out, announces, protests, curves itself, rises, designs and remakes the world . . . and its importance has to do with a certain sensualism . . . contained by the body, even in connection with cognitive ability. I think it's absurd to separate the rigorous acts of knowing the world from the passionate ability to know (1993, 87).

Precisely this "sensualism" with its revolutionary potential for the dialectical empowerment of students as both individuals and social beings is systematically stripped away from the educational experience of students in public schools. Conservative ideologies of social control, historically linked to puritanical notions of the body as evil and passion or sensual pleasure as corrupting the sanctity of the spirit, continue to be reflected in the pedagogical policies and practices of schooling today. Hence, it should be no surprise to learn that domesticating educational policies and practices that ignore the experience of the body and reinforce abstract, fragmented, and decontextualized theories of teaching and learning seldom function in the interest of oppressed populations. More often than not, students are socialized and conditioned into passive roles that debilitate, and can eventually annul, their sense of social agency within schools. Consequently, the very real and present physical, emotional, and spiritual needs of students are generally ignored or rendered insignificant, which facilitates efforts to obtain their obedience and conformity to the dominant culture of the schooling process.

Yet in spite of major institutional efforts to control the desires, pleasures, and physical mobility of students in public schools, students from subordinate populations do not completely or readily acquiesce to authoritarian practices. Instead, many of them engage in the construction of their own cultural forms of resistance—and these may or may not always function in their best interest. As a consequence, teachers (irrespective of their politics), who are under enormous pressure to follow particular prepackaged curricula within the context of daily teaching practice, will generally experience an uphill battle in meeting their school district's standardized mandates.

As a consequence, the majority of teachers, consciously or unconsciously, reproduce a variety of authoritarian classroom-management practices in their efforts to maintain "control" of their students. On the other hand, teachers who struggle to implement more liberating strategies often are forced to become masters of deception—telling the principal or district office what they wish to hear while pursuing behind close doors an emancipatory vision of education. Unfortunately, having to shoulder the hidden (or perhaps not-so-hidden) stress of existing in such duplicity can drive some of the most effective teachers away from their chosen vocation, irrespective of their political commitment. Others who begin to feel defeated in frustration begin to execute authoritarian approaches to manipulate and coerce *cooperation*, while *justifying the means* in the name of helping students succeed academically. What cannot be overlooked here is the way authoritarian practices are designed not only to "blindfold students and lead them to a domesticated future" (Freire 1970, 79), but teachers as well. Concerned for the need to restore greater freedom, joy, and creativity in their classrooms, Freire urged progressive teachers to

> . . . critically reject their domesticating role; in so doing, they affirm
> themselves . . . as teachers by demythologizing the authoritarianism

of teaching packages and their administration in the intimacy of their world, which is also the world of their students. In classrooms, with the doors closed, it is difficult to have the world unveiled (1998a, 9).

Paulo Freire (1970, 1987, 1993, 1997, and 1998) repeatedly affirmed in his work that the perception of our students as integral human beings is paramount to both a liberatory classroom practice and the development of critical consciousness. Freire recognized the unique capacity of human beings to respond to their learning environments simultaneously by way of the intellect, body, and emotions, as well as spiritually. All of these aspects of our humanity with their particular pedagogical needs are present and active in the context of the classroom—all aspects of our humanity are activated and integral to the teaching and learning process. Hence, to perceive a student (or even oneself) solely in terms of cognition can often result in objectifying and debilitating experiences for students, irrespective of their intellectual capacities.

I want to clarify here that I am not suggesting that teachers necessarily become immersed in the personal lives of students outside the classroom, although there may be moments when this is absolutely necessary and appropriate. Rather, I am confirming that a student comes into the classroom as a whole person and should be respected and treated as such. However, the degree to which this is possible is directly linked to a teacher's willingness and ability to be fully present and in possession of the capacity to enter into dialogical relationships of solidarity with students, parents, and colleagues.

As is likely evident, this view of the student-teacher relationship goes hand in hand with obliterating the myth that the classroom isn't "the real world." For teachers who aspire to a revolutionary practice, anywhere where human beings are congregated and engaged in relations of power (as they are in schools) constitutes a real-world experience. Freire strongly refuted the perception that life in the classroom is somehow removed from the real world.

What we do in the classroom is not an isolated moment separate from the "real world." It is entirely connected to the real world and it is the real world which places both powers and limits on any critical course. Because the world is in the classroom, whatever transformation we provoke has a conditioning effect outside our small space. But the outside has a conditioning effect on the space also, interfering with our ability to build a critical culture separate from the dominant mass culture (Shor and Freire 1987, 25–26).

Whether we are talking about preschool children, youth, or adult learners, traditional pedagogy assumes the posture that teaching and learning are solely cognitive acts. According to this view, teachers need not concern themselves with the affective responses of students, unless they are deemed "inappropriate," in which case the school psychologist is summoned to evaluate the "problem" student. But in fact, it cannot be denied that learning, as well as teaching, can be very exciting, painful, frustrating, and joyful—all affective and physical responses. Freire often referred to these very human responses when he considered the process of studying. "Studying is a demanding occupation, in the process of which we will encounter pain, pleasure, victory, defeat, doubt, and happiness" (1998, 28).

Freire (1993) considered it a pedagogical necessity for teachers to be honest with students about the arduous task of studying. Just as strongly as he refuted authoritarian practices of conservative teachers, he rejected liberal approaches that essentially "coddled" students through a deceptive emphasis on learning as "fun," while disabling the development of their responsibility for the act of studying. When these students were confronted with more difficult processes of studying and learning, the hypocrisy of the "fun" approach often functioned to generate disillusionment as they discovered the truth, causing them to retreat from studying as the material became increasingly difficult. Instead, Freire urged teachers to support their students through the difficulty of intellectual perseverance and critical discipline, to help them not only build greater self-confidence in themselves as knowing subjects but also discover the beauty inherent in the act of studying.

Knowing is a difficult process indeed, but the child has to learn that, because it is difficult, the process of studying becomes beautiful.

I also think it would be wrong to tell the child that there is only joyful compensation for the act of studying. It is important that the child realize, from the beginning, that studying is difficult and demanding, but it is pleasant [as well] (1993, 90).

Along the same lines, when our students must contend with difficult information or concepts that are culturally, cognitively, or theoretically unfamiliar, they often feel fear of being stupid, shamed, or humiliated. This fear can provoke responses of frustration, insecurity, and hopelessness, which can then lead students to withdraw or become openly resistant to the teaching and learning process, which debilitates their capacity to achieve academically. A teacher's unwillingness to acknowledge and support students through these very real emotional and physical responses, so that they may develop the necessary discipline to overcome their fears, can inadvertently set students up to fail—a failure that usually is blamed on the student.

Freire recognized the debilitating nature of such fears and argued strongly (1998b) that a revolutionary pedagogical practice had to consciously engage these fears in both students and teachers, in order to support the emancipatory development of intellectual discipline and to prevent students from abandoning their studies.

For this reason, studying requires the development of rigorous discipline, which we must consciously forge in ourselves. No one can bestow or impose such discipline on someone else. The attempt implies a total lack of knowledge about the educator's role in the development of discipline. Either, we adhere to study with delight or accept it as necessity and pleasure, or it becomes a mere burden and as such, will be abandoned at the first crossroads. The more we accept discipline, the more we strengthen our ability to overcome threats to it and thus to our ability to study effectively (ibid., 28–29).

This is particularly the case within the university, where there seems to be little pedagogical tolerance for the emotional needs of the adult learner. The expectation is that both professors and students compartmentalize themselves within the classroom, without any serious concern for the manner in which the very essence of university education is often tied to major moments of life transitions. This is a time when students are being asked to make commitments and investments related to the direction of their very uncertain futures. Simultaneously, students are expected to engage in their studies and research as objective, impartial observers, even when the objects of their study are related to conditions of human suffering. The academic expectations of the university affirm "that feelings corrupt research and its findings, the fear of intuition, the categorical negation of emotion and passion, the belief in technicism [which] all ends [up] convincing many that the more neutral we are in our actions, the more objective and efficient we will be [in our knowing]" (Freire 1993, 106). Hence, students are slowly but surely socialized to function as uncritical, descriptive scholars, fragmented, dispassionate, and decontextualized in their intellectual understanding of the world. This is an *antidialogical* way of knowing that seldom leads students to critically challenge the oppressive structures that sustain human suffering in the first place.

THE CHALLENGE OF DIALOGICAL PEDAGOGY

In *Pedagogy of the Oppressed*, Paulo Freire (1970, 59) provided an energetic critique of what he called "banking" education, where students are treated like passive receptacles of learning into which teachers deposit knowledge. Further, he surmised that such education *at the service of capitalism* stimulates naïve thinking among students and generates greater failure. Freire argued that teachers had to "abandon the educational goal of deposit-making and replace it with the posing of the problems of [human beings] in relation with the world" (66).

In contrast to "banking" education, a liberatory educational process is one where teachers seek to help students learn how to problem-pose or "problematize" their reality, in order to critique it and discover new ways to both individually and collectively work to change their world. One of the major tasks of problem-posing education is to effectively tap into the existing knowledge and hidden strengths of students' lived histories and cultural experiences, in the process of their critical development. More important, through the

development of their critical abilities students begin to unveil ideological beliefs and practices that function to inhibit their democratic
voice and participation.

It is virtually impossible to speak of a revolutionary practice of
problem-posing education outside the dialogical process, since dialogue is truly the cornerstone of the pedagogy. Central to Freire's concept of education is an understanding of dialogue as the pedagogical
practice of critical reflection and action, which nurtures students' curiosity and imagination toward a greater critical capacity to confront
dialectically the content of their study and the task of constructing
new knowledge. This process of problem-posing serves to enliven,
motivate, and reinforce creativity and the "emergence of critical consciousness" in the learning process, as students grapple critically to
better understand the past, present, and future in making sense of the
world. Freire noted that "whereas banking education anesthetizes and
inhibits creative power, problem-solving education involves a constant unveiling of reality. The former attempts to maintain submer-
sion of consciousness; the latter strives for the emergence of consciousness and critical intervention in reality" (1970, 68).

Freire's political project encompassed his desire to articulate a
process of teaching in concert with an emancipatory vision of society, by which teachers could critically interrogate traditional teaching methods and approaches and move toward reinventing their
classroom pedagogy in the interest of liberation. Such a transforma-
tional vision clearly requires that teachers abandon authoritarian
structures and relationships that silence students and condition
their uncritical acceptance and conformity to the status quo. In his
work, Freire pointed out the manner in which "the banking method
emphasized permanence and becomes reactionary" (ibid., 72) in ac-
cordance with its hidden political intent—the conservation of class
domination. He urged teachers to embrace a "problem-posing education which accepts neither a 'well-behaved' present nor a pre-de-
termined future. [But instead] roots itself in the dynamic present and
becomes revolutionary" (72).

Hence, a revolutionary pedagogy "sets itself the task of de-
mythologizing" (ibid., 71) and reinventing reality through its em-

phasis on dialogue, critique, and transformative action. Key to Freire's view is the conviction that all human beings "subjected to domination must fight for their emancipation" (74), for freedom is not a gift but a right that is earned through committed struggle. He posited that this process of emancipation could begin when students began to eject false perceptions and debilitating myths about themselves and their world "that confuse people's awareness and make them ambiguous beings" (Freire 1985, 89). Furthermore, this required students to confront their individual and collective contradictions—the ways "human action can move in several directions at once . . . [containing] itself and its opposite" (Shor and Freire 1987, 62)—in search of greater clarity and coherence in consciousness and political commitment.

Freire referred often to the importance of dialogue and its role in the process of *conscientização,* or "conscientization," of students—the process of their becoming conscious—and the transformation of life in schools and society. Dialogue represents a powerful and transformative political process of interaction between people. Dialogue requires the interactive and ongoing participation with and among people. We cannot be involved in dialogue alone and in isolation. Moreover, "as a democratic relationship," Freire wrote, "dialogue is the opportunity available to me to open up to the thinking of others and thereby not wither away in isolation" (Freire 1998c, 250). In the face of dialogue, individualism goes right out the window. Within a dialogical educational practice, students are expected to reflect on that which they know, their lived experiences, and on how these impact the way they read their world. Through dialogical relationships, students learn to build learning communities in which they freely give voice to their thoughts, ideas, and perceptions about what they know and what they are attempting to understand, always within the context of a larger political project of emancipation.

Clearly, this process requires engaging not only with shared values and beliefs but also with the ways students differ and even find themselves experiencing conflict and tension. It is important for teachers to note that this is not uncommon or unusual given the underlying nature and purpose of dialogue.

> Dialogue does not exist in a political vacuum. It is not a "free space" where you may do what you want. Dialogue takes place inside some kind of program and context. These conditioning factors create tension in achieving goals. . . . To achieve the goals of transformation, dialogue implies responsibility, directiveness, determination, discipline, objectives (Shor and Freire 1987, 102).

By creating ample opportunities for students to problematize the conflicts they experience, teachers create conditions for students to reflect on their lived histories, so they may consider what needs to change and what actions need to transpire in order for that change to become a concrete reality in their lives. As students participate consistently in dialogue, they become skilled at posing problems, defining the limit-situations associated to those problems, and identifying the best strategies for action. ("Limit situations" is the term Freire used to describe conditions that limit the expression of the practice of freedom.)[1] And once the action is put into motion, coming back together to reflect on its outcome in comparison to their original intent. Dialogue provides a space to interrogate both our individual and collective actions; to consider the most effective approaches to both study and struggle; and to consider if there is something that we can do differently to improve our efforts to know and participate in our world.

Freire repeatedly stressed that dialogue could not exist without a teacher's "profound love for the world" (1970, 77). In his view, love was not only the basis for true dialogue but also a loving commitment to our students and our political dreams. Most important, he insisted that dialogue only takes place to the extent teachers have the capacity to teach with humility and have faith in the students. "Faith in their power to make and remake, to create and recreate, faith in their vocation to be more fully human, which is not only the privilege of the elite but the birthright of all" (79). Such love, faith, and humility are vital if students are to overcome their domestication and fear of conflict. Through dialogue and solidarity, teachers and our students can discover new ways to contend with conflicts and differences in the interest of creating greater instances of democratic life in their schools and communities.

However, it is important that teachers recognize that there are significant distinctions between critical dialogue and everyday conversation: "Dialogue must not be transformed into a non-committal 'chewing the fat' to the random rhythm of whatever happens to be transpiring between teacher and [students]" (Freire 1998c, 249). Both friendly chats and intense debates and arguments contradict the fundamental purpose of dialogical interaction. Friendly conversations are extremely enjoyable activities, but are generally free-flowing and are not dialogue, interactions that are purposefully focused on the development of critical consciousness or transformative social action. Debate—competitive in nature—is the predominant style of communication within traditional academic circles and is generally focused on the precise articulation of clear oppositional points of view; its primary purpose is winning points and gaining advantage over the opponent. Yet solidarity is essential to dialogue, so debate is clearly at cross-purposes with dialogue. Dialogue is collaborative, bringing participants' focus on critical engagement of similar, differing, and contradictory views in order to understand the world together and forge collective social action in the interest of an emancipatory political vision.

Although the process of dialogue can inevitably lead to collective social action that is oppositional to the status quo, our challenge is to live our politics and our pedagogy without objectifying, dehumanizing, or demonizing those who oppose our liberatory efforts. Freire (1997b) warned that "it is fundamental not to give in to the temptation of believing the 'ends justifies the means'" (63) within a revolutionary educational practice, for the dialectical relationship between the "means" and the "ends" is a key concern. The construction of a social and economically responsible world must begin with the way we relate, from the moment we intend its formation. This is a feat more easily said than done, particularly within the alienating and debilitating structures of public schooling in this country. Along the same lines, Freire (1970) warned that "in the revolutionary practice, [teachers] cannot utilize the banking method as an interim measure, justified on the grounds of expediency, with the intention of later behaving in a genuinely revolutionary fashion. They must be revolutionary—that is to say dialogical—from the onset" (74).

Freire often acknowledged this challenge to be particularly great for those who believe strongly that they are one of the few struggling for that which is "just and right"—a ripe breeding ground for self-righteousness. It is imperative that progressive teachers not fall into replicating the very dynamics that produce exploitation and domination in the first place, and think that we will get a different outcome. Hence, a constant question we must be asking ourselves is how to best strive for a dialogical practice within the context of our classrooms.

This also represents an essential question in efforts to support the development of voice in students. Teachers cannot legitimately talk about the development of voice outside of a dialogical context that nourishes and cultivates its development, movement, and full expression. For it is precisely within the experience of dialogue that students begin to experience the process of *conscientização*. Through this process, students discover themselves as reflective beings; where they develop their ability to give voice to their ideas and impressions; where they practice the process of critique; and where they savor the joy and anguish of becoming socially responsible subjects within their world. Inherent in such a purpose is the realization that dialogue is not solely about the development of student voice as self-expression. To stop there falls seriously short. Instead, a critical understanding of voice entails "a process that turns experience into critical reflection and political action" (Macedo 1994, 182). This constitutes a political process whereby students come to recognize that their voices and participation are politically powerful resources that can be collectively generated in the interest of social justice, human rights, and economic democracy.

Freire was steadfast in his belief that a revolutionary pedagogy must begin, first and foremost, with

> ... the students' comprehension of their daily life experiences, no matter if they are students of the university or kids in primary school. ... My insistence on starting from *their* description of *their* daily life experience is based on the possibility of starting from concreteness, from common sense, to reach a rigorous understanding of reality (Shor and Freire 1987, 106).

Furthermore, Freire was thoroughly convinced from his years of experience that when teachers listened closely and respectfully to how students spoke and how they understood their lived histories, we could move with them "towards the direction of a critical, scientific understanding of the world" (ibid., 106).

A primary challenge for progressive teachers in public schools is the creation of dialogical opportunities for students, particularly under circumstances where there are requirements and expectations to use pedagogical strategies that are in direct opposition to goals of dialogue. Yet there are a variety of activities that teachers say are particularly useful for stimulating dialogue and reinforcing the development of critical development in their students. Many teachers use journals to encourage students to be more reflective about their experiences in and out of the classroom. Students are asked to reflect on their assigned readings, texts, or activities, and are also asked to consider how the material connects to their actual lives.

Teachers also use pedagogical activities linked to the production of poetry, prose, art, drama, and photography to stimulate creativity and artistic imagination in their students, as well as the capacity to critique their surroundings. Through such classroom activities, students can work on school, family, or community projects that encourage them to develop their voices and enhance their critical participation together in the larger world. Freire strongly encouraged teachers to create classroom libraries composed of personal histories, written and illustrated by the students. These student books have been found to have a powerful impact in students' developing a better sense of themselves as historical beings. Along the same line, developing projects of study and investigation that are grounded in questions, issues, and interest generated by students themselves is another effective critical educational practice. Of course, the inclusion and effectiveness of these activities is closely tied to a teacher's willingness to critically engage students' issues and concerns openly and honestly as they move through the required subject matter.

In efforts to increase classroom dialogue, a revolutionary teaching practice must also strive to provide opportunities for parents to be involved in substantive ways. The issue of parent involvement was a significant issue for Freire (1993). While still in leadership at the Municipal Secretariat of Education in Sao Paulo, he wrote:

> It is impossible to democratize schools without really opening them to the real participation of parents and the community in determining the school's destiny. To participate is to discuss, to have voice, acquiring it through the educational politics of schools and the reorganization of their budgets (124).

There is little question but that the participation of parents in the lives of young students is important, but it is also of great benefit in the upper grades. Moreover, teacher-parent dialogues can provide excellent opportunities to establish working alliances to further our efforts to transform the oppressive structure of public schooling. To ignore the impact of parents both to their children and as members of a school community is contradictory to a liberatory educational process, for precisely through our relationships of solidarity with parents, greater possibilities for school and social transformation can be realized.

For example, teachers involving parents and students in letter-writing campaigns about issues that are important to the well-being of the community. This is a highly useful exercise in cultivating and supporting an ethics of voice, participation and social responsibility. Parents and students are also encouraged to participate in cultural, educational, and political events that reinforce the importance of community involvement, critical citizenship, and solidarity.

It is undeniable that a revolutionary practice requires the full presence and involvement of teachers in their teaching. Teachers must constantly be assessing their students' interactions and be willing to engage them openly when difficult questions or issues surface. Large and small dialogues are commonplace within these classrooms, providing opportunities for lively participation and the exchanges of ideas, values, and beliefs among students and teachers. To reinforce a participatory student learning process, many teachers will use large sheets of butcher-block paper or poster boards around the classroom and have students write down their ideas as the class pursues these large or small dialogues. This documentation serves as future reference and gives students a clear message that their thoughts, ideas, and input are valuable in the collective process of knowledge construction.

Teachers committed to a revolutionary practice must often search for and bring in alternative materials, articles, and textbooks to juxtapose with those required by their districts. This gives students an opportunity to consider multiple readings within a subject area. Conflicting representations of history, for example, provide students an excellent opportunity to consider why such conflicts would exist and how different readings are tied to issues of power, privilege, and entitlement. Along the same lines, teachers utilize alternative assessment methods that include students and parents in the process, in contrast to those generally utilized by their districts. These dialogical alternatives are essential in order to compile more accurate and valuable information regarding students' true academic needs. This is a significant resource particularly given Freire's concern regarding the manner in which student (and teacher) assessments work, more often than not, against the interest of subordinated students.

> We want a truly competent public school system: one that respects the ways of being of its students, their class and cultural patterns, their values, their knowledge and their language—a school system that does not assess the intellectual potential of lower-class children with evaluation tools created for those whose class conditioning gives them an undeniable advantage over the former (Freire 1993, 37).

These alternative methods are useful pedagogical tools for the establishment and implementation of critical dialogue. Ongoing participation in dialogues that are linked to a variety of activities is very helpful to students, both in the process of coming to greater critical consciousness and in their academic development. The dialogical process helps to renew students' understanding of the world and reinforces the need for solidarity and community in our development as full human beings. Within a revolutionary practice, this effort must be central to our teaching, for it is through ongoing participation in dialogue that students begin to discover and experience their sense of empowerment.

Empowerment is a process that we as individuals must willingly and freely undertake for ourselves. Within the classroom, this entails participation in pedagogical relationships in which students experience the freedom to break through the imposed myths and illusions that stifle their empowerment as subjects of history and the space to take individual and collective actions that can empower and transform their lives.

This dialogical process of student empowerment is not just an individual phenomenon, but takes place within the solidarity of relationships with others. Freire (1970) often reminded us that "while no one liberates himself [herself] by his [her] own efforts alone, neither is he[she] liberated by others" (53). Teachers do not "empower" their students, but they are in a position to support their process by creating the dialogical conditions, activities, and opportunities that nourish this developing process within students, as both individuals and social beings.

Even with alternative methods, no revolutionary practice of education can work towards a democratic vision of life without a dialogical process that supports students as integral human beings. Lilia Bartolomé (1994) found in her study with classroom teachers that teachers who use traditional methods coupled with a humanizing pedagogy are actually more effective than teachers who use progressive methods but fail to truly respect the values of their students. She argues that what is most important in the classroom is not the method but the creation of a pedagogical process that makes education more humane, a process that truly respects students as subjects of their learning. These findings are an affirmation to the centrality of dialogue within Freire's concept of a revolutionary practice. In short, such a pedagogy is enlivened and given meaning by the spirit of solidarity and a political commitment to social justice, human rights, and economic democracy. But more important, it is inspired by our deep love of and commitment to teaching and the world—a love and commitment that also give us the courage to face our fears and "do the right thing" in the midst of painful and difficult situations.

NEGOTIATING POWER AND AUTHORITY

It is impossible to forge a revolutionary practice without the will-ingness of teachers to grapple with the dialectical tensions at work in negotiating power and authority in the classroom. For a teacher to proclaim that she or he gives students all the power is simply not true. The teacher's authority and power cannot be transmitted as if they were objects. Authority exists within a relational process that is manifested according to the contextual structure of power and the relational contingencies at work. Thus, teachers must crit-ically utilize their power in the interest of democratic life or "*on the side of* freedom" (Freire 1998c, 74) to authorize dialogical con-ditions within the classroom. These conditions support and culti-vate the knowledge and experience that students bring to the classroom and their efforts to learn, study, and produce meaningful knowledge.

When antidialogical conditions exist as a consequence of either authoritarian or excessively permissive dynamics, the authority of students' lived experiences is seriously compromised. As a conse-quence, students can experience trepidation, fear, self-doubt, de-pendency, intellectual insecurity, or even a false security related to their knowledge production. These are all responses that can func-tion ultimately not only to repress the personal and collective free-dom of students to act upon their world, but to interfere with their critical development.

The question of teacher authority and power within the class-room is also strongly linked to the issue of "directivity," the act of directing students in their learning process. Often progressive teachers voice tremendous angst over the quantity and quality of direction they provide to their students. Many feel very insecure about using any lecture format for concern that they will be guilty of reproducing the "banking system" of education. This seems to be strongly influenced by fear of being authoritarian on one hand and being excessively permissive and unfocused on the other. In dis-cussing the issue in *Pedagogy of the City*, Paulo Freire (1993) clearly affirms both the directive nature of education and the validity of these concerns.

Beginning with the fact that all educational practice is directive by its very nature, the question that coherent progressive educators must deal with is what do they need to do to diminish the distance between what they say and they do so as not to allow directivity to turn into authoritarianism or manipulation. By the same token, in avoiding directivity they need to prevent losing themselves in the lack of clear limits that often leads into a laissez-faire approach (116–117).

Rather than placing emphasis strictly on the directive quality of instructional methods (e.g., lecture, worksheets, vocabulary list, science manuals, etc.) that may be employed for the introduction of required content in different subject areas—an absolutely legitimate and necessary component of teaching and learning—a revolutionary practice is concerned with the underlying intent and purpose of the knowledge that is being presented and the quality of dialogical opportunities by which students can appropriate the material to affirm, challenge, and reinvent its meaning in the process of knowledge production. Freire again speaks to the heart of this issue.

> From the progressive teacher's point of view, it is not some magic understanding of content by itself that liberates, nor does disregard for subject matter liberate a student. We cannot neglect the task of helping students become literate, choosing instead to spend most of the teaching time on political analysis. However, it is equally impossible to spend all of the class time on purely technical and linguistic questions, trusting the critical consciousness will follow as a result of being literate. . . . Progressive and reactionary teachers do have one thing in common—the act of teaching course content. [The difference in] teaching from a progressive point of view is not simply the transmission of knowledge . . . which is intended to be mechanically memorized by students [but] that learners penetrate or enter into the discourse of the teacher, appropriating for themselves the deepest significance of the subject being taught (Freire 1987, 212–213).

More than almost any other issue, questions related to the teacher's directivity within the classroom have caused tremendous misconceptions that have led to heated debate and conflict among progressive educators. Nevertheless, Freire argued that directivity is always at work in the process of teaching and learning. So, irrespective of conservative or liberal myths about schooling that shroud themselves in the cloak of neutrality, no educational endeavor is ever a neutral affair. The particular questions that are posed are intimately linked to the direction that knowledge production will take and the ideological interests that will ultimately be preserved or challenged by such a direction. This is why a revolutionary practice insists that the purpose and intent that underlies a teacher's pedagogy must be explicit. Freire described his thinking on this issue in the following manner:

> On the one hand, I cannot manipulate. On the other hand, I cannot leave students by themselves. The opposite of these two possibilities is being radically democratic. That means accepting the directive nature of education. There is a directiveness in education which never allows it to be neutral. We must say to the students how we think and why. My role is not to be silent. I have to convince students of my dreams but not conquer them for my own plans (Shor and Freire 1987, 157).

Freire was also quick to point out that it is precisely the "possibility of directivity" within education that permits teachers to engage social injustice. The way they direct the content of study, students' responses to the content, and the political consequences of particular practices and relationships within schools all influence the outcome.

Similar to teacher directivity, teacher authority is always present, whether it be veiled or clearly articulated. Again, it is important that teachers distinguish between authority and authoritarianism. Authority refers to the power teachers possess to influence (direct) learning, thought, and behavior through their responsibility to educate students; authoritarianism is linked to the expectation that students should and will blindly accept and submit to the concentration of power in the hands of the teacher as the exclusive knowing subject. In the simplest terms, authoritarianism results when authority has run amuck. The point here is that teachers must recognize that there exist no human relationships, let alone educational practices, without the explicit or implicit existence of authority. What often cannot be reconciled here, to the detriment of an emancipatory political vision, is the dialectical relationship between authority and freedom. What is essential is that teachers comprehend that authority expresses itself in a multitude of ways within the context of human relationships—some more overt or well defined than others. Hence, revolutionary practice embraces the expression of directivity and authority in the interest of a humanizing pedagogy that functions to break down the hidden, and not-so-hidden, authoritarian structures within public schooling, which objectify and domesticate human beings into social complacency, silence, and false security.

In addition, we must recognize how students also express their authority, although they possess distinct levels of power and responsibilities within the classroom. Although the following is a very simple illustration, hopefully it can shed light on the complex ways authority manifests itself in student-teacher relationships. When a student announces to a teacher that her name is Maria, this is an action that she does with authority because she knows for certain the name by which she has been known since birth. When the teacher responds by using the student's name, he or she in turn uses authority to honor and respect the child's knowledge. On the other hand, when a teacher, instead, renames the student Mary, the teacher has utilized his or her authority in an authoritarian manner to undermine the certainty or knowing of the student.

Questions linked to certainty and knowing are highly significant, particularly to relationships between teachers and students where there exists a power differential. For Freire, this relationship is deemed liberatory only when both the teacher and the students are free "to be critical agents in acts of knowing. . . . The teacher and students *both* have to be learners, *both* have to be cognitive subjects, in spite of being different" (Shor and Freire 1987, 33) with respect to the level of power held. However, "If the dichotomy between teaching and learning results in the refusal of the one who teaches to learn from the one being taught, it grows out of an ideology of domination. Those who are called to teach must first learn how to continue learning when they begin to teach" (Freire 1998c, 114).

Hence, certainty and doubt must be respected as recurring moments in the process of teaching and learning for all human beings. There is necessarily knowledge that a teacher brings to the classroom; but no matter how valuable, that knowledge must be open to questioning. There must necessarily be room for interrogation, if we truly accept all knowledge as historically produced, contextual, and always existing in a partial state of development. In simple, practical terms, Freire described the relationship in the following manner. "Many things that today still appear to me valid . . . could be outgrown tomorrow, not just by me, but by others as well" (1985, 11). This view of knowledge production is lived out by the teacher through humility and openness to be questioned and to respond to student inquiries with respect. Students must be listened to and expected to engage in a similar manner. This is indeed a challenging process, given the shift in perspective required, because "the domination of the official curriculum rests on many things, but surely fixed, expert knowledge is one pillar. If the dialogical teacher announces that he or she relearns the material in the class, then the learning process itself challenges this unchanging position of the teacher" (Shor and Freire, 101). The effective accomplishment of this shift necessitates, first of all, the willingness of the teachers to take responsibility for what they know: "It does not mean that the educator first denies what he or she knows! It would be a lie, an hypocrisy. He or she has on the contrary to demonstrate his or her competency to the students" (Shor and Freire 1987, 101). On the other hand, teachers must also reveal what they do not know, with a recognition that knowledge is always contextual and hence, seldom absolutely certain. Freire (1997) explained this aspect of the challenge in the following way:

> I have been always engaged with many thoughts concerning the challenges that draw me to this or that issue or to the doubts that make me unquiet. These doubts take me to uncertainties, the only place where it is possible to work toward the necessary provisional certainties. It is not the case that it is impossible to be certain

about some things. What is impossible is to be absolutely certain, as if the certainty of today were the same as that of yesterday and will continue to be the same as that of tomorrow (30–31).

What this brings to mind is the objective/subjective dialectical nature of knowledge and its connection to questions of authority and educational directivity. It would be foolish to pretend that there exist no forms of objective knowledge or information that students require in order to transverse effectively through their world. Moreover, all cultures claim funds of objective knowledge that have been historically produced, expanded, and transformed over time. What is problematic is when these funds of knowledge are not only privileged but also presented as absolute, fixed truths, fragmented and decontextualized from the historical, economic, and political conditions that produced them. These reified "truths" are often transmitted both in form and intent in an authoritarian manner, which precludes all possibility of dialogical inquiry. The hidden curriculum here is that students should blindly submit to the teacher's direction and knowledge, without questioning the underlying interests.

Unfortunately, such an oppressive pedagogical process can also take place even within a supposedly politically progressive educational context—one where students' rights to reflect, question, and act upon the objective knowledge presented are manipulated, repressed, or prohibited. Thus, a teacher can be politically correct in content, but pedagogically off the mark. To avoid falling into such contradictions, teachers must develop a deeper critical understanding and analysis of pedagogical form and intent. Here again, Freire's insistence on not focusing on specific teaching formulas or recipes of practice speaks to the danger of simply replacing one ideology for another yet leaving the structural relations of oppression intact. Within his conceptualization of a revolutionary pedagogical practice, it is above all the prohibition or oppression of students' rights to participate, engage, question, and act upon the text, curriculum, or lecture material that constitutes an antidialogical moment. This is in contrast to judging a teacher as antidialogical simply because she or he has utilized a particular textbook, curriculum, or method or has presented material in a lecture format.

Often such criticism is tied to partial or unclear understanding of Freire's critique of "banking" education. As a consequence, the issue of lecture formats or expository lessons has generated much controversy and confusion among progressive teachers. In *Pedagogy of Hope* (1993), Freire addresses himself to this issue:

> The real evil is not the expository lesson. . . . This is not what I have criticized as a kind of "banking." I have criticized, and I continue to criticize, that type of [teacher-student] relationship in which the educator regards himself or herself as the [student's] sole educator—in which the educator violates, or refuses to accept, the fundamental condition of the act of knowing, which is its dialogical relation . . . and therefore establishes a relation . . . in which educator transfers knowledge. . . to a [student] considered as recipient (189).

In *Education for Liberation* he explained:

> The question is not banking lectures or no lectures, because traditional teachers will make opaque whether they lecture or lead discussions. A liberating teacher will illuminate reality even if he or she lectures. The question is the content and dynamism of the lecturer, the approach to the object to be known. Does it critically reorient students to society? Does it animate their critical thinking or not (Shor and Freire 1987, 40)?

Although a dialogical situation presumes the absence of authoritarianism, Freire urged teachers to recognize the manner in which the dialectical relationship between authority and freedom is always at work in classroom dialogues. "Dialogue means a permanent tension in the relationship between authority and liberty. But, in this tension, authority vis-à-vis permitting student freedoms which emerge, which grow and mature precisely because authority and freedom learn discipline" (Shor and Freire 1987, 102). It is just this tension between authority and freedom that is permanently at work in the process of classroom dialogues. Moreover, Freire (1998c) argued that when teachers attempt to superficially break this tension, it "inevitably leads to teaching without dialogue" (159).

So, for example, when teachers, in an effort to stimulate critical thinking, practice dialogue to mean, "everyone involved *has* to speak," they inadvertently create a contrived or false sense of democracy in their classrooms. In the name of reinforcing equality or the development of critical voice, they dogmatically pressure students to speak, even when students may not feel they have anything they wish to say at that time. Such a practice ultimately functions as an imposition upon students and converts dialogue into a form of coercion that prevents open, genuine exchange. Speaking to this issue, Freire (Shor and Freire 1987) insisted adamantly, "In dialogue, one has the right to be silent" (102)! And he was quick to point out that this did not mean that students had the right to sabotage dialogue through refusing to speak. In the latter instance, the teacher has the responsibility to engage the student's resistance in a meaningful and respectful manner. The ability to negotiate the tension between freedom and authority effectively is not always an easy process, but can result in powerful learning experiences for both teachers and students.

It is vital that teachers recognize that this ability to effectively negotiate the dialectical tension between authority and freedom is essential to the development of critical consciousness. Paulo Freire (1998b) firmly believed that the inability of teachers to engage this tension gravely interfered with the development of political discipline and ethical responsibility, key ingredients to democratic participation. He expressed much concern for the manner in which many teachers, seeking to avoid authoritarianism, fumble around with the issue of student discipline, as a result of the enormous ambiguity they experience regarding the use of their authority and power within the classroom. As a consequence, most students experience teachers who go back and forth between "the absence of discipline by the denial of liberty and the absence of discipline by the absence of authority" (89). The debilitating consequences of this pedagogical contradiction betray a revolutionary practice and cannot be resolved until teachers come to terms with the dialectical relationship or tension that exists between the exercise of freedom and authority.

For Freire (1998b), the struggle for liberation entails on one hand a deep responsibility to exercise individual discipline freely and on the other the need to exercise authority freely in the interest of democratic life. He associated this process to our ultimate ethical responsibility to struggle against the oppressive structures of capitalism that prevent the function of democracy. "Let's make clear that people mobilizing, people organizing, people knowing in critical terms, people deepening and solidifying democracy against any authoritarian adventure are also people forging the necessary discipline without which democracy does not function" (89). Moreover, such ethical responsibility can only develop effectively within a classroom culture that respects the humanity of all students and is founded on a deep and abiding faith in their capacity to become conscious revolutionary subjects of history.

THE CULTURAL POLITICS OF THE CLASSROOM

A revolutionary pedagogy is intimately linked to the conditions teachers create for their students within the classroom. Here, a significant focus of our work involves the enactment of a classroom culture where students come to clearly perceive and experience themselves as historical subjects of their world. Students come to understand that "history, like us, is a process of being limited and conditioned by the knowledge we produce. Nothing that we engender, live, think, and make explicit takes place outside of time and history" (Freire 1997b, 32). As students engage their cultural identity and understand themselves as political beings of history, they begin to discover that through their individual and collective intervention in their world, they can and will change the course of history. Most important, students come to see the power that is inherent in their ability to define themselves and give meaning to their world.

By understanding the classroom as a cultural context in which history is produced, students can begin to reflect on how their actions affirm, challenge, or interrupt the prevailing social forms or patterns of relationships in their lives. As they build a critical understanding of how their individual and collective actions can change what transpires within classroom life, students can begin to break through their conditioned and static notions of history. They begin to critically comprehend the social construction of culture and the way it impacts their view of the world.

Freire (1998) often spoke of teachers as cultural workers, for in every way that teachers engage or do not engage students, we are teaching values—values about what it means to live in this world and what it means to relate to other human beings. All teachers bring their beliefs and values into the classroom and these are transmitted in how we teach and what we teach, as well as the relationships we establish (or fail to establish) with our students and their parents. Hence, teachers must consistently reflect on their practice, so they can become more socially conscious about what they believe. Freire (1993) firmly believed that through consistent reflection on our practice, teachers could work to "diminish the distance between what we say and what we do" (22). Such reflection entails posing critical questions: What do I believe about the purpose of education? What do I believe about the students I teach? What do I believe about their parents? What do I believe about the community in which I teach? For Freire, overall, "The question before us is to know what type of politics it is [we hold], in favor of what and of whom and against what and for whom is it realized" (22). Beyond asking critical questions, teachers must be willing to be critically vigilant about what they actually do, so they might discover where their utterances and their actions lose coherence.

This question of coherence is a central ethical principle in Freire's (1993) work. He considered it to be an "indispensable virtue" of progressive teachers to practice coherence between their discourse and practice:

> To diminish the distance between these represents an exercise that we should require of ourselves. It is one thing to speak and write about democratic relations between teachers and students, it is another to repress students because they ask the teacher uncomfortable questions. It is one thing to speak of teachers' seriousness, the academic rigorousness, the necessary ethics, the other to in-

clude in the bibliography books recently published but which the teachers themselves haven't read (119).

So to "walk our talk" requires that we struggle to become critically conscious about our practice. To work and live coherently within the context of a revolutionary practice requires that teachers consistently think critically about what they do in their classrooms, through both individual reflection and ongoing dialogues with peers, students, and students' parents. Freire (1993) believed this was important, particularly given the way the "hidden curriculum" impacts the practice of teachers in the classroom. "A teacher can be theoretically clear concerning his or her duty of respecting his or her students, their cultural identity, but the power of the authoritarian ideology with which he or she has been previously inculcated ends up winning, forcing him or her to contradict the theoretical discourse" (119–120).

For example, when teachers, in their desire to motivate students to write, decide to organize an essay contest, what cultural values are being reinforced in our students? What values are living in the discourse of what may appear as a small, simple educational activity? Does this type of activity reinforce a sense of cooperation and collaborative spirit or does it reinforce competitiveness among students? What are the consequences of perpetuating the values that underlie such a contest? Might there be other forms of educational experiences that would reinforce a stronger regard for community action and solidarity, rather than an activity with one winner? How are competition and competitive motivation tied to the interest of the market economy?

The concept of education as cultural politics and teachers as cultural workers can be more clearly illuminated through a critical analysis of how teaching practices are influenced and shaped by both the dominant values of the school and the worldview of the teacher. "No matter what a teacher's politics, each course points in a certain direction, towards some convictions about society and knowledge. The selection of materials, the organization of study, the relations of discourse, are all shaped around the teacher's convictions" (Shor and Freire 1987, 33) and the policies mandated by school districts.

Hence, as teachers struggle to become more coherent in their practice and politics, it is helpful to consider the arrangement of the learning environment; the relations of interaction between teachers and students; how teachers interpret student behavior and respond to that behavior; how decisions are made about what is deemed legitimate knowledge; what relationships, activities, and materials are judged appropriate; what issues and which students teachers believe worthy of their attention, and what and whom they ignore. Through a critical understanding of these practices as limit-situations, teachers can begin to discover effective ways to intervene and transform their pedagogy.

Such questions can also help teachers recognize how cultural values inform knowledge construction in their classroom. For example, within the traditional practices of public schooling there is an emphasis on mandated and sequential content in the construction of lesson plans—content that is often disconnected from the actual educational needs or interests of students. For instance, on one occasion, a very good teacher was involved in doing the science lesson for the month. It required the children to study the parts of flowers. She had wonderful visuals and experiential activities for the children. But the children's curiosity had become focused on some new books that had recently arrived on whales. The children were all very excited about this topic and not terribly interested in flowers. Meanwhile, the teacher, who was making a great effort to direct the children's attention away from the whales, promised them that they would study whales sometime next month. The children, after much disquieted protest, finally acquiesced, and reluctantly moved back into the lesson on flowers.

In this example, the teacher unwittingly used her authority to "inanimate" the learning process of her students by redirecting their attention from the object of their curiosity. Rather than placing the emphasis of her teaching on the process of student participation in constructing and directing their knowledge production, she placed the emphasis on the importance of sticking to the prescribed content of study. Thus, despite the creativity of the teacher's lesson on flowers, the traditional cultural value of teacher as knowing subject and students as passive objects was inadvertently reproduced. It is important to clarify that this critique in no way constitutes a blanket criticism against teachers providing direction in the teaching process. Instead, the example shows how an opportunity for young students to initiate learning stimulated by their curiosity and desire to know can be overshadowed by a very good teacher's internalization of the dominant culture's expectation of prescriptive teaching.

It goes without saying that the cultural values that inform the hierarchical and authoritarian foundation of "banking" education are in diametrical opposition to those of a revolutionary practice. Traditional teachers participate in "banking" in that they place major emphasis on the quantity of content memorized. Freire, however, argued that the most powerful learning is learning that is meaningfully connected to the curiosity and imagination of those who are learning and well anchored upon their lived experiences. He argued that one of the most powerful motivations for learning is an object of study that is linked to the curiosity and imagination of students. Consequently, Freire (1998b) expressed deep concern for the way students were stifled by the "banking" approach: "Children learn early on that their imagination does not work. Using their imagination is almost forbidden, a kind of sin. . . . Nothing, or almost nothing, is done toward awakening and keeping alive children's curiosity. . . curiosity which needs to be stimulated in the students by the teacher" (31). He also said (1997b), "The important thing is to educate the curiosity through which knowledge is constituted as it grows and refines itself through the exercise of knowing . . . only an education of question can trigger, motivate and reinforce curiosity" (31).

When teachers fail to recognize the epistemological significance of curiosity and its powerful connection to learning, they can miss excellent opportunities to use their authority in the interest of the students' right to experience the joy of being subjects of their world. Significant teaching and learning moments in which children's interest, attention, and motivation can be fully engaged are inadvertently deactivated, rendering students passive. Unfortunately, this occurs only too often. Teachers, besieged by the politics of expediency and the standardization of knowledge, feel little freedom to practice the flexibility to permit the learning process to emerge

organically with students. Needless to say, public-school teachers are
under tremendous pressure to "cover the material" and to move
their students "successfully" through standardized tests—serious
pressure that to one extent or another is constantly at work in the
pedagogical decisions they make in their classroom. Ira Shor sums
up teachers' situation well:

> They are oppressed by this race to the end of the term. They are
> under pressure to use certain textbooks or to cover certain man-
> dated topics in a prescribed order . . . with too many students.
> There will be mandated exams at the end and the next course in
> the curriculum will expect the previous course to have covered
> certain material. Teachers who deviate from this procedure worry
> about looking bad if their students do poorly on standard tests or
> in the follow-up courses. Their reputations could decline. They
> could be fired (Shor and Freire 1987, 87–88).

Such realities have remained constant in the United States, despite the last thirty years of efforts to reform the cultural context of
schooling so that it might reflect more substantively the realities of
students who attend public schools. As a consequence of these pressures, often teachers who are working with students from subordinate populations and who possess limited understanding of these
students' cultural values, language, and lived experiences inadvertently interfere with their ability to construct knowledge. This
should not be taken to imply that, say, children of color, can be
taught only by teachers from their own cultural communities, but
rather to highlight Freire's argument that we must take as the starting point "the social and historical particularities, the problems, suffering, visions, and acts of resistance, that constitute the cultural
forms of subordinate groups" (Giroux 1985, xxi).

Moreover, for Freire culture constitutes a complex phenomenon
rooted in historical processes as they are shaped and influenced by
the means of production within society. As such, culture does not
lend itself easily to simple homogeneous explanations; its fundamental nature is to exist as a terrain of struggle and contradictions
within the dialectical tension of subordinate and dominant relations

of power. It is precisely for this reason that cultural conflict, class an-
tagonisms, and social contradictions reveal themselves so markedly
within the context of public schooling. In the United States, where
inequality so readily resists transformation, competing interests are
always at work, as defined by the particular power relationships that
control any particular school site at any given moment in time.
Freire (1985) concluded,

> The more you have freedom to criticize, the more necessary is the
> sacredness of the domesticating social order for its self-preserva-
> tion. In this sense schooling at whatever level plays one of the
> most vital roles, as an efficient mechanism for social control. It is
> not hard to find educators whose idea of education is "to adapt the
> learner to his environment," and as a rule formal education has
> not been doing much more than this (116).

Hence, given the politics of cultural and class subordination,
Freire asserted the need for both teachers and students to interrogate
critically their values and beliefs and their consequences for a larger
emancipatory political vision—a vision that is committed to the ful-
fillment of social justice and economic democracy.

What does this mean at the level of classroom practice? It means
that teachers committed to such a vision must consistently involve
themselves and their students in ongoing critical analysis of the cultural and class prejudices, language uses, and contradictory beliefs
that reproduce racism, sexism, homophobia, and other forms of structural inequalities in their classrooms. It is impossible for students
from subordinate populations to intervene within the context of
classroom life if they don't have real opportunities to fully integrate
themselves in their learning process. Freire understood this well. In
his teaching of Portuguese to subordinate students, he accepted the
responsibility of interrogating his own privilege and remained ever
cognizant of the cultural struggles his students faced, particularly
with respect to the issue of subordinate/dominant language usage.

> What mattered . . . was my refusal to install the language of the
> professor as the valuable idiom in the classroom. My language

counted, but so did theirs. My language changed and so did theirs. This democracy of expression established a mutual atmosphere which encouraged the students to talk openly, not fearing ridicule or punishment for being "stupid." I wish I could repeat to you their surprise at my interest in their words, their culture. Very rarely had a professor taken them seriously, but the truth is that they never had taken themselves so seriously either (Shor and Freire 1987, 23).

For Freire, the dialogical relationship with his students served as the cornerstone of his educational praxis—a process of learning founded on speaking the word, critical reflection, and action. "Having the 'dialogical relation' as priority generates respect for the students' culture and for the valuation of knowledge the learners bring to school" (ibid., 102). Through the dialogical process, the culture of the classroom itself is democratized and sets the stage for teacher and students to participate in the critical unveiling of the world.

CULTURE, LANGUAGE, AND LITERACY

Language and culture represented to Freire the two most significant factors in the development of a revolutionary pedagogical practice. He firmly believed that in a society like that of the United States where such culturally diverse populations must coexist within the context of glaring political and economic inequality, teachers had to be cognizant of the impact that culture and language have upon teaching and learning. No matter what age or grade level, the language and cultural identity of the students played a pivotal role in their learning process. Respect for students had to translate into respect for their language and their cultural identity.

> For us progressive educators, it does not matter if we teach biology, the social sciences or the national standard language, it is fundamental that we respect the cultural identity that passes through social classes of students. It is necessary to respect the students' language, its syntax and its semantics. It is this respect that is not

present when we disregard or minimally regard the discourse of children from subordinate classes. Particularly when we more than insinuate and make our dislike obvious for the way those children speak, the way they write, the way they think, by labeling their speech inferior, and incorrect. It is precisely this that takes place in the so-called multicultural societies where language and hegemonic culture smash and belittle the language and culture of so-called minorities. (1993, 134–135).

This is particularly at issue in the literacy process of young students. In states like California, where the right of minority language students to be educated in their primary language has been repealed, bilingual teachers experience great anxiety and frustration in their efforts to execute a critical literacy process. In some schools, teachers are strictly forbidden to use any language except English when speaking to students and their parents or are restricted in their freedom to inform minority-language parents about bilingual waivers (parents' legal right to request bilingual education for their children). Such administrative policies to carry out English-only practices place many bilingual teachers in tremendous conflict—forcing them to execute "behind closed doors" tactics in their efforts to meet the needs of limited-English-proficiency students. Such policies were of great concern to Paulo Freire (Freire and Macedo 1987) because he believed that "the exclusive use of [English] in education would result in a strange experience characterized by [English] as a superstructure that would trigger an exacerbation of class divisions" (111) and result in greater inequality.

Highly aware of the oppressive consequences of traditional educational policies toward minority language development in subordinate populations, Freire in his life work placed a great emphasis on the development of literacy among oppressed populations. He insisted that "literacy and education are cultural expressions," for how students are taught is directly influenced by the cultural and class values of the teachers and other educators who develop and implement educational practices. Unfortunately, many traditional educators still remain suspicious of the legitimacy of primary culture and language instruction and its positive impact on the academic development of students from subordinate-language communities.

Freire strongly emphasized that "culture is not an autonomous system, but a system characterized by social stratification and tensions" (Freire and Macedo 1987, 51). Although culture is a dynamic and complex historical phenomenon, many teachers today still conceive culture in reified, classless terms. Moreover, culture represents social processes that are intimately linked to class, gender, sexual and racialized formations, upheld by particular social structures, such as those which we find in public schools. Cultural processes then are not neutral endeavors but rather are tied to the reproduction of power relationships through social organization. Thus, cultural values and belief systems, which are transmitted through language, constitute significant sites of difference and struggle among people (Johnson 1983). The dialectical implication of this critical perspective of culture is multidimensional. On one hand, teachers must comprehend that "language is also culture" and hence, "the mediating force of knowledge" (Freire and Macedo 1987, 53). On the other hand, they must understand that "the presence of the cultural factors alone does not explain everything" (70).

In the teaching of literacy, Freire argued tirelessly that a significant relationship exists not only between language and culture but also between language and class. How we speak is inextricably linked to the particular values, relationships, and survival strategies that are historically reproduced within the context of particular material conditions and modes of production. Thus, where we're born, where we grow up, where we are schooled, where we work, and where we live all impact our linguistic expression. Those who have worked in a variety of schools and communities have found that the language of the students differs depending on their class background, even in the case of English-speaking Chicano students, or of Euro-American students, for that matter.

The reason for this is that students' expressions of values and beliefs, as well as their cognitive styles of learning and relating in the world, are inextricably tied to culture *and* class, all which are transmitted through the language or languages spoken within a community. Freire (1993) stressed in his work that

... the way we are—the manner in which we eat, what we eat, the way we dress up, the way we behave in the world, how we find ourselves with others and the way we communicate, the levels of education, our class position in the society to which we belong— all these things end up being part of our language, our thinking structure that in turn, conditions us. We experience ourselves in language, we socially create language, and finally we become linguistically competent (134).

The stories, jokes, music, poetry, all incorporate very particular affective linguistic expressions that are tied to deeply internalized historical responses—responses that are shaped by the particular dynamics of class formation and class struggle, whether it be by choice or simply dire necessity. Thus, language, one of the most powerful transmitters of culture and mediators of class relations, both transmits and reinforces the rules for community as these relate to collective notions of identity and histories of survival within particular moments in time. Language invokes in students particular emotions and feelings, distinct poetic sensibilities and political perceptions of society, as well as different understandings of what it means to be human.

Moreover, students who must communicate in a second language face a further obstacle. It is often difficult for them to relax or be spontaneous in their learning process. The tension generated heightens the feeling of dissonance between their external reality and their internal world. Hence the connection between experience and language, so vital to the construction of knowledge, is compromised.

Freire viewed language "not only as an instrument of communication, but also as a structure for thinking. . . . It is culture" (1985, 184). Hence, within the context of our primary language we come to know our world through sounds, intonations, and cadences that give meaning to our being. This implies a relationship between language and the material realities that students must negotiate daily. Thus, problems of language and the teaching of literacy always involve ideological questions. It is through language, then, that students forge deep unconscious connections tied to both concrete and imagined experiences of shared history, class, culture, and community, experiences that invoke individual and collective memories of who they believe themselves to be in the world. For Freire (1997b), this constituted a sense of being "rooted" within a social location from which students could extend themselves outward, so as to eventually become citizens of the world. "No one becomes local from universal" he wrote; "the existential road is the reverse" (39).

Freire taught that the capacity of oppressed students to "develop a collective consciousness of their own constitution or formation . . . as well as an ethos of solidarity and interdependence" (McLaren 2000, 153) is deeply connected to their collective process of empowerment. This development of critical consciousness could be supported by teachers through their ability to honor and integrate the cultural experiences of students in the teaching of literacy. This does not of course imply that teachers should take all such experiences at face value, but rather that teachers recognize that

> . . . it's impossible to talk of respect for the dignity that is in the process of coming to be, for identities that are in the process of construction, without taking into consideration the conditions in which they are living and the importance of the knowledge derived from life experience, which they bring with them to school. I can in no way underestimate such knowledge. Or what is worse, ridicule it (Freire 1998a, 62).

But although Freire recognized and respected the value of subordinate students' primary culture and language, he did not believe that teaching children from oppressed communities solely in their primary language was sufficient—a belief for which he was much criticized and maligned. For Freire, like Antonio Gramsci before him, "the problems of language always involved ideological questions and along with them, questions of power" (Freire 1998b, 74). He strongly urged that children from subordinate cultural groups also be educated in whatever was considered the "educated norm" of the society in which they lived. It was "fundamental that they learn the standard syntax and intonations so that . . . they diminish the disadvantages in the struggle to live their lives, [as well as] gain a fundamental tool for the fight they must wage against the injustices and discrimination targeted at them (74). Freire felt that students from subordinate cultures have to be *armed* with the ability to engage the dominant language, so as to prepare them to struggle effectively with institutional societal rules, laws, policies, and practices that function against their democratic interests.

It is also true that a common language can forge deep connections, critically or uncritically, and has served socially and politically as a unifying force in the world. This is evidenced historically not only in the efforts of nationalist liberation struggles to retain their primary language but also in the overwhelming efforts of colonizers everywhere to impose their language upon colonized populations, a practice carried out most effectively through the public educational system.

> The colonizers spent centuries trying to impose their language. The colonized people were told either verbally or through message systems inherent in the colonial structure that they did not possess effective cultural instruments with which to express themselves. This language profile imposed by the colonizers eventually convinced the people that their language was in fact a corrupt and inferior system unworthy of true educational status (Freire and Macedo, 118).

The destructive effects of imposing a dominant language at the expense of the students' primary language are still felt even today by the large numbers of minority-language students who have lost their right to bilingual education. Consequently, Freire noted, "To continue to use the language of the colonizer as the only medium of instruction is to continue to provide manipulative strategies that support the maintenance of cultural domination" (ibid., 117).

Freire(1993) was convinced that "it is not possible to discuss language without discussing power, or without thinking about social classes and their contradictions" (133). For example, the sentimental connections and the hegemonic meanings that are ascribed to particular language forms are also evident in the way that "the power of language" has been used to politically manipulate poor and working-class Latinos and other minority-language parents against their own interests. This phenomenon was definitely at work in the discursive practices of teachers such as Gloria Matta Tuchman, who were active Spanish-speaking supporters of the Proposition 227 "English for the Children" campaign. These individuals addressed Spanish-speaking parents during this ghastly campaign, beseeching them to abandon their support for bilingual education for the sake of their children's well-being and future success. The campaign utilized all the familiar rhetoric that invokes deep emotional responses tied to parents' desires for a better life for their children. Unfortunately, this is a life tied to meeting the interest of the marketplace rather than students' rights to cultural and linguistic self-determination. In 2000, we saw the same phenomenon repeated in the Latino community in the campaign for the conservative presidential candidate, George W. Bush.

The central point being made here is that language, like culture, is not monolithic, but rather a deeply contested ideological terrain. For instance, Freire (Freire and Macedo 1987) explained, "The big problem with the Spanish language is the multiple discourses. . . . These discourses, in my view, are linked to the differences among various social classes" (107) and the historical formations linked to distinct regions of Latin America. Precisely for this reason teachers cannot establish a deeper understanding of language and the literacy needs of the large majority of bilingual students in the United States without a class analysis. For only through such a critique are we able to distinguish more clearly the manner in which language is shaped by contradictory expressions of culture. These are contradictions generated in a variety of ways by the mediation of both cultural and class conflicts, particularly within communities that must contend with overwhelming forms of racialized and economic inequalities.

Freire (1993) argued that "words, sentences, articulated discourse do not take place up in the air. They are historical . . . social" (58) and cultural constructions. Only through such an understanding of culture, language, and literacy can teachers truly appreciate the inextricable relationship that also exists between language and the formation of identities. It is precisely because language rises out of historical relationships of culture, gender, sexuality, religion, etc., as defined by class status, privilege, and material conditions, that a revolutionary pedagogy of literacy must begin wherever students are linguistically situated. By utilizing the strength of students' existing linguistic knowledge, teachers can support students in expanding their appropriation of the dominant language, in ways that are meaningful and ultimately emancipatory. Freire (1998b) recognized the difficulties many teachers might experience in accomplishing this; nevertheless he believed it was indispensable to students' academic development:

> When inexperienced middle class teachers take teaching positions in peripheral areas of the city, [cultural and] class-specific tastes, values, language, discourse, syntax, semantics, everything about the students may seem contradictory to the point of being shocking and frightening. It is necessary, however, that teachers understand that the students' syntax, their manners, tastes, and ways of addressing teachers and colleagues; and the rules governing fighting and playing among themselves are all part of their cultural identity, which never lacks an element of class. All that has to be accepted. Only as learners recognize themselves democratically and see that their right to say "I be" is respected, will they become able to learn the dominant grammatical reason why they should say "I am" (49).

There is no question but that Paulo Freire (1993) believed that "language represents one of the most important aspects in the process of democratization of societies" (135). He insisted that "teaching literacy is, above all, a social and political commitment" (115). A fierce advocate of a critical view of literacy, Freire argued that the primary purpose for a critical linguistic approach is to support students in developing their abilities to analyze and challenge the oppressive structures of the larger society, so that a more just, equitable, and democratic world could be forged. Fundamentally, this requires a social and political commitment to teaching literacy dialogically, so that teachers and students together can work to decode the ideological dimensions of texts, institutions, social practices, and cultural forms that conceal the hidden structures of oppression (Macedo 1994).

TEACHING AGAINST THE GRAIN

Given the political principles that inform a revolutionary practice of education, progressive teachers must contend daily with the tensions of teaching against the grain. There are clearly some very fundamental ways in which a pedagogy inspired by Freire's work is diametrically in conflict with that traditionally found in public schools. The ability, then, to identify opposing perspectives that create considerable tension for progressive teachers can prove valuable during difficult moments. It is also important to distinguish, in spite of the inherent political conflicts between a revolutionary and a traditional teaching practice, that the actual degree of tension produced will be greatly determined by the local arrangement of formal and informal power relations within any particular school. This is in keeping with our understanding of education as both a terrain of struggle and a perpetually incomplete hegemonic condition.

Traditional practices of public schooling perpetuate a functional and instrumental view of knowledge that is primarily concerned with whether the student can perform the basic skills and do well on official standardized tests. As such, traditional teaching practices reinforce the superiority of the dominant cultural belief systems and language, at the expense of the cultural values and language of subordinate populations. It is significant to note that this includes the privileging of an imaginary "middle-class" norm that is linked to the perpetuation of a capitalist political economy, while subordinating the cultural sensibilities, aesthetics, and linguistic patterns of working-class populations, irrespective of their ethnicity. Traditional practices of schooling negate the historical conditions, cultural and linguistic competencies, and lived experiences of a large percentage of students who attend public schools. As such, students from subordinate cultural communities continue to be perceived as culturally deprived, albeit in more sophisticated terms. Moreover, the ideology that informs traditional schooling practices denies the political nature of schooling and its function within the society at large, while its promulgators assume a moral posture of victim blaming (Freire and Macedo 1987).

The traditional pedagogy views the teacher as a neutral, objective, and benevolent agent of the state who is there to impart solely the basic information required for students to survive within capital-ist America. Unfortunately, more often than not this results in edu-cational practices that work against the interests of a large majority of students from working-class and subordinate cultural communi-ties and precipitates their expulsion. Such a perspective defines in absolute terms what is legitimate, appropriate, and acceptable knowledge and teaching practice, without consideration for the contextual conditions and particular needs at work in different cul-tural and class communities or the oppressive outcomes. And as im-plied earlier, traditional educational ideology obscures issues related to class, while traditional curricular practices and materials are pro-foundly steeped in the values of the marketplace. Thus, schools rein-force a "commonsense"[2] notion of capitalism and democracy as not only synonymous, but as a fixed and naturalized phenomenon to be uncritically accepted and defended.

In contrast, a revolutionary practice of education begins with the view that all human beings participate actively in producing meaning and thus reinforces a dialectical and contextual view of knowledge. Educational practices are recognized as political and cul-tural acts. Therefore, a revolutionary practice enhances the educa-tional process of oppressed populations by focusing on students' be-coming literate about their cultural histories and lived experiences, in addition to their learning, engaging, and interrogating subject content. A revolutionary educational practice supports students in appropriating the codes of power within educational institutions for the purpose of transforming their world. Such a practice stimulates students to critically reflect upon their own lives and social relation-ships within the larger social context, so that they may come to un-derstand how power moves and shapes the condition in which their communities exist. It is an educational practice that demystifies the artificial limits imposed upon particular class and cultural groups and recognizes the worldview of different cultural communities as inher-ently valid forms of existence, when understood as social formations rooted within the material conditions in which different popula-tions have evolved historically.

Moreover a revolutionary practice reinforces a language of possi-bility that enables learners to recognize and understand their voices within a multitude of social discourses. It is a critical practice of schooling that encourages the curiosity, imagination, creativity, risk taking, and questioning of students; doubt and resistance are perceived as necessary and useful to their critical development. Furthermore, it is a practice carried out with the explicit recognition that the educator is not neutral, but rather a historical and political subject of change. As such, teachers carry the responsibility for creating the conditions for students to achieve academically through a process that provides them the intellectual, emotional, and physical space to develop their capacity to reflect, critique, voice, and participate with the purpose of constructing new avenues for authentic democratic life.

Given the opposing values between these two educational perspectives, it should not be surprising that when progressive teachers get out into public schools and begin trying to live a revolutionary pedagogy, they experience a great deal of resistance and conflict, which can cause enormous stress, particularly for new teachers. This resistance may come from a variety of sources: resistance from students, resistance from colleagues, resistance from administrators, and resistance from parents. Consequently, a major question for progressive teachers is how to develop their practice in the midst of debilitating forms of opposition. To develop effective strategies for teaching in the midst of great contradictions requires that teachers recognize that resistance is often generated by internalized traditional expectations of schooling linked to the perpetuation of the status quo. But resistance can also be generated by conditioned uncritical responses to anything or anyone perceived as potentially oppressive or limiting—even when the resistance may function against the individual's or group's interest.

Students may be so "long-habituated to passive schooling" that they feel a teacher has "no right to make critical demands on them" (Shor and Freire 1987, 25). Nevertheless, when students respond with resistance, their responses and the particular ways they act out their resistance can provide significant information about how students see their world and their place within that world. Rather than perceiving resistance as a pedagogical impediment, teachers can engage with it as a meaningful process in the development of student consciousness. Often teachers will experience with working-class students a self-imposed expression of "anti-intellectual" attitudes that manifest as resistance to learning or participating in whatever the teacher proposes. For many of these students, such resistance constitutes the only effective mechanism they have found to protect the self from the alienation they have experienced for years as a consequence of academic oppression. Often, working-class youths struggle with the fear that if they achieve academically they will betray their friends and be left completely isolated outside their peer community. It goes without saying that one of our greatest challenges here is to create opportunities and relationships within the classroom that will provide students the space and time to work through issues related to their personal histories of schooling. This requires creating opportunities for students' views and ideas about education to be examined, affirmed, challenged, and transformed, in a way that makes learning a meaningful and relevant process—meaningful and relevant because it frees them to identify and challenge the internalized belief that they are unworthy of a place in the world.

Student resistance can manifest itself in highly passive forms. Some students resist entering into critical forms of inquiry, preferring to be told very concretely what is expected and exactly what they must do to receive a passing grade. Sad to say, this type of student resistance is found in classrooms from elementary·school to doctoral programs. In fact, it is not unusual for students enrolled in teacher education programs to exhibit this form of resistance. The passivity that informs such classroom resistance must be linked to the way students have been historically conditioned to be passive learners who receive into their "mind banks" the information doled out by the teacher.

This issue constitutes a major challenge that requires teachers to dialogically engage a student's passivity so they can develop the ability to critically engage in a participatory process of learning. It is not always an easy process for students to break with past pedagogical conditioning and expectations. Progressive teachers, even with experience, can be criticized by students who question their competency.

This is particularly prevalent with older students, although parents of younger students may also make similar accusations. In *Learning to Question*, Freire and Faundez (1989) acknowledge the difficulty teachers may experience.

> Knowledge is a process, and thus we should engage in it and achieve it through dialogue, through breaking with the past—that is not accepted by the great majority of students, who are used to the teacher's, the wise one's, having the truth, hierarchically, and thus do not accept dialogue. For them, dialogue is a sign of weakness on the part of the teacher: for them modesty of knowledge is an indication of weakness and ignorance (32).

In direct conflict with a revolutionary pedagogy that seeks to engage students critically in unveiling the world, public schools are predominantly focused on the standardization of knowledge and authoritarian approaches to teaching content, with little regard for involving students critically or substantively in the process of knowledge production. Instead, the emphasis is on the sequential memorization of descriptive content, irrespective of whether the student comprehends what she or he is "learning." Nowhere is this more evident than in the current "transfer of knowledge" mania behind such approaches as teaching-to-the-test and the "Open Court" literacy curricula. Freire and Shor (1987) provided a decisive critique of this educational approach:

> The transfer-of-knowledge approach [is] the most suitable pedagogy for sustaining elite authority. The transfer method is thus no accident or mistake. The inequality and hierarchy in our corporate society simply produce the curriculum compatible with control from above. That chain of authority ends in the passive, transfer pedagogy dominating schools and colleges around the country. It also ends in teacher burn-out, student resistance and the continual eruption of reforms. . . . The standard transfer curriculum is a mechanistic, authoritarian way of thinking about organizing a program which implies above all a tremendous lack of confidence in the creativity of students and the ability of teachers (76–77).

In light of this critique, it can be easily understood why the role of teaching content also generates heated controversy. First of all, it is important to clarify several issues. Freire (1993) firmly believed that teaching content is an important and necessary aspect of the pedagogical process. Moreover, he insisted that progressive teachers needed to be competent and constantly studying within their particular fields, not for the purpose of "transferring knowledge" but rather to teach content always in connection to a "critical reading of reality. One teaches how to think through teaching content" (24). But he strongly refuted the notion of "teaching content by itself, as if the school context in which this content is treated could be reduced to a neutral space where social conflicts would not manifest" (24).

Progressive educators who teach dialogically are often falsely accused by reactionary colleagues or administrators of simply being ideologues who "damage students" by their failure to teach the "knowledge" necessary for their students to succeed academically or on standardized tests. Many reactionary educators make such accusations because they truly believe that if you just fill students up with content, eventually they will somehow "magically" learn how to think. Freire (1997b) fiercely opposed such a perspective. Instead, he argued for a "critical education":

> I must insist and re-insist on critical education. The argument that the teaching of content, deposited in the learner, will sooner or later bring about a critical perception of reality does not convince me. In the progressive perspective, the process of teaching— where the teaching challenges learners to apprehend the object, to then learn it in relation with the world—implies the exercise of critical perception, perception of the object's reason of being. It implies sharpening of the learners' epistemological curiosity, which cannot be satisfied with mere description of the object's concept. I must not *leave* for a random tomorrow something that is part of my task as a progressive educator right now: a critical reading of the world, alongside a critical reading of the word (75).

For progressive teachers to engage this issue effectively in their classrooms, they must be not only absolutely convinced of the validity of their revolutionary project but also highly skilled and competent in their field of study. Throughout his life, Freire was very clear and consistent about this issue. The only way to effectively critique a subject is to know that subject well. However, to engage students in rigorous forms of dialogical study is to expect them to be actively involved in their learning. This may feel so unfamiliar to students that they will respond by judging the teacher as lacking rigor for not presenting "monologue" lectures of descriptive content for which they need only listen and take notes to prepare for the exam that will follow.

In contrast with an authoritarian notion that perceives rigor as rigid and absolute adherence to the dominant knowledge base, to think critically is a rigorous act which requires students to take responsibility for their learning. Moreover, Freire (Shor and Freire 1987) reminds teachers to stay cognizant of the fact that

> . . . [students] are so used to following orders that they don't know how to be responsible for their own formation. They have not learned how to organize their own reading of reality and of books, understanding critically what they read. Because they are dependent on authority to structure their development, automatically they think that liberating or dialogical education is not rigorous, precisely because it asks them to participate in their own formation (77).

To contend effectively with such issues of student resistance, Freire strongly urged teachers to develop their teaching practice grounded in an unbending faith in the capacity of students to learn and become critically conscious human beings. The absence of such faith can generate unnecessary tensions and frustrations. For example, progressive teachers are at times worried that their students will be negatively affected or hindered by their participation in a critical pedagogical classroom, once they return to a more traditional classroom environment. This concern fails to recognize how the year or semester the students spend within an emancipatory environment provides them a living example of another way of life, another way to express their humanity, and another way they can be, know, and act in their world. And this experience, like all meaningful experiences in our lives, stays with them. Thus, we are advised at such moments to teach with far more faith in our students than we often do. For no revolutionary practice can be constructed without the love that generates an unwavering faith and willingness to not give up on students, colleagues, or even ourselves during moments of adversity.

Progressive teachers often express deep concern and frustration over the difficulties they experience in trying to implement a liberatory pedagogy in the context of school schedules and time constraints that seem at cross purposes with the critical formation and emancipation of students. The despicable conditions of many school facilities and the quality (or lack of quality) of books, equipment, and materials give teachers and students very clear messages about their worth and value in the world. Unfortunately, public schooling places greater priority on expediency and social control than on the development of ethical and socially responsible citizens of the world. The use of domesticating language, authoritarian practices, and alienating physical arrangements can erode a teacher's sense of well-being and hope, causing deep feelings of disempowerment in teachers. The fear of losing one's job because one is not tenured is an effective means by which new teachers are socialized and conditioned into institutional compliance. Without concerted personal effort and a teaching community of solidarity, teachers can too easily become caught in the bureaucratic web of public school culture. Freire (1998c) strongly advised teachers to fight against becoming bureaucratized. "Bureaucracy annihilates creativity and transforms persons into mere repeaters of clichés. The more bureaucratized they become, the more likely they are to become alienated adherents of daily routine, from which they can never stand apart in order to understand their reason for being" (117). Such difficult issues again highlight significant limit-situations that teachers must creatively confront in their efforts to transform the debilitating conditions so prevalent in public schools.

As in other institutions, the issue of political backlash is highly relevant to public schools. Teachers who speak out against oppressive policies and practices or establish strong relationships of solidarity

with their students and parents can face conflict and hostility in
their relationships with school administrators and reactionary colleagues. There is oftentimes a reticence and unwillingness to listen
and support teachers who critically voice their concerns and seek to
transform their work within their schools and districts. Many of the
most progressive teachers can find themselves chastised and singled
out as troublemakers. This generates debilitating experiences of being alienated and isolated, even when they have the support of parents and community members on their side. But Freire's (1998) response to this was to quickly point out that "the so-called
troublemakers represent a form of resistance against those who ag-
gressively oppose [institutional change]. For me, the immorality and
the lack of ethics rests with those who want to maintain an unjust
order" (68). Just as students and their parents are expected to remain passive and politically dormant, particularly within subordinate communities, teachers too are expected to simply accept willingly the domesticating regimen prescribed for them by school
officials. These teachers often end up disappearing from the scene by
being fired, transferred to a different school, or simply "pushed-out"
by intolerable conditions. Those "who speak out, organize or deviate
from the official curriculum are made an example of, and the example of their disappearance is not lost on those who remain" (Shor
and Freire 1987, 59).

Unfortunately, when young progressive teachers finally get out
into the schools and start to live their dream, it does not take long
before they begin to feel very discouraged, angry, and frustrated.
These feelings generally arise as a result of difficulties the teachers
face as they attempt to practice a pedagogy that can genuinely support the social, cultural, and political empowerment of their students. These teachers consistently feel great doubt and despair in
the face of institutionalized expectations that they acquiesce to educational policies and practices that clearly subject their most vulnerable students to further marginalization. These policies and practices
include the administration of testing, curricular, grading and assessment requirements that systematically negate and overlook the very
strengths and abilities that can actually assist subordinate students
to become academically proficient and successful. Under the guise of

political neutrality, benevolent control, and educational expediency, these policies and practices continue to perpetuate the class-based and racialized ideological structures that historically have permitted the exploitation and domination of over two-thirds the world's populations.

There is no question but that once teachers immerse themselves in any form of political struggle within schools or communities, they must constantly make tough decisions. They must make decisions about what they are willing to risk, what battles they will take on, and how far they are willing to stretch the boundaries of what is considered legitimate teaching practice within their schools. How far a teacher can stretch is a very personal issue and no one has the right to make such a decision for another. Ultimately, each person must take responsibility for his or her own decision—a critical process that will sustain them when the consequences of such a decision must be faced. Each of us must attempt to clarify for ourselves what we are willing to do. How far are we willing to go? It is also imperative that teachers choose their battles carefully—any battle requires enormous energy, time, and commitment. We must consider critically the nature of the risks we take, their purpose, and their potential for real change. Reflecting on the risks connected to decisions teachers might be called to make, Freire (1997b) cautioned that "risk only makes sense when it is taken for a valuable reason, an ideal, a dream beyond risk itself" (73).

Freire strongly encouraged progressive teachers to develop the courage, security, and confidence necessary to make hard decisions—decisions that could result in the rupture of political and collegial relationships. Progressive teachers often have to confront fear and pain, as they contend with heart-wrenching experiences of mean-spirited attacks and accusations of being "ideological," "egotistical," or "uncaring toward their students" whenever they challenge the negative impact of school practices. Educators who dare to speak out to the contradictions and inconsistencies can experience a sort of "internal exile" within their schools—"repression by colleagues and administrators . . . the uneasiness of having to be restrained and only speak half-truths" (Freire 1997, 68). In their personal struggle for coherence, some teachers are forced to leave public schools. For many, the hope is that by leaving they will be able to recuperate the meaning of their work and recommit themselves more fully to the struggle for authentic democracy. Paulo Freire's (1993) words upon his departure from his leadership position with the Municipal Secretariat of Education in São Paulo echo the sentiments of many teachers who leave: "I am not leaving the fight, but simply moving to another front. The fight continues on the same. Wherever I am I will be as engaged as you in favor of democratic public schools" (140).

As so many teachers know only too well, at times the pressures, tensions, and stresses of becoming isolated or alienated within a school can become overwhelming. The pressure to acquiesce and "get with the program" can also give rise to tremendous feelings of doubt and insecurity in teachers. Along with personal and public fears of reprisals and retaliation by reactionary administrators and senior faculty, progressive teachers can also experience potentially immobilizing fear of being co-opted, utilized, or tokenized within educational institutions in ways that move counter to our revolutionary dreams. To counter these fears or gain "command of our fear," teachers must recognize that it is very concrete and normal to experience such fear when one confronts the institutional power of the status quo. Freire (1998), very concerned with this issues, stressed:

> When we are faced with concrete fears, such as that of losing our jobs or of not being promoted, we feel the need to set certain limits to our fear. Before anything else, we begin to recognize that fear is a manifestation of being alive. I do not need to hide my fears. But I must not allow my fears to immobilize me. If I am secure in my political dream, having tactics that may lessen my risk I must go on with the fight. Hence the need for control of my fear, to *educate* my fear, from which is finally born my courage (41).

Through the containment of our fears and the development of courage, teachers can more easily remain critically vigilant about the issue of power and the consequences of our participation and contribution within schools—fully cognizant of the overarching complicity of education in the reproduction of social and economic injustice. However, Freire (Shor and Freire 1987) repeatedly warned that to act alone "is the best way to commit suicide" (61). He insisted, "It is impossible to confront the lion romantically! You have to know who you can count on and who you have to fight! To the extent . . . you know that, you can begin to be *with* and not to be alone. The sensation of not being alone diminishes fear" (61). Hence, we can only struggle against our fears through an uncompromising acceptance of our historical and ethical responsibility to transform the social, political, and economic structures at work in schools and society—a struggle that can never be waged in isolation.

To break the alienation and isolation teachers so often experience within public schools is impossible without creating avenues of solidarity through which they receive the political sustenance and support they require in order to deal with the many difficult issues they face daily. Teachers require opportunities to sit together and reflect on their practice. They need a place where they can openly and consistently engage their concerns about the effectiveness and sustaining quality of what they are doing with their students in the classroom; a place where they can freely continue to learn and develop as teachers. Teachers also need the intellectual space where they can map out ideologically the particular arrangement of power relations that structure and shape life in public schools, and assess the power dynamics at work in their particular schools, so as to make wise decisions regarding their practice.

Nevertheless, it must be kept in mind that there are no pat formulas or recipes for constructing a necessary pedagogy of resistance. Our assessment of possible strategies and tactics for intervention must be rooted in the actual lived conditions of teachers and the particular problems they are facing. But the ability to critically read power relationships, articulate pedagogical alternatives, and assess the outcome of our interventions can only be strengthened and expanded in connection to an ongoing political praxis.

Given the need for sustained praxis, teachers must work together to build their own organizations of study where tough issues can be faced, understood, and transformed. Freire was a strong advocate of teachers taking their practice into their own hands. He firmly believed that

. . . teachers whose dream is the transformation of society have to get control of a permanent process of forming themselves, and not wait for professional training from the establishment. The more an educator becomes aware of these things, the more he or she learns from practice, and then he or she discovers that it is possible to bring into the classroom . . . moments of social [change]" (Shor and Freire 1987, 47).

Historically, it has often been during painful moments of struggle and adversity that teachers begin to recognize they cannot fight the struggle within schools alone. During such moments, teachers reach out and take civic responsibility for creating places within their communities where they can meet and engage freely and openly with questions linked to the transformation of oppressive and alienating structures and relationships within schools. Freire consistently encouraged teachers to come together across differences to challenge practices and policies that serve to perpetuate the exploitation of their labor. In *Teachers as Cultural Workers* (1998b) he wrote:

Thus I can see no alternative for educators to unity within the diversity of their interests in defending their rights. Such rights include the right to freedom in teaching, the right to speak, the right to better conditions for pedagogical work, the right to paid sabbaticals for continuing education, the right to be coherent, the right to criticize the authorities without fear of retaliation . . . and to not have to lie to survive (45–46).

Anchored in this realization, progressive teachers have established networks of struggle to challenge the educational status quo, in terms of both their rights as teachers and the needs of students and their communities. Currently, many progressive organizations around the country—Rethinking Schools, The Pedagogy of the Oppressed Conference, Socialist Teachers Forum, Teachers for Democracy, California Consortium for Critical Educators, and Coalition for Social Justice—have been established by teachers to support their work within public schools. More important, these teachers seek to link their local work in public schools to the larger political struggles for social justice, human rights, and economic democracy in this country and around the world.

Freire (1993) also strongly encouraged critical educators who teach in teacher-education programs to support the development and ongoing needs of progressive teacher networks, in their efforts to better ground their revolutionary practice as academics in the day-to-day realities faced by teachers in schools. This is particularly important for new teachers. It is a tremendous disservice to prepare student teachers in critical pedagogical theories of social justice and economic democracy and then send them out into difficult environments without the necessary support or teaching community to sustain them through hard times.

Through study groups and other progressive teacher networks, public-school teachers develop effective pedagogical and political strategies for interventions within their workplace and communities, with the critical intent to change the nature of public schooling. Moreover, through such relationships of solidarity teachers as cultural workers and educational activists also develop a more rigorous understanding of human beings. This helps to prevent *errors of struggle* that result when one "underestimate[s] the power of the dominant [and] ignore[s] the deep-seated presence of the oppressor" (1997b, 66) in all of us. Through relationships of solidarity, teachers can help one another to shorten the distance between what they say and what they do. This coherence develops through ongoing dialogues where the human connection to others can help teachers to move past their fears and develop a critical consciousness well grounded in lived experiences. It is precisely this ongoing process that is essential to our establishment of solidarity across our many differences.

In the development of study groups and teacher networks, it is important to recognize the differences in teachers' experiences and levels of commitment. For example, I'm certain that there are teachers who, if they were called to participate in acts of civil disobedience in the interest of transforming public schools, would not think twice, and there are others who would hesitate, given the realities of their lives. But in social struggle, it is seldom a black and white issue.

No matter our decisions, what's important is that we act consciously, with commitment and purpose. We must accept that relationships of solidarity are not built to eliminate tensions in an effort to create consensus—such artificial processes can result in sectarianism. For Freire, the "role of liberatory pedagogy is not to extinguish tensions. The prime role . . . is to lead [us] to recognize various tensions and enable [us] to deal effectively with them. Trying to deny these tensions ends up negating the very role of subjectivity. The negation of tensions amounts to the illusion of overcoming these tension which are really just hidden" (Freire and Macedo 1987, 49).

Given the many challenges and tensions of life in public schools, our relationships of solidarity must be founded on both a shared political vision *and* our sincere willingness to move together across our different readings of the world. By connecting our dreams of liberation, we can build together new paths to a world where all life is sacred and all children are born with the freedom to live, learn, love, and dream. There is no question but that our struggle is arduous. This also makes it more clear why Paulo Freire, at the risk of appearing foolish, repeatedly insisted throughout his life that *teaching is an act of love*. A love that Peter McLaren (2000) so rightly described as "the oxygen of revolution, nourishing the blood . . . [and] spirit of struggle (172). Undoubtedly, it is only through the power of such love that teachers can embrace a revolutionary pedagogy and remain uncompromisingly committed to the restoration of our humanity.

NOTES

1. For more on this concept, see Chapter 3 of *Pedagogy of the Oppressed*.

2. The term "commonsense" is used in the Gramscian sense. It recognizes the realm of human consciousness, where both authentic and distorted notions of reality coexist. Without the critical benefit of interrogation, they both mystify and legitimate the material world through ideas of accommodation and resistance. For a discussion of this concept, see Giroux, *Pedagogy and the Politics of Hope*, Chapter 3.

CHAPTER 4

LIVING THE PEDAGOGY: TEACHERS REINVENT FREIRE

The dialectic between practice and theory should be fully lived. . .

PAULO FREIRE,
Teachers as Cultural Workers (1998)

I want to assert that it was the intersection of Paulo's thought and the lived pedagogy of the many black teachers of my girlhood who saw themselves as having a liberatory mission to educate us to effectively resist racism, that has had a profound impact on my thinking about the art and practice of teaching.

BELL HOOKS,
Teaching to Transgress (1994)

More than any other educator of the twentieth century, Paulo Freire left an indelible mark upon the lives of progressive educators—teachers from different ethnic locations who openly commit their lives and work to changing the structures of social and economic injustice. I am a Puerto Rican working-class woman who lived in poverty for the first twenty-five years of my life. Freire's writings were the first to touch so resoundingly many of the deeper political issues of my life and our historical struggles for democratic schooling in Puerto Rico, New York, California, and other regions of the country. Freire's language is direct in its discussion of oppression, formidably linking the conditions our children face in school with the politics of cultural domination and economic exploitation. More important, it was the first time that I felt that the plight of students from subordinate cultural communities was addressed from the perspective of the social reality of our subordination, rather than of the projected images and myths of dominant cultural interpretations.

I have been struck with the dramatically similar powerful impact that *Pedagogy of the Oppressed* has had upon the intellectual and political development of the teachers I have had the privilege to work with in the past. The ability not only to theorize about critical pedagogy or a liberatory education but also actually to live it in the classroom is key to the purpose of this volume. For this reason, this chapter is solely dedicated to the voices of eight teachers who have worked for many years, in a variety of ways, to "reinvent" Freire's philosophy of education within the context of their classrooms. Through Paulo Freire's work, these teachers gained or renewed their critical understanding of class, culture, and language—and sought actively to integrate this understanding in their teaching practice and everyday lives.

I echo here Paulo Freire's (1997a, 1998c) use of "reinvention" because it was a concept that he used in his efforts to steer teachers away from reducing his ideas of pedagogy and political project into a "method" (Freire 1998b). Freire's literacy project has been often mechanized into a "method" and stripped of its revolutionary intent. In their foreword to *Teachers as Cultural Workers* (1998), Donaldo Macedo and Ana Maria Araujo Freire discuss Paulo Freire's serious concern with such reification of his work. In a conversation with Macedo, Freire emphasized, "It is impossible to export pedagogical practices without reinventing them. Please tell your fellow American educators not to import me. Ask them to re-create and rewrite my ideas" (xi).

I believe that the concept of "reinvent," as Freire proposed, is true to the spirit of a liberatory pedagogy. First of all, to say "reinvent" extends an open invitation of solidarity and pronounces a deep faith in the capacity of teachers to draw on his work and freely recreate it, as if for the first time, in their efforts to meet the particular needs of their own students. Further, reinvention is an act of empowerment that can be accomplished only when teachers truly recognize themselves as subjects of history and as ethically responsible for their practice. Reinvention is seldom permitted to students or their teachers in public schools. There, reproduction is more sought after, leading to "teacher-proof" methods and the standardization of knowledge. These are antithetical to the creativity inherent in reinvention, for reinvention entails imagination. Unfortunately, imagination is often a suspect or prohibited quality in public schools.

To reinvent requires teachers who will willingly risk doing their labor as full knowing and creative subjects; who can reflect critically on Freire's ideas, grounded within the specificities of their concrete lived experiences in schools.

In *Mentoring the Mentor*, Paulo Freire (1998a) strongly urged progressive teachers to "always be moving out on [their] own, continually reinventing me and reinventing what it means to be democratic in [their] own specific cultural and historical context" (308). In solidarity with his proposal, the eight teachers whose narratives are featured here constitute living examples that Paulo Freire's ideas are not only pedagogically sound but also absolutely paramount to our reinvention of public schooling in this country today.

TEACHING AS THE PRACTICE OF FREEDOM

GINA M. CASTILLO: PRIMARY SCHOOL TEACHER

I grew up speaking Spanish and English. The ability to speak and understand two languages brought with it a certain amount of responsibility. Because I was bilingual, at times I acted as a translator for my maternal grandmother during our outings into town. Even though I was very young at the time, the memories of my daily walks during those hot summer days in Ontario, near Los Angeles, with Mama Chencha and my sister, Lisa, are etched vividly in my mind.

My grandmother came to the United States from Jalisco, Mexico, after she married my grandfather at age sixteen, but she never learned to speak English or drive a car. When Mama Chencha had to go to town and there wasn't anyone else to go with us, I would translate for her. Our *mandados* (errands) took us to Crocker Bank to get a money order, to Hamilton's Drug Store to buy medicine, and sometimes to Alpha Beta to buy groceries. I will never forget the way the teller at Crocker Bank looked at my grandmother, eyes full of contempt because she could not speak English. I'll always remember the curtness in the voice of the produce man at Alpha Beta, acting as if he did not want to be bothered by a small child and an old woman who did not speak English.

When I got older, these images and feelings followed me. At times, the pain of these memories made me feel ashamed of speaking Spanish, but eventually, I understood the gift that I had been given. My ability to speak two languages gave me entry into two worlds. As I negotiated my place between them, my path turned to education. My experiences of being marginalized motivated me to search out a more just and equitable system where those of us who spoke a different language or who looked different could be respected. I discovered the possibility of teaching in a bilingual setting and then understood that my life's work would be dedicated to supporting other children through their struggle of negotiating two languages, two identities, and two cultures.

Over the last seven years, my work as an educator has revolved around working with the Latino immigrant community in the Pomona-Ontario Inland Valley in Southern California, where I grew up. Because I came into education with a definite purpose and goal, which was to work with a Spanish-speaking community, I chose a geographic area with a majority Latino population.

My path crossed Paulo Freire's during my teacher credential program. That year, I heard him speak and I also read *Pedagogy of the Oppressed*. Freire's work profoundly influenced and inspired me to go beyond the traditional role of teacher. It affirmed my decision to become a teacher. Freire's writings seemed to provide the theoretical framework for my teaching and anchored my hopes to become an agent of social change within a larger sociopolitical context. In Freire's work, the concept of education went far beyond the classroom walls to become more broadly defined and to serve a larger social purpose. Freire's work described the teaching and learning process in terms of people becoming socially conscious in order to become socially and politically active.

During my time as a classroom teacher, I tried to be mindful and respectful of the lived experiences of my students and their families. I recognized that for social transformation to take place, students had to understand and give voice to their struggles. We engaged in dialogues about violence in the neighborhood, economic difficulties at home, family situations, and discrimination and racism. Often, colleagues would marvel at the topics that were discussed in my kindergarten and first-grade classrooms. However, critical pedagogy had taught me that student experience and lived reality were integral to developing more equitable teacher and student relationships. To disallow those conversations would be to pretend that children don't see what they see or hear what they hear. I, as a child, understood that people treated me differently because I spoke another language, just as my students understood the same thing. Through my teaching, I discovered that talking to five- and six-year-olds about discrimination and racism helped the children understand their reality, while cultivating the hope necessary to change their future.

Freire in the Classroom

When I started my first assignment as an elementary bilingual teacher in the fall of 1991, it was my hope to become a teacher who was responsive and mindful of the needs and realities that students, but particularly students of color, faced. As a person of color, my own educational experience had been one that did not reflect nor integrate the social, political, economic, and historical perspectives that defined the Mexican/Chicano/Latino community in California. For this reason, I saw my purpose in the classroom as being not only to teach children to read and write but also to provide what Darder (1991) calls a "bicultural mirror" (69). My role as a bicultural mirror would be to model the constant negotiation that a person of color must undergo as a member of a subordinate culture living within a dominant culture. My reasons for being in the classroom were political in that I did not just want to be a role model; I also wanted to actively affirm and include the cultural and linguistic attributes of the students in my class in order to foster a positive bicultural identity. Furthermore, I wanted to help children and their parents to understand that they had the power to influence and potentially change the structures and institutions that oppressed them. With this in mind, I attempted to create learning environments that not only affirmed kindergarten and first-grade children who were bilingual and bicultural, but also made their parents feel welcomed and wanted. It was my sincere desire that my classroom would be a place where social transformation could occur.

Understanding that critical pedagogy in the classroom involves first and foremost an examination of power, I had to learn how to read the existing power relationships within the school system in which I was teaching. And since schools operate within a certain hierarchy of authority, I as a classroom teacher had to recognize the rules of this hierarchy and be willing to challenge those traditional norms in an effort to make a space for the development of different voices within the schooling process. Specifically, this involved a willingness to break down the authoritative role of teacher and open myself up to accepting suggestions and contributions for the development of new teaching practices from people who were usually marginalized in the school community—namely, students and parents. The vulnerability inherent in this action was most connected to the fact that I had to place myself in a continuous process of redefining what it meant for me to be a teacher. As a teacher using critical pedagogy, I had to struggle to move beyond the authority of the teacher's role in the classroom to transcend the boundaries of school, in order to become an active member of the larger community by affirming that school *is* part of a larger societal context.

Although integrating the principles of critical pedagogy can be done through different aspects of daily classroom practices, for me, one excellent way to do so is through the creation of a student-driven curriculum. By encouraging students to contribute to the development of the curriculum, I as the teacher began to share the power of the class with students, which enabled them to negotiate their role in the teaching and learning process. Moreover, these contributions reinforced for all of us the idea that alternative forms of knowledge are legitimate and have a place in classroom life. What I mean by student-driven curriculum is the creation of educational activities where students come to see their daily lived experiences reflected in the classroom. This also includes opportunities for students to participate in critical dialogues with their teacher and classmates about issues that intimately affect them, their families, and their communities.

One way to include students' experiences in the curriculum is to create opportunities for students to share or write about their everyday lives and family experiences. Freire taught us that, for social transformation to take place, it is important for students to understand and give voice to their personal struggles. Although we as teachers may not like to hear about the private lives of children, the realities children face are important factors in their social and academic development. In my classroom, daily "sharing circles" provided students with many opportunities to voice their thoughts or concerns on a particular subject. Using the curriculum guidelines and expectations of the grade level, I transformed routine practices into critical tools. "Daily news" was a regular morning activity in which three students shared something that had happened to them. During this time students would talk about special occasions such as birthday parties and family events. They also talked about some of the tough conditions they experienced, such as violence in their neighborhoods or the fears and hopes they held. Although these discussions often lasted only a few minutes, the conversations provided a window into the lives of my students. These discussions allowed me to ask students how they felt about a particular incident or issue, while simultaneously letting them know that their teacher wouldn't ignore what they had to say, but would listen to them. Furthermore, the dialogues that ensued created the space for other children to contribute their own experiences, while giving me the opportunity to connect their experiences to a larger social context and pose questions about what steps they could take to change their future.

Journal writing and drawing pictures were other ways for children to describe or reflect on their experiences. Journal writing was used to develop reading and writing skills, and students were free to draw and write about any subject they chose. In addition to writing about birthdays, toys, and play activities, students would draw pictures of struggles or sacrifices they were experiencing. For example, when students drew the apartment in which they lived, they would also often share that they lived with many people or that they had to sleep on the floor. At times they would also write and draw about the presence of the police in their neighborhoods or the fact that their families didn't have much money and couldn't buy toys or things for school.

When children shared these experiences and conditions, I was able to understand issues and difficulties in the classroom that I might not otherwise have understood about my students. For instance, when children came to school sleepy, there was usually a valid reason, such as having had to sleep on the floor; if a child was quiet, withdrawn, or distracted, it might often have to do with their worries and anxieties about something happening at home. Being watchful for the difficulties my students might face has made me not only more sensitive to their needs as human beings but also more aware of how those needs could affect their ability to learn.

In my classroom, students had opportunities to engage in "activity time," during which they could choose an activity they wanted to pursue, such as reading, drawing, or playing with Legos or blocks. An outside observer of my classroom might only perceive activity time as "playtime," but in actuality, activity time gave students an opportunity to develop oral language or storytelling skills openly and freely. Activity time also provided me with insights into the lives of my students, because while involved in creating block or Lego constructions, they would usually create stories to go with their constructions—stories that often echoed their real-life experiences. In my classroom, it was not unusual to find Lego constructions that immigrant children connected to their U.S.-Mexico border crossings at San Diego; or playhouse activities that mimicked real-life scenarios about the day the landlord came for the monthly rent, or struggles of families to provide enough to eat for their children.

The combination of these three classroom activities provided me with opportunities to address some of the inequities that my students faced. It should be noted that when students discuss personal or painful topics, it is extremely important that we, as teachers, be mindful and respectful in how we respond to their experiences. Furthermore, I found that it is equally important that the teacher guide discussions around these issues, so that the students might better understand the context in which they live. When classrooms provide such forums for children to talk and write about their world, teachers affirm that their world has meaning. Often, colleagues would marvel at the topics that were discussed in my kindergarten and first-grade classrooms. However, Paulo Freire's work taught me that student experience was integral to developing more equitable teacher-student relationships. To disallow those conversations would be to pretend that children don't see what they see or hear what they hear. My own experience during my childhood showed me that people treated me differently because I spoke another language. Making sense of the situation would have helped me understand why people treated me differently. It would have helped to not carry the burden of others' prejudices as if there was something terribly wrong with me that I had to correct. Consequently, I believe that talking to five- and six year-olds about discrimination, racism, and poverty actually helps children to understand their reality and to know that their reality is valid. These discussions also provide children with hope and cultivate their belief that they and their families do in fact have the power to change their world.

Acts of Solidarity
One of the most important insights I gained from listening to the children's stories also made me painfully aware that social, economic, and political changes need to take place outside of school if the conditions children face are to change. Freire (1970) taught us that school should not be viewed in isolation, but rather as an important part of the larger society. He wrote, "Education as the practice of freedom—as opposed to education as the practice of domination—denies that man is abstract, isolated, independent, and unattached to the world; it also denies that the world exists as a reality apart from

men" (69). Hence it is impossible to separate the child from her or his lived experiences. For this reason, we must challenge ourselves to create practices that link schools to community and society. Beyond our efforts toward inclusive curriculum, establishing relationships with parents and community members can help us to facilitate the link between school and society. Recognizing the importance that parents and the community play in a child's academic success validates their contribution to the educational process.

I found that I had to make a conscious decision to extend my responsibilities as a teacher to include working with my students' parents. This involved abandoning the traditional expectations of work duties and work hours. In addition, this challenged me to put aside my assumptions about parents and their abilities and accept them as significant people in a child's life. Moreover, I recognized that, since parents *are* their child's most important teachers, I had to make an effort to create an environment that welcomed and invited parents to become active participants in their child's school-based education.

At Back to School Night I would tell parents that I considered them an important part of their child's education. Many times when I made this statement, I was greeted with looks of utter amazement. Many parents had never thought of themselves as important to the education of their children. They were accustomed only to being told to do things, such as sign the homework, get their kids to school on time, and turn in library books on time to avoid fines. Consequently, when they heard the words, "Parents are a child's most important teachers," they responded with interest, enthusiasm, and gratitude. In my efforts to break with the traditional "banking" model of education, I had to dramatically redefine the relationship between the teacher, student, and parent. I invited students and parents to contribute their own stories and knowledge to create learning opportunities that were relevant and meaningful. I talked to parents willingly, not just about their child's academic progress but also about life, about family, and about politics. Recreating my traditional role as a teacher, I brought myself fully to the classroom and became involved in my students' lives in very different ways than most traditional teachers did at my school. Parents called me by my first name and phoned me regularly at home. I developed relationships with families outside of school and began to be invited to special occasions at their homes. I assisted them with problems unrelated to school and attempted to find them health, economic, and emotional resources, whenever possible.

As I began to establish relationships with the parents, I began to realize that most parents had little understanding about how schools function. It was not that parents were not interested but rather that they had not been given the opportunity to learn or acces important information regarding the school system. In general, I found that most parents were very eager to contribute to their child's education and with a little guidance and support, they could become active members of the school community. Monthly newsletters, phone calls, and home visits kept the lines of communication open. In addition, I took advantage of the time before and after school to just talk to parents. After establishing a level of trust, parents began to engage in more honest dialogue with me about their fears, their hopes, and their wishes for their children's future.

Once the parents began to share their struggles, concerns, and hopes with each other, they began to hold informal gatherings, which they called *pláticas*, or "chats." The *pláticas* turned into regular meetings for the purpose of identifying problems at the school and for parents to define their role in the school community. The parents took their responsibility so seriously that shortly thereafter, a group of parents, students, and teachers founded a formal group that worked in solidarity to identify oppressive school practices in an effort to transform the educational structure of the school. However, our group was not well received at the school. It seems that when immigrant or working-class parents really take an interest in school policies and practices, the traditional school authority within the community is threatened. The balance of teacher authority is turned around when parents are allowed to voice opinions, critique practices, and make suggestions. Rather than supporting parents to reach a new level of consciousness (and power), schools prefer that parents just follow the rules. To say the least, the level of parental involvement that evolved from this group was not appreciated by school personnel. It was even more distasteful for school officials when school struggles were put into the larger social-political context of anti-immigrant rhetoric and Proposition 187, a 1994 California ballot initiative the aim of which was to eliminate public services to undocumented immigrants.

Engaging in this type of practice required honest dialogue between the parents and me. It required recognition of the consequences of taking on active roles in the school community that challenged existing policies and practices. It is naïve to think that one can challenge the status quo without experiencing any consequences. Parents and teachers who work in concert in school communities must understand that when they engage in activities that upset the traditional balance of power in schools, there often are consequences. For many of us, the consequences may involve marginalization among colleagues owing to the perception that critical behavior is "unprofessional." This marginalization may result in our removal from leadership positions or an increased surveillance of our daily practices inside and outside the classroom. The parents may be viewed as troublemakers and may be shunned by other parents. Consequences could extend to their children, who may be unduly reprimanded for playground or classroom behavior as a direct result of their parents' involvement. These outcomes are real and should not be minimized, but they are not reasons to avoid challenging oppressive school practices. Rather, such backlash serves as an indicator that one is on the right path.

Constant critical reflection enables us to reassess our purpose and intended goals. Sometimes it makes sense to move ahead, and at other times, to retreat. Therefore, it is important to see a retreat not as failure but as a moment to understand the context of the particular struggle and learn how to start again with renewed hope. Freire (1973) wrote of this in relation to his experience in Brazil: "Thus the dynamic of transition involved the confusion of flux and reflux, advances and retreats. And those that lacked the ability to perceive the mystery of the times responded to each retreat with tragic hopelessness and generalized fear" (9). The ability to reflect is an important aspect in our work as critical educators. In my case, reflection and retreat taught me to take a "time-out" and step back from my practice in an effort to change it, if necessary, in order to ensure that

I was truly meeting the needs of my students. This constant cycle of action and reflection challenged me to constantly rethink curriculum and renegotiate relationships in the school community as changes occurred in the larger school and community setting. I believe that this responsiveness on our part as teachers demonstrates to our students, parents, and colleagues our willingness and commitment to transforming the nature of schooling.

Whenever possible, I share my story with new teachers in hopes that they will begin to incorporate critical pedagogy into their own classroom practices. In my work, I am often asked what are the practical applications of critical pedagogy—is it realistic to think we can create social transformation in a system that perpetuates the status quo? My answer is that because teaching and learning are ongoing processes there are no "recipe lesson plans" for critical pedagogy. Instead, our practice and relationships within our classrooms need to be rooted in a philosophy that promotes social justice as a daily lived experience.

One of my greatest impetuses for implementing critical pedagogy in the classroom is the knowledge that if I remain silent I become an accomplice to those who perpetuate educational inequality and allow schools to remain undemocratic. There is no question but that schools are failing not only students of color, but all students. Schools should be places where teachers, students, and parents can critically reflect and enter into dialogue together, not places where we stifle creativity and silence each other.

Paulo Freire (1973) greatly inspired me with the following words:

> Democracy and democratic education are founded on faith in [people] on the belief that they not only can but should discuss the problems of their country, their continent, their world, their work, the problems of democracy itself. Education is an act of love, and thus an act of courage. It cannot fear the analysis of reality or, under pain of revealing itself as a farce, avoid creative discussion (38).

Freire understood intimately that the construction of a democratic society relies on the understanding and participation of its people. In order for our global society to hope for a future that is more equitable and just, education must be perceived as an exercise in freedom and democracy. To view education as anything less is to diminish its power and its potential to reshape our future.

FREIRE AND THE EDUCATION OF YOUNG CHILDREN

ALEJANDRO SEGURA-MORA, PRIMARY SCHOOL TEACHER

Yo no le cuento a mi hija sobre lo que está pasando con la migra que golpeó a los inmigrantes. Sobre todo lo que está haciendo ese Pete Wilson y de como nos quiere sacar de aquí. Pobresita. Ella está muy chiquita para que se preocupe de esas cosas. No quiero que se asuste.

I don't tell my daughter about what is happening with the police beating up the immigrants. Especially what this Pete Wilson is doing and how he wants to deport us all. Poor child. She is too young to be worrying about those things. I don't want her to get frightened.

Parent of Stephanie, third-grader

My husband and I are very concerned with what you are teaching our child. Last night during our Thanksgiving dinner, she kept asking my husband and me how come we celebrated Thanksgiving if the Pilgrims who initiated the tradition had also killed many Indians. Last month during our Columbus Day picnic she kept asking us how come Christopher Columbus had a holiday if he did so many awful things to the Indians who lived here. You are confusing her!

Parent of Sandra, second-grader

These statements were made by parents of two of my students. As a critical educator, I consider these comments extremely important because they describe the familial context in which my students live. Parents often are concerned with sheltering their children from negative experiences, including those that would interfere with their family's belief and value system. Some believe that we should not subject young naïve and innocent students to political and ideological issues. In addition, many of my students' parents have internalized the belief that schools are neutral grounds of knowledge; hence, they perceive critical pedagogy as both openly political and anti-educational.

Alongside parent concerns are school practices that, more often than not, promote sanitized versions of historical struggles. While "higher-order thinking skills" are proposed as essentials for all students, the reality remains that authentic critical inquiry is widely discouraged and commonly prohibited altogether in many schools and classrooms (Fine 1991; Macedo 1994). This impediment to critical understanding is carried out by the censoring of students' difficult questions about race, class, culture, and sexuality, and many other issues of power and social struggle. Unfortunately, for students of color this type of educational experience can promote success in school at the expense of cultural identity and self-determination.

It is not unusual to find that the young children I teach have been repeatedly bombarded with one-dimensional images and decontextualized historical accounts of "happy Pilgrims" sharing a Thanksgiving dinner, and a "happy Christopher Columbus" discovering a continent inhabited by "happy Indians." From the beginning of their schooling experience and through a process of memorization and daily repetition, these students begin to internalize the misconception that there is "liberty and justice for all" in this country. Students, particularly the impressionable young, are often fed a steady diet of myths which ultimately help to shape their identity and support their participation in the unjust asymmetrical power relationships within the classroom and society. Paulo Freire (1970) exposed these myths in his writings:

> It [hegemonic control] is accomplished by the oppressors' depositing myths indispensable to the preservation of the status quo: for example, the myth that the oppressive order is a "free society"; the myth that all men are free to work where they wish . . . ; the myth that this order respects human rights and is therefore worthy of

esteem; the myth that anyone who is industrious can become an entrepreneur—worse yet, the myth that the street vendor is as much an entrepreneur as the owner of a large factory; the myth of a universal right to education . . . ; the myth of the equality of all men . . . ; the myth of the heroism of the oppressor classes as defenders of "Western Christian civilization" against "materialist barbarism"; the myth of the charity and generosity of the elite . . . ; the myth that the dominant elite . . . promote the advancement of the people . . . ; the myth that rebellion is a sin against God; the myth of private property as fundamental to personal human development (so long as oppressors are the only human beings); the myth of the industriousness of the oppressors and the laziness and dishonesty of the oppressed, as well as the myth of the natural inferiority of the latter and the superiority of the former (135–136).

Thus, we are left with a key question: How can we practice critical pedagogy—a pedagogy of liberation, of love and hope—in our work with young students? Or can we?

I firmly believe that we can and should implement critical pedagogy with young students. Antonia Darder (1995) describes this pedagogy as "a set of guiding principles for the enactment of an emancipatory classroom culture—principles that are intimately linked to an emancipatory paradigm, or a way of thinking, about human beings, culture, knowledge, power, and the world" (42–43). Freire (1970) describes this teaching/learning approach as a dialogical paradigm in which the teacher enters into dialogue with the student, who, by nature of being alive, comes to the classroom with valuable knowledge and experiences. This is the antithesis of what he calls "banking" education, in which the teachers see themselves as the owners of knowledge and the student as an empty vessel into which teachers deposit their knowledge. My teaching experience has shown me that young children are capable of engaging in dialogue on important issues, and are often very willing to do so. Moreover, Freire challenges us to have faith in our students and their power not only to become actors in their own lives but also to transform their world. He referred to this as "faith in the oppressed."

Faith in the Oppressed

I can't help but feel bad for these students. I can share critical issues with them, but for what? They won't be able to do anything about it.

Veteran teacher

If I share critical issues with my students, they're going to become frustrated and maybe even overwhelmed—I think even hateful of the dominant culture.

Young teacher

During my last six years as a teacher in public schools, I have come across many teachers who seem to see no connection between issues of social justice or economic democracy and their work with young students. It is not surprising to find many teachers who see the issue of social justice as a political one and their job as teachers as anything but political. I have also met teachers, like the two quoted above, who, despite having been introduced to and claiming to agree with critical pedagogy, still hesitate to create a space where their students can engage in critical issues. The first teacher demonstrates a lack of faith in her students to use their power as social actors to transform their lives and the world they live in. The second teacher seems to be afraid of the possibly debilitating consequences of his students' coming to a better understanding of unequal power relationships in society. The primary goal seems to be one of sparing students the anguish of coming to a clearer awareness of our social reality. In any case, the consequence of not creating this dialogical space is in fact to promote an inability in students to "link societal themes" (Freire 1970). Macedo comments: "This inability to link the reading of the word with the world, if not combated, will further exacerbate already feeble democratic institutions and the unjust, asymmetrical power relations that characterize the hypocritical nature of contemporary democracies" (Macedo 1994, 15).

Linking Societal Themes

No es duro ser Indio y Europeo porque puedes escojer uno, o Indio o Europeo.

It's not hard being Indian and European because you can choose one, Indian or European.

Erick, third grade

Yo quiciera que los Europeos jamas hubieran venido a nuestra tierra.

I wish that the Europeans had never come to our land.

Estela, fourth grade

Maestro, yo no sabía que parte de los Estados Unidos eran de México antes. ¿Por qué nadie me había dicho antes?

Teacher, I didn't know that part of the United States belonged to Mexico before. Why did no one tell me this before?

Fernando, third grade

Comments such as these are among those we hear when young students are free to express what they are experiencing while they attempt to make sense of their world. It is a challenge to confront these issues with any student, and I believe it is a special challenge when teaching young students. The primary reason for this is that teachers must be ready to respond to the questions parents may have upon hearing some of these comments made by their children. Therefore, the space for dialogue that we create in our classrooms for young students must be extended to their parents. This provides an excellent opportunity for establishing solidarity with parents, particularly those who have strong cultural identities. Doing this may pose a greater challenge with parents who, despite their cultural heritage, are appalled at having their child identified as a person of color or as an *Indio*.

In a society that tends to see most issues in dichotomous terms, it is common for people to hold polarized judgments. For example, we hear these types of judgments often in debates over the use of whole language versus phonics. Often, educators feel compelled to choose one methodology over the other, seldom rupturing the polarization to consider that elements from both might be useful. It is equally common to hear a young student like Erick come up with a dichotomous solution to the problematic contradiction inherent in mestizo identity. Erick, one of the lightest-skinned students at his school, decided he was an Indian and not a European. After a dialogue about the genocide of many indigenous communities by European settlers, Estela wrote in her journal that she wished Europeans had never come to her land. Another student, Fernando, wrote that he did not know that a part of the current United States had once been part of Mexico, and wanted to know why no one had told him the truth.

As a teacher, I realize that I could have chosen not to deal with any of the above issues in the first place. If I had not done so, it is very likely that my students would not have come to these realizations at that time, nor would they have shared them with me. Chances are they would not have linked societal themes related to the invasion of these lands by Europeans with the genocide of many indigenous communities and with the subsequent loss of land by indigenous populations. In such dialogues, young students often make comments that many teachers would prefer to avoid. Unlike such teachers, I try never to discourage student comments, however negative or disturbing they may seem. The reality is that these issues affect young students in very profound ways. Given this, their candid commentaries provide great teaching moments that must be seized rather than discouraged.

By fostering an open dialogue with my students, I can assist them in the formation of greater critical understanding and help them overcome debilitating forms of resistance. An example of this type of resistance occurred following a history lesson on the United Farm Workers' struggle. One of my young students commented, "*Todos los gringos son malos!* (All white people are bad)."

Creating a critical space in which students feel safe to express themselves provides us the opportunity to both support and challenge our students to transcend reductionist conclusions which distort their reading of the world and can interfere with their process of empowerment.

Child Development and Traditional Ideology

It has been important for me to understand that traditional studies and recommendations by acknowledged leaders in child development have been shaped by their particular ideologies—ideologies generally masked with claims of "objective" science. For example, child psychologists such as Piaget, who studied his own white middle-class children, have fostered notions of childhood development as "raceless" and "classless." More recently the psychologist Mussen (1983) has written an extensive four-volume *Handbook of Child Psychology* that deems invisible the experiences of children of color. In her critique of Mussen's work, Margaret Beale Spencer (1987) wrote, "Not only is there no section on the experiences of African-American children, or minority children in general . . . but research by fewer than 10 minority scholars is referenced in a volume that cites thousands" (105). This narrow notion of early childhood development has been perpetuated by child psychologists who consider identity issues related to race, class, gender, and ability unimportant, instead of recognizing these significant markers of identity as pivotal components of early childhood development. Their failure to engage these issues has advanced the notion that to focus on such issues with young children is detrimental to their healthy development.

Moreover, the acritical views held by traditional leaders in the fields of child development and early childhood education have resulted in an overwhelming conviction among teachers that young children should be sheltered from critical and controversial issues (Alexander 1984). In Hatcher and Troyna's (1993) view, this sheltering by traditional educators is the result of a set of "commonsense assumptions about childhood innocence which constitute one of the main tenets of the ideology of primary education" (21). This view of childhood is fairly widespread and has helped to discourage many K–12 teachers, especially in the primary grades, from involving their students in discussions about race and other "controversial topics." This refusal to deal with critical issues constitutes a refusal by educators to provide their students with the skills they need to read their environment—one shaped by the devastating effects of racism and other forms of social and economic injustices.

Nonetheless, in recent years, there has been a steady increase in research that challenges dominant notions of traditional child psychology. The research indicates that early childhood identity formation is informed by notions of race and ethnicity (Clark and Clark 1947; Cross 1991; Derman-Sparks, Higa, & Sparks 1980; Glover 1990; Goodman 1964; Katz 1976, 1987; Katz and Seavy 1973; Ogbu 1985; Spencer 1985); by societal conceptions of gender (Aboud 1987; Huston 1983; Wickens 1993); and by notions of social and economic class (Ramsey 1987).

Critical Dialogue with Young Students

The current research brings us to another important question: How do we engage young students in critical dialogue? I do plan activities purposely, but I have found that the most interesting dialogues have emerged from learning experiences initiated by my students. In fact, I seldom know exactly how I will carry out a critical dialogue with my students. Practicing critical pedagogy with young students is a difficult task because I must try to facilitate authentic dialogue based on issues that are relevant to my students. This way of teaching is almost always more rewarding, although more demanding, than following a prescribed curriculum.

I have discovered that I must be on the lookout for golden opportunities, instances when a student might say and do something that reflects a belief or a value related to questions of social justice. According to Nancy Jean Smith (1995), "We miss many opportunities, which are intensely rich teachable moments, when we fail to listen closely to the intentions behind children's thoughts, or decline to read the entire environment that the child is reading" (243). Once a teachable moment arises, I recognize it as an experience that can potentially transform us together. As a teacher, I often struggle with myself at junctures where I am faced with making a choice. Do I deal with the issue at hand for the benefit of my students, or do I give in to the pressure by the school culture to turn away and stick to the state-prescribed curriculum. The reality is that often, critical educators are marginalized by their coworkers when the latter discover that these teachers are disrupting the flow of "business as usual." However, I have found that my willingness to address hard issues when they arise with my students has brought me a greater sense of dignity as a teacher and as a human being.

The best way I can illustrate how I have engaged my young students in critical dialogue is by sharing an experience that took place in my kindergarten classroom last year. Most of my kindergarten students had already been picked up after school by their parents. Two of them still sat on the mat in the cafeteria lobby, waiting. Occasionally, one of the children would stand to look through the door's opaque windows to see if they could make out a parent coming.

Ernesto, the darkest child in my class, unexpectedly told me in Spanish: "*Maestro*, my mom is giving me pills to turn me white."

"Is that right?" I responded, also in Spanish. "And why do you want to be white?"

"Because I don't like my color," he said.

"I think your color is very beautiful and you are beautiful as well," I said. I tried to conceal how his comment now saddened and alarmed me, because I wanted to encourage him to continue sharing.

"I don't like to be dark," he explained.

His mother, who is slightly darker than he, walked in the door. Ernesto rushed to take her hand and left for home.

A Childhood Memory

Ernesto's comment took me back to an incident in my childhood. My mom was holding me by the hand, my baby brother in her other arm, my other three brothers and my sister following along. We were going to church and I felt happy. I skipped all the way, certain that I had found a solution to end my brothers' insults.

"You're a monkey," they told me whenever they were mad at me. I am the only one in my family with curly hair. In addition to "monkey," my brothers baptized me with other derogatory names such as *Simio* (Ape), *Chineca* (an unpleasant image of curliness, made even more negative by feminization with an "a" at the end), and *Urco*, the captain of all apes in the television program *The Planet of the Apes*.

As we entered the church, my mom walked us to the front of the altar to pray before the white saints, the crucified white Jesus, and his mother. Prior to that day, I hadn't bought into the God story.

After all, why would God give a child curly hair? But that day there was hope. I closed my eyes and prayed with a conviction that would have brought rain to a desert.

"God, if you really exist, please make my hair straight," I prayed. "I hate it curly and you know it's hard. So at the count of three, please take these curls and make them straight. One, two, three." With great suspense I opened my eyes. I reached for my hair. Anticipating the feel of straight hair, I stroked my head, only to feel my curls. Tears stung my eyes. As I headed for one of the benches, I whispered, "I knew God didn't exist." For Ernesto, the pill was his God; for me, God was my pill. Even now, I wonder how Ernesto will deal with the failure of his pill in the future.

A Teachable Moment

As teachers we are cultural workers, whether we are aware of it or not. If teachers don't question the culture and values being promoted in the classroom, we socialize our students to accept the inequalities of our society along lines of race, class, gender, and ability. Yet teachers can—and should—challenge white-supremacist values and instead promote values of self-love.

I am grateful for Ernesto's sincerity and trust in sharing with me. Without knowing it, Ernesto opened the door to a lively dialogue in our classroom about racism. To resurface the dialogue on beauty and skin color, I chose a children's book that challenges white privilege (a category with very few selections). The book is *Niña Bonita* (*Beautiful Nina*), written by Ana María Machado and beautifully illustrated by Rosana Faría. The book tells the story of an albino bunny that loves the beauty of a girl's dark skin and wants to find out how he can get black fur. I knew the title of the book would give away the author's point of view on the little girl, so I covered the title. I wanted to find out, before reading the book, how children perceived the cover illustration of the dark-skinned girl.

"If you think this little girl is pretty, raise your hand," I said. Fourteen hands went up.

"If you think she is ugly, raise your hand," I then asked. Fifteen voted for ugly, among them Ernesto.

I was not surprised that half my students thought the little girl was ugly. Actually, I was expecting a higher number, given the tidal wave of white dolls that make their way into our classroom on Fridays, our Sharing Day, and previous comments by children in which they have indicated that a dark complexion is ugly.

After asking my students why they thought the girl on the book cover was ugly, the following discussion took place:

One student responded, "Because she has black color and her hair is really curly."

Ernesto added, "Because she is black-skinned."

"But you are dark like her," Stephanie quickly pointed out to Ernesto, while several students nodded in agreement. "How come you don't like her?"

"Because I don't like black girls," Ernesto quickly responded.

Several students affirmed Ernesto's statement with a "yes" and a "that's right."

"All children are pretty," Stephanie replied in defense of all children.

Carlos then added, "If you behave good, then your skin color can change."

"Are you saying that if you are good, you can turn darker?" I asked, trying to make sure the other students had understood what he meant.

"White!" responded Carlos.

"No, you can't change your color," several students responded. "That can't be done!"

"How do you know that your color can change?" I asked, hoping Carlos would expand on his answer.

"My mom told me," he said.

"And would you like to change your skin color?" I asked.

"No," he said. He smiled shyly as he replied and I wondered whether he may have wished he was not dark-skinned but didn't want to say so.

Carlos's mother's statements about changing skin color reminded me of instances in my family and community when a new baby is born. "Oh look at him, how pretty and blond-looking he is" is a common expression if the baby has European features and coloring. And if the babies came out dark, like Ernesto? The comments are often *"Hay, pobrecito, salió tan prietito"*—"Poor baby, he came out so dark."

In our school's staff lounge I hear similar comments from coworkers. A typical statement: "Did you see Raul in my class? He has the most beautiful green eyes." Is it any surprise that so many students must fight an uphill battle against racism, while other students choose not to battle at all.

Challenging My Students

In an effort to have students explain why they thought the black girl in *Niña Bonita* was ugly, I asked them, "If you think she is ugly for having dark skin, why do you think her dark skin makes her ugly?"

"I don't like the color black," volunteered Yvette, "because it looks dark and you can't see in the dark."

"Because when I turn off the light," explained Marco, "everything is dark and I am afraid."

Although most of my kindergarten students could not articulate the social worthlessness of being dark-skinned in this society, I was amazed by their willingness to struggle with an issue that so many teachers ignore, avoid, and pretend does not exist. At the same time, it was clear that many of my students had already begun to internalize notions of white privilege.

At the end of our reading and discussion of the book, I took another vote to see how students were reacting to *Niña Bonita;* I also wanted to ask individual students why they voted as they did. This time, eighteen students said the black girl was pretty and only eleven said she was ugly. Ernesto still voted for "ugly."

"Why do you think she is ugly?" I asked. But this time, I must confess, the students didn't volunteer responses. Perhaps they felt that I did not value negative answers as well as I did comments by students who fell in love with *Niña Bonita.* In their defense of dark skin, some students offered explanations such as "Her color is dark and pretty"; "All girls are pretty"; and "I like the color black."

Our discussion of *Niña Bonita* may have led four students to modify their values of beauty and ugliness in relation to skin color, or maybe these four students just wanted to please their teacher. But one thing is certain: the book and our discussion caused some students to look at the issue of skin color in a new way. Equally important, *Niña Bonita* became a powerful tool to initiate discussions on an issue that will affect my students, and me, for a lifetime.

Throughout the school year, the class continued to engage in critical dialogues on the notions of beauty and ugliness. (Another story that sparked much discussion was Hans-Christian Andersen's *The Ugly Duckling*. This popular fairy tale—whatever the original intent of its author—was repeatedly interpreted by my young students as the story of a little duckling that is "ugly" because his plumage is dark. Happiness comes only when the duckling turns into a beautiful white swan. I chose to use this book because it mirrored the way in which mainstream children's stories may inadvertently reinforce racist views in young children. Given the impact such stories can have on my students' sense of self, I want my students to know that they can disagree with and challenge such views.

I am very aware that, when I have such discussions with my students, I often feel like instantly including my opinion. But I consistently try to allow my students to debate the issue first. After they have spoken, I ask them about their views and encourage them to clarify their statements. One of the reasons I enjoy working with young students is that teaching is always like an experiment where the students constantly surprise me with their candid responses—responses that require me to be ready to modify how I move through the day.

I do, however, struggle with knowing that as a teacher I am in a position of power in relation to my young students. I am only too aware of how easy it is to persuade or manipulate students to stop using the dominant discourse and adopt the discourse of the teacher. In a society in which we have been accustomed to dealing with issues in either/or terms, children (like many adults) tend to adopt one discourse in place of another, but not necessarily in a way that requires them to actually think through the issues carefully. I struggle to create a space where my students can begin to look critically at the many forms of unequal power relations that shape their lives—relations that, even at the age of five, have already begun to determine whether they love or hate their skin color and, consequently, themselves.

At the end of our discussion of *Niña Bonita*, I shared my feelings with my students. I told them that, in my opinion, the girl in the story is beautiful. I said that my skin color is beautiful. I caressed my face and kissed my cinnamon-colored hands several times happily and passionately, so that they could, concretely, see my love for my skin color. I told them that Gerardo, a light-complexioned student, has beautiful skin color and so does Ernesto. I told them that Gerardo cannot be out in the sun for a long time because his skin will begin to burn. I can stay out in the sun longer because my darker color gives me more protection against sunburn. But Ernesto, I told them, can stay out in the sun longer than both of us because his beautiful dark skin gives him even more protection.

Despite our class discussions on beauty, ugliness, and skin color, Ernesto did not appear to change his mind. But hopefully he will not forget our discussions. I hope that every time Ernesto pops one of his magic pills into his mouth, which his mother later explained to me are Flintstones Vitamin C pills, he will remember how his classmates challenged the view that to be beautiful, one has to be white. I want Ernesto always to remember, as will I, Lorena's comment: "Dark-skinned children are beautiful and I have dark skin too."

A Final Reflection
Tell the children the truth.

Bob Marley

My experience with Ernesto and my other kindergarten students is significant in that it demonstrates the permanency of the struggle to engage students in liberatory education. This is not work that can be done in a single school year. It is a lifelong process. Although I will probably not be these students' teacher in the future, I hope that the critical skills of dialogue and reflection I have tried to share with them will help them survive the uphill battle in our assimilationist educational institutions. At such a young age, students' self-concepts have already been tainted by the same culture of racism and economic inequality that has shaped the identities of their parents and of teachers who will continue to socialize them in school and at home.

One of the most powerful lessons that I have learned is that even young children are able to reflect on issues that impact their identity and their lives. The world of children is governed by the same values and beliefs that govern the world of adults. For this reason I firmly believe that Freire's contributions to critical pedagogy are equally valuable and applicable to the education of young students. As critical educators, we must build the courage to deal with critical issues that affect the lives of bicultural students, and all students in general, whether these be racial epithets or other forms of social injustice. I believe young students can benefit greatly when encouraged to express their concerns openly—not as an end to the dialogical process, but as a powerful beginning of what undoubtedly will be a rich learning and growing experience for both teacher and students. When students are encouraged to make moral judgments about social issues, their discussions are engaging, while at the same time students begin to develop a voice, a fundamental catalyst to feeling empowered in the world.

Furthermore, it is crucial that we also seek ways to develop critical dialogue with students' parents about the asymmetrical power relations that shape their lives and the way these affect the identity formation of their children. Through participatory parent projects, more parents can empower themselves to take a liberating role in their own development, as well as in their children's education. Through a variety of educational projects that bring parent knowledge to the classroom and to curriculum development, students, parents, and teachers, can engage together in what Freire called "praxis"—a combination of theory and practice, leading to purposeful action that can transform our world.

TEACHING HOPE TO CHILDREN IN SPECIAL EDUCATION

BARBARA S. C. GOLDSTEIN,
PRIMARY SCHOOL SPECIAL EDUCATION TEACHER

Paulo Freire continues to be a living presence in my classroom and in every other place where I interact with students. He has influenced the educational experiences of the students who have passed some part of their lives with me; yet most of them, particularly those who experience the effects of difference as oppression, do not know his name. Freire's life and work shaped their classroom experience, including curriculum, methodology, assessment, management, discipline, parent participation, and student-teacher interaction. Freire was present in their daily classroom life because his work informed and shaped my basic educational philosophy and approach to teaching from the beginning of my teaching career.

As a teacher who worked to imbue my practice with critical pedagogical principles, I struggled with the daily, practical issues of running a classroom. Keeping attendance, assembling portfolios, passing out lunch tickets, remembering rainy-day and block schedules, sitting through faculty meetings, and finding time for a bathroom break when it's our week for yard duty, tend to use up whatever energy is left after several hours of teaching. Seldom do I find the time to reflect, discuss, question, and share ideas about my practice with my coworkers. Seldom are we provided with the time to remember why we became teachers in the first place. For many of us, it was to change the system, contribute to our communities, make a difference in the lives of families and children, and in some way make the world a better place. Unfortunately, all this gets lost in the middle of the hubbub, and so we search and struggle to create a space where we can renew our vision of the possibilities.

Discovering Freire

It was in the midst of just such a search that I first heard Paulo Freire speak at the International Institute's Escuela Laboral in East Los Angeles. I felt at that time that the idea of the "community school" could be maintained in the public school system. The idea of students determining the scope and content of their curriculum was certainly not new, but the idea of a dialogical pedagogy with the purpose of making education truly liberatory was one that I felt should not be reserved only for adults or older students. Unfortunately, my discussions about this issue with like-minded colleagues were helpful but did not sufficiently assist me to address the needs of my young students.

Nonetheless, I knew through my personal experiences as a student, teacher, female, and working-class Chicana from a nontraditional family, that young students, like older students, were also silenced and coerced into blind obedience. Often, when a spark of resistance or rebelliousness emerged, they were shamed back into desk chairs with lowered eyes, or were insulted or intimidated and humiliated by adults in authority. Students who dared to speak out (talk back), engage in dialogue (speak to others without permission), and follow their own ideas, thoughts, and interests in their assignments (not following directions) were labeled troublemakers, delinquents, or slow learners. Many of these children eventually disappeared from the classroom, weeded out in a process so insidious that even the most well-intentioned teachers did not (and do not) recognize their pivotal role in this economic and social maintenance of the status quo.

When I read *Pedagogy of the Oppressed* (Freire 1970), I was struck at the ease with which I connected the stories and ideas in this book to my family's own social, political, and cultural development. I knew that my teaching practices and my own distrust of the system in which I worked was fueled in large part by my knowledge of the struggles that members of my own family had encountered in schools, most particularly those encountered by my father. However, I remember how reading the text embued my perception of familial historical events with clarity and a sharp focus regarding the oppressed's willingness to participate in their own oppression. This lack of consciousness regarding the internalization of one's supposed inferiority became vitally important in my development as a teacher. Moreover, it helped me to understand the ambivalence over cultural, linguistic, and ethnic identity that I had inherited—and which I also recognized in my young students.

My subsequent years of teaching English and English as a second language were characterized by examinations of literature that depicted how individuals and groups of people dealt with many different types of struggles for self-preservation, growth and development, and liberation. I found that I could engage my high school and junior high school students in discussions about historical narratives that were relevant to their lives and maintain their interest through the use of literature and related individual and group projects anchored in their everyday lives. Student-generated projects that were directly connected to the histories of their neighborhoods, communities, and families provided powerful learning opportunities that resulted not only in their acquisition of critical modes of inquiry, but also the acquisition of skills and methodologies valued by traditional education. Thus, my young students learned how to read the *word* as well as the *world*.

Critical Pedagogy and Young Children

In my teaching, I have found that children who come from families who are struggling to survive economically, culturally, and politically can benefit from teaching practices that are rooted in critical theory because these children already have an awareness that all is not just in their world. Often these children serve as cultural and linguistic mediators for their families, trying to reconcile two very different worlds. Moreover, their school and home generally represent two different worldviews, often with conflicting rules and norms. From a very early age, many of my young students must learn to juggle multiple worlds and ways of being.

What has often been missing for these students has been a place to discuss, question, and analyze these interactions with peers and with a "teacher." Here is where I believe that Freire's ideas related to the development of critical consciousness are relevant to the young child. Critical consciousness can best be understood as a process that can be nurtured commensurate with the cognitive and linguistic capabilities and development of the young child. Consequently, it becomes vitally important to provide children with opportunities to begin to develop critical consciousness and hence their critical voice, even at a very young age. I discovered with my elementary school students ways to foster, nurture, and enhance the critical voice, so often stilled during their first years of schooling.

Perhaps one of the reasons few teacher-researchers have written about Freire's work in relation to young children is because "conscientization," the development of critical consciousness, requires the ability to reflect and critique one's thoughts, actions, and motivations. It requires ongoing dialogue with peers and mentors. It demands awareness of self and environment in a particular place and time, within a historical and cultural context, and a particular political landscape. The development of critical consciousness requires the ability to analyze these features within a community of learners and to discover the relationships among these features and their impact on our lives.

And, finally, it requires the ability to translate these discoveries into action, to transform some aspect of our lives to one that is more just. It is assumed that young children do not have the cognitive, linguistic, or even the emotional development required to engage in this type of pedagogy because we are used to thinking of them as limited in their ability to understand "complex" matters. Most teachers view the problem-posing nature of critical dialogue and action as being "for mature audiences," and the topics that emerge as too intense for younger sensibilities.

Special Education and Social Justice

In special education, I have found that efforts to provide a critical educational experience for young children requires our willingness to address an additional dimension of difference—a dimension that is intimately connected to issues related to quality of life and social justice. When I design opportunities for critical dialogue and analysis, I also have to keep ever present in my mind the strengths and needs of special learners and the life concerns unique to this community. Early intervention that assists my young students with special needs to analyze, to the best of their ability, their unique situation in society, both as individuals and as a community, is just as important as early intervention in language, academics, and health needs. If my students with special needs can begin to see themselves as subjects rather than objects, they will have greater opportunities to contribute to their own liberation from oppressive conditions that stem from societal ignorance and prejudices concerning differences due to disability.

Most of my special education students were first- and second-graders. They were in an educational program for students with learning and language disabilities. Most of them came from families that were struggling economically. They were primarily Spanish speaking and were learning English as a second language. I believed that Freire's work was and is a direct response to the lives of my students, who because of their age, developmental differences, social and economic obstacles, and the ethnic and linguistic prejudice they face are truly oppressed. Hence, the pedagogy that Freire describes is germane to their liberatory education. My challenge was to discover how to accommodate and modify the communicative structures and modes of analysis required to successfully work through problem-posing situations and dialogical interactions that would tap in to my students' strengths. I also needed to create a way to integrate basic skills, individualized educational plans, and the general education curriculum into a critical educational setting.

However, the key issue here is that the children, who had been labeled as the most difficult to teach, demonstrated an ability to engage in modes of analysis, critique, and dialogue that resulted in praxis, reflection, and action, which ultimately transformed some aspect of their lives. They learned not only how to read and write, but also to speak their minds, challenge assumptions, and make generalizations and connections. They learned that study is hard work, that it takes time and effort, and that it also can be "joyful and rigorous." These children learned that they are living history and that people write books. They learned that they can tell their own stories. Most important, they learned that they have potential to change their lives, and that to change structures and systems they need to work in community. My students were able to push each other through their supposed limitations and, through sustained effort, build an environment where it was safe to practice autonomy and self-regulation, critique each other's work and ideas, and propose changes to the teacher's plans.

I believe that critical pedagogy enables special education teachers to examine theories and models of diagnosis, assessment, instruction, and evolution of special education with respect to the context in which it has developed and is practiced today. Further, it makes explicit the social context in which a child is identified as a special education student.

Rather than focusing on neurological pathways, skills, or consequent behavior, a critical perspective of language/learning disabilities emphasizes the development of critical consciousness and critical literacy that can result in praxis. Students' difficulties are also examined in light of historical conditions of cultural and linguistic subordination; the effects of racism on their communities; and the impact of poverty and discrimination on their educational experiences. All diagnoses of learning difficulties must involve a critical analysis of this educational history and experiences. To carry out this type of student assessment, it is up to teachers to establish an atmosphere of collaboration between family members, educational staff, and the student— one that includes alternative and interactive assessment practices as well as an assessment of the curriculum, instructional program, and instructional approaches. Reading and language-development activities should be based on student narratives that can be woven into the study of children's literature and that reflect students' concerns and experiences regarding self, family, and community. Learning experiences are most effective when they are characterized by authentic tasks as part of action research requiring critical analysis and reflection. The goal of a special educational program based on a critical pedagogical perspective is a liberatory, transformative educational experience that enables students and their families to become knowing subjects and full creators of and participants in a socially just and democratic society.

Critical Emergent Curriculum

The curriculum that emerged from my attempts to weave Freire's work into my practice within the special day-class setting integrated a holistic/constructivist approach with critical pedagogy and traditional special education instruction designed for children with learning disabilities (Goldstein 1995). The key feature of the reading/language arts component, which addressed the language and literacy development of the students' Individualized Education Plans (IEPs), was units based on children's literature and the students' original narratives. Instruction for specific skills was presented as minilessons for reading and writing. In addition, students had access to a computer reading, decoding, and vocabulary program entitled "Writing to Read" (1982). Afternoons were devoted to an integrated pattern of study whose content—which included material from social studies, art, music, dance, song, science, physical education, and English as a second language—was connected to the literature unit being studied.

The study of selected children's literature provided my students with the opportunity to become familiar with story grammars (sequence and story components), new vocabulary and sentence structures, and reading for pleasure. I selected stories for study that encompassed social themes, characters, events, or places that the students might relate to personally. Students would read or listen to a story and respond to the story in discussions and illustrations or by dictating a sentence or two about their observations. Students also kept class charts and individual logs that contained information regarding the story grammars, key vocabulary they had identified, and unanswered questions they had about the story.

Subsequent discussions about the book, other related storybooks, and their own discussion items generated book and content comparisons. Questions about the storybook went from literal to inferential and discussions grew more complex. Students began generating their own stories related to the ideas and social issues they had identified in the storybook and their own discussions. Students then returned to the original storybook and engaged in a critical rereading of the text in light of their own personal stories. Comparisons of similar issues, problems, and solutions eventually led to action planning as a reaction to the issues identified by the students' narratives. Action projects were designed and implemented and later evaluated as part of the action design. Reflective discussions about the plan, action, and results enabled students to develop a deeper understanding of the issues they identified. It also gave them opportunities to examine the problems from multiple perspectives, that is, from the points of view of storybook authors, their characters, and the students as authors of their own stories.

In summary, my students responded to the literature by demonstrating their literal comprehension of the literature story and retelling the story. They also discussed and wrote about their initial reactions to the story. Students then began to discuss their inferential and interpretive comprehension of the story features and eventually participated in a writers' workshop where they wrote their own original stories. With time, students began to critique both the literature story and the personal narrative stories. They began to identify assumptions that inform the texts. They used generative words and codifications to illustrate ideas and vocabulary or phrases. Students generated a course of action inspired by their critique of the literature story and their personal stories. They conducted a power analysis of the plan and identified obstacles and resources for each plan generated. Students outlined their plan and implementation. Finally students reread and critiqued the literature story and the personal stories in light of the action outcomes. They reviewed the power analysis charts and logs. They conducted an evaluation of the critical story unit that included evaluations for the activities, discussion, and supporting texts. Students analyzed their portfolios consisting of generative words, word banking lists, codifications, story grammar charts, and reaction journals.

The assessment process I used was collaborative and was conducted both individually and in groups. I held a conference with each student to identify areas of growth and need. Throughout the course of study activities tied to specific academic skills were included. Students incorporated their "Writing to Read" activities into their personal writing and reading of texts. It is important to note that each approach to the individual children's literature unit varied depending upon the context in which it occurred. In other words, the process changed in form and sequence depending on both teacher and student strengths and weaknesses, and their responses to one another's interests and reactions.

My use of storybooks provided students with an effective way to understand the concept of a story. Their work with grammar provided a scaffold upon which the students could organize their own story in order to make it comprehensible to others for sharing and for dialogue. Because many of the students in my classroom had difficulties with expressive and receptive language, providing them with an easy to follow framework for story building was crucial to their success with the activity.

Many of the storybooks that I used in my classroom were books written by authors with the intent that social themes not ordinarily dealt with in primary grades would be presented in developmentally appropriate ways for younger children. Although I knew it intellectually, in reading and discussing my students' personal stories I became acutely aware that these children were already well acquainted with the social themes depicted in these storybooks, including homelessness, prejudice, poverty, and confusion regarding their bicultural identities. Their stories and discussions often gave voice to their feelings and thoughts about issues that they lived but seldom named.

Children who had been identified as the most difficult to teach demonstrated an ability to engage in modes of analysis, critique, and dialogue that resulted in praxis, action, and reflection that somehow transformed some aspect of their lives. Students who had a history of failure learned to read and write. They also learned to speak their minds, challenge assumptions, and make generalizations and connections. We all learned that study—that is, teaching and learning as one event—is hard work and that it takes time and effort, but that it can also be joyful. My children taught me that we all could tell our stories and that in the telling we are transformed; and in the action and reflection we have the ability to transform structures, systems, and lives.

Most important, my students showed me that they could support each other's efforts and challenge each other's supposed limitations. Through their sustained effort, they learned to build an environment where it was safe to practice autonomy and self-regulation, to critique each other's work, and to speak of and act for possibilities for change. If it is true that we make the road by walking, then my students have already begun to clear a path of hope for me, so that I may share it with you.

TEACHING AGAINST PRISON PEDAGOGY

EDUARDO F. LOPEZ, HIGH SCHOOL TEACHER

I became a teacher because I see teaching as a political necessity, particularly at this historical juncture. We are living in dangerous times. Capitalism is currently undergoing dramatic and profound transformations, changes that have had a cataclysmic impact on the entire globe. For those of us who have chosen teaching as our profession, I believe that it is our ethical and moral obligation to urgently engage the devastating impact of these changes.

Democracy is quickly becoming (if it is not already) a state of virtual reality. Our current political and economic systems attempt to sell and market "illusions of wealth . . . to the poor, illusions of freedom to the oppressed, dreams of victory to the defeated and of power to the weak" (Galeano 1988, 116). Equality and justice are becoming an unattainable fantasy (did they ever exist?) as we see the disparity between the rich and the poor grow to such a state that even the middle class has now become cynical of reaching the ever-elusive "American Dream."

We live in an age in which global capitalism seems to be the only site where the slogan "*un mundo sin fronteras*"—"a world without borders"—is truly practiced. Multinational corporations no longer deem it profitable enough to exploit the poor, women, and people of color in the United States and thus have sought new markets and a cheaper labor pool in overexploited countries, especially along the U.S.-Mexico border. Domestically, these same corporations are "downsizing" and in the process are displacing an unprecedented number of workers through the introduction of new technology, including robotics, the information superhighway, and the computer.

Teaching within these conditions is not an easy task. It is difficult because most critical educators do not have access to the material resources or decision-making power to oppose and transform the impact of changing class conditions in schools. Consequently, teaching is often a frustrating and both physically and spiritually draining experience. As someone who is relatively new to the teaching profession, I was quickly introduced and immersed in this reality.

I have been teaching for two years now. For about a year and a half, I taught English as a second language to adult Latino immigrants through an organization called the Community Learning Network. Currently I find myself teaching at an all-boys private Catholic school in South Central Los Angeles. I teach sociology to twelfth-graders and Intercultural Studies to tenth-graders. Although I am still struggling to find my own teaching style, my views about education and my political commitment to socioeconomic change are grounded in my own personal history.

My parents were born in Mexico. Like all the thousands who continue to come to "El Norte," they sought better economic opportunities. They established themselves in East Los Angeles and raised five children. Despite racism and economic inequality, they somehow managed to teach their children to love, to be proud of their culture, to value knowledge, to be politically conscious, and to work toward social and economic transformation. I have attempted to apply these lessons to my work as a high school academic counselor, activist, organic intellectual, poet, and educator.

Beyond my personal history, my efforts to integrate critical pedagogy in my work in East Los Angeles have required that I take into account the radical transformation of the inner city by the "postindustrial" economy. Moreover, I had to learn to recognize how institutions such as the educational system are increasingly employing the use of "prison pedagogy" in order to render servile and closely control and regulate inner-city youths of color. Young people respond to this by resisting and internalizing prison pedagogy—as I was soon to discover.

Facing the Impact of Prison Pedagogy

Excited about the possibilities critical pedagogy offered, I looked forward to working with the young men at the private all-boys Catholic school. The school has developed a strong reputation for its athletic program, but in the last few years its academic reputation has been slowly declining. From being one of the areas' best college-preparatory high schools, the school has shifted its function, as one instructor recently commented at a faculty meeting, "The school serves now as a continuation high school."

For the past four years, the school has been thrown into constant chaos. In this time span, the school's principal has been replaced three times. Each administrative change has brought a different educational philosophy and pedagogical approach. Teachers came and went, some staying only for a few months. Last year, approximately eleven teachers left, in part because of all the school's "discipline" problems.

As the school saw itself deteriorate, it increasingly shifted its focus from academics to discipline. The school increasingly began to become preoccupied with the surveillance and control of students. For example, the first thirty pages of the parent-teacher handbook are only about discipline and the actions the school will take when rules are violated.

Before the start of the 1998 academic year, a new principal and vice-principal were hired. Rather than placing a heavy emphasis on discipline in order to create effective school reform, the new principal and vice-principal initiated some new strategies: class sizes were reduced to twenty students, teaching across the curriculum was stressed, the curriculum was diversified in order to have more college preparatory courses, and the position "dean of discipline" was renamed "dean of respect," and this person's functions were restructured. The most dramatic change occurred during the first two weeks of school. During this time, students did not have assigned courses or textbooks. Teachers were assigned a group of students from each grade level and were asked to evaluate students' intellectual, spiritual, moral, and social skills. The administration felt that there was a wide gap between what students' report cards stated and their actual skill levels. Therefore, instructors needed to conduct alternative assessments in order to identify the skills of students.

It was in this context that I met, struggled with, and learned from my first sophomore class in Intercultural Studies. The course is designed as a one-semester elective course. It provides students with an introduction to some of the major historical and political events that have shaped the Latino and African American communities. I was hoping to engage in some exciting dialogue about the material and historical forces that have oppressed these communities and the ways in which they have also resisted, opposed, and mediated these forces.

Since I also had attended an all-boys Catholic school, I thought I was well prepared to deal with young men from poor and working-class communities. Yet during the first weeks, I came across such powerful resistance that I was unsure and confused as to how to teach in this context. A power struggle between the students and me emerged over control of the classroom. Students proudly and defiantly told me how they had been able to get rid of eleven instructors last year. They recounted stories of a student peeing in a classroom, students who had stolen books and materials from instructors, and how sometimes books and batteries were thrown at teachers. Several young men smiled as they informed me that teachers had been unable to control them and it would be only a matter of time before I, too would leave the school. Since students figured I would eventually abandon them in desperation, they figured it didn't make any sense to listen and participate in class. They refused to pay attention and instead talked excessively. Often, students would get out of their chairs and sit next to their friends in order to have a conversation. Once, in order to show their defiance, a group of students suddenly began to rap. I stood in front of the class amazed as I watched most of the class join in on the song and start clapping.

It was an extremely frustrating experience for me. I found myself using about 90 percent of my energy attempting to control students and only 10 percent on content. At the end of the day I was exhausted. I simply wanted to come home and sleep. What I found most disturbing was that many students began to ask me if I used to be a police officer. Some even suspected I was an undercover officer. For someone who considers himself as a progressive, this revelation was disturbing. But at the time I was unable to understand, nor willing to engage this idea because I was more concerned about "classroom management." However, about the fourth week of classes, an incident occurred that made me deeply reflect on not only students' perceptions of me but also the organization of the entire course. It was shocking, frustrating, and humbling to realize that their perceptions of me were more accurate than I had initially realized or was willing to admit.

The Internalized Oppressor Unmasked

On one particular day, I had finally reached the end of my patience with one of my students who constantly talked in class. I was determined to make an example out of him. I walked up to him and told him to get out of the class. Several students turned to me and asked why I was only kicking out that student, since there were other students also talking. I did not care because I wanted to make an example of him. I was determined to have discipline in my classroom, even if I had to use force.

As the student got up to leave the room, I noticed that he was taking his book bag with him. I feared and suspected that this student would leave the campus, so I instructed the student to leave his book bag in the room. The student refused and continued to walk out the room. As he walked past me, I suddenly grabbed the student's bag and again instructed him to leave it.

Like two mortal combatants, we stood in the middle of the class, desperately pulling on the book bag. The rest of the class looked on and wondered who would eventually win this tug-of-war. As I looked back and forth between the class and the student, I suddenly became horrified at what I was doing. I let go and the student took his bag with him.

The students were right; I had become the police officer. My main objective in the classroom was policing, not teaching. Because I was so determined to establish discipline in my classroom, I accepted the dominant ideology on how to deal with these students. Pedagogically I was only thinking about control, surveillance, classroom management, and quick and swift punishment.

It was at this point that I turned again to Paulo Freire for some sort of guidance. These were troubled and sleepless nights for me, as I attempted to confront and wrestle with my internalized oppression. For someone who believes himself to live his life from a left political standpoint, it was difficult to admit that twice now, I had aligned myself with traditional and dominant forms of teaching. In these reflections, I began to see how in those moments of uncertainty or frustration, I would blindly turn to oppressive forms of pedagogy. I naïvely believed dominant forms of pedagogy would offer me salvation, when in reality, these practices were fundamentally dehumanizing. Paulo Freire compared the process of liberation to childbirth, a painful process. However, if one is authentic, then reflection and a critical engagement with one's practice can serve as powerful tools in the struggle for our humanization. On that day, I decided to change my relationship with students and the structure of the course.

Toward a Pedagogy of Love and Liberation

A few days later I approached the student I had kicked out of class and apologized to him. He was surprised to hear a teacher apologize to him and I assured him things were going to change. When students arrived for class, I asked them to rearrange all the seats into a circle. I informed them that from now on, I was not going to give out any detentions. It was a frightening decision to make, since I figured many would take it as a license to continuously disrupt class. Many of the students looked confused and I proceeded by explaining I had come to this school to teach. I cared about them too much to continue treating them in the way I had been doing. A young Latino student challenged me by saying he did not believe me and that no teacher had ever said they cared about them. I agreed with the student and said he had every right not to believe me at this moment. In the following weeks, students would have to decide for themselves whether I was truthful and sincere.

In order to create a more meaningful educational experience for these young men, I decided to eliminate exams. I made this decision because students were not studying for exams. Students would come in on exam day, write their names on the test, give it back to me, and proceed to talk with their friends. Others would simply try to cheat. Instead I assigned weekly two-page papers which were due every Friday. In addition, during the week I presented and lead discussions on stereotypes, racism, and economic inequality and examined some of the major historical factors that shaped the Latino and African American communities.

Students were encouraged to write and explore topics from their cultural backgrounds. When their papers were due, I informed students that they would be required to give an oral presentation on the information they had researched. My initial fear that students would not take the assignment serious quickly disappeared. The young men would stop me around campus in order to inform me that they were working on their papers and they seemed excited. On the first Friday the papers were due, we gathered in a circle and I anxiously waited to see what type of work was produced. One by one, students began to read their papers. Although a few students still continued to talk, for the most part everyone was listening. Presentations were made on the Mexican American War, George Washington Carver, Cesar Chavez, the Emancipation Proclamation, Malcolm X, El Salvador, Simon Bolívar, Rosa Parks, and Louis Armstrong. What was most striking about students' work was that most of these young men had chosen to write about people who had acted as social agents against oppression. Through this process, students began to become immersed and involved in the development of an oppositional collective memory of struggle, resistance, and hope. For example, one Latino student wrote about El Salvador. Though he had been exposed to and had to endure the brutal oppression in El Salvador, this student still wrote about the people's struggle for freedom:

> My reflections upon the readings is that Salvadorians suffered a lot for their freedom. Many people died for their freedom, the government always got their way. They didn't listen to the people. They slaughtered many people. . . . Many people fought for their rights and were exiled or killed. The government fought against the people for many years and a civil war broke out. The U.S. helped the government with supplies.

On several occasions, students wrote or wanted to write about figures that I found problematic. One student wrote about the Colonel Charles Young, who was the first African American to graduate from West Point Academy and rode with Roosevelt's Rough Riders in Cuba. Another student wanted to write about the richest African American in the United States. While these men were exceptional in their ability to rise above society's restrictions, their stories mask the ugly reality of U.S. imperialism and how our society is organized along class lines. I therefore found it necessary to include a critical historical perspective in order to challenge and problematize many of the internalized assumptions of students. For example, when we began looking at the Mexican-American War, this event was examined from the perspective of U.S. expansionism, "Manifest Destiny," and capitalist formation. Many of the young men were amazed and did not know about these events.

For homework, I asked students to write reflection papers. An African American student wrote:

> My view of history is different because I did not know the land I or we lived on was once Mexican land. I did not know that the president of Mexico was Santa Ana, so now I will treat Mexican Americans different.

Another African American student wrote:

> This view of history affects my view of American history drastically. I was not aware that the U.S. took most of Mexico's land by force. Knowing this today we would be considered illegal immigrants. In this day people are trying to prevent immigrants from coming to America, but we are the true immigrants! America has a very bad history. They hide the truth so that we do not know. They are ruthless conquers who did not care who they ran over in the process.

A young Latino student wrote:

> At first, I did not care about the Mexican-American War but now I know what happened. America stole the land. They took advantage while Mexico was weak. Also I did not know this part of Mexican and American history but now I know.

Through dialogue, love, and a critical engagement with history, the classroom became a site where students were able to recreate and reclaim history from an emancipatory standpoint. A new learning community was being created as our relationships began to change. They learned from me as much as I learned from them. Not only did I learn from the presentations, but I also began to learn about the students' everyday reality. For example, I learned that the reason why the student I had earlier kicked out of class refused to leave without his book bag was that students often steal or play tricks on each other and hence they always take their bags with them.

But perhaps the most painful realization I learned from these young men, was the horrifying amount of violence they are exposed

to on a daily basis (Lopez 1998). Several students have seen someone get shot. For example, in the third month of class, one of my
student's best friend was gunned downed. Some live in situations
where adults openly and freely use drugs. All of the students see the
police as a source of intimidation and terror.

It is important not to frame these observations from a conservative political perspective that seeks to blame the problems of the
inner city on the people who live there. One needs to take into
account the "postindustrial" context of inner-city social problems.
Mike Davis (1990) illustrates how the inner city, in particular South
Central, has been the site of tremendous upheavals in the last few
years. Thousands of manufacturing jobs have been lost in the inner
city. In their place, service-sector jobs have become the primary
means of employment. Where manufacturing jobs at least promised
a steady income and benefits, service-sector employment only offers
part-time jobs paying the minimum wage and with no benefits. In
addition to the economic devastation, Mike Davis argues that the
inner city has increasingly become a site where there is an intensified police presence, a growing reliance on private security companies, an increase in the prevalence of gated communities, and an expansion of the for-profit prison industry.

The sociologist William Julius Williams (1997) contends that
many of the problems associated with the inner city, such as crime,
the breakup of families, poverty, and low levels of social organization, are a consequence not only of racism but also the disappearance of work. Many inner-city African American and Latino young
men, unable to find work, turn to drugs and the underground economy in order to make money. The nihilism that Cornel West
(1993) speaks about so eloquently when he says that young people
feel a "profound sense of psychological depression, personal worthlessness, and social despair" is very real for the young men in my Intercultural Studies course.

The intensification of racism and capitalism has had a detrimental and dehumanizing effect on working-class youths of color. When
social cohesion breaks down, love, nurturing, and care become elements that are hard to find in the lives of these young men. I see this
social reality in the way students relate to each other and teachers,

and the way they approach the educational process. Students constantly hit and push each other. They steal from classmates and throw batteries at teachers. Because some students have low reading and writing skills, their discomfort with critical work manifests itself as classroom disruptions.

Developing a curriculum of liberation and teaching in a critical manner is not an easy task. I only work with a given group of students for a limited amount of time. When the class period is over, students return to a world that does not value them, except as cheap labor. In addition, I am still struggling with my own internalized oppression. There are many pitfalls in this journey.

Yet it is a struggle we urgently need to wage, particularly in a world where the advancement of capitalism reigns unchecked and triumphant, while more and more of the world's population is relegated to "disposable" workers within the greedy ethos of a globalized international economy, yet all is not hopeless. While capitalism has been able to colonize many aspects of everyday life, it has yet to effectively commodify love. I believe this is where critical pedagogy can create a truly revolutionary space in order to teach against prison pedagogy. Critical pedagogy is a necessary and important tool in creating and fostering the conditions in our classroom for democracy, liberation, and love.

SHARING THE MAP: TEACHERS AS CRITICAL GUIDES

KATRINE J. CZAJKOWSKI, HIGH SCHOOL TEACHER

I came to Southern California in 1990, having recently graduated from the Edmund A. Walsh School of Foreign Service at Georgetown University. My degree in international politics encompassed an interdisciplinary focus that included science and technology. Initially I became a teacher because I felt disillusioned by what I had experienced at Georgetown while interviewing for positions with some of the country's most elite corporations and government agencies. At the time, I explained my decision by saying that I could not see myself sitting in front of a computer all day, generating money for someone else. Today, I'm amazed that I had so little awareness that such a dilemma is born of privilege.

Perhaps I though I was taking the easier route when I entered a teacher credential program. My first teaching experience was at a junior high school located four miles north of the U.S-Mexico border. It provided me with a whole new understanding of "international politics." Schools in this country by no means serve a common purpose. Today I am a teacher because I recognize the critical role of schools that serve students from cultural communities that have been historically oppressed. For the past nine years, I have worked with students who differ greatly from people I knew when I was their age. As a teacher working in one of San Diego's poorest communities, I have been taught the meaning of humility and respect by the young people and parents who struggle to hold on to the myth of the "American Dream." When I first read Paulo Freire's *Pedagogy of the Oppressed*, it truly represented for me an accurate articulation of the phenomenon I was both witnessing and experiencing in my life. This caused me to begin thinking about my teaching and my students in a completely new way. As a consequence, I focused my graduate studies on critical pedagogy and forged ahead to develop more personal and well-grounded relationships with my students.

Blazing beneath the banners of standardized tests and legislative rhetoric, public education is a war pursued by a host of unseen enemies. Poor students and students of color are often its unwitting victims. Schools face a shortage of well-trained teachers from all communities. Through Paulo Freire's work, I came to understand that teachers from privileged backgrounds have a particular role to play in the struggle for social justice in schools. In my experience, this issue of privilege is seldom addressed, and when it is, it is often sugar-coated with a vapid liberalism that is condescending and deceitful. Yet in my experience with my students, they tell a strong kind of truth, for they often know more about what they need than the teachers who so easily dismiss their voices. So I have learned to listen and to search for ways to mediate the clash between the world in which they live and the world they find within the schools that they are forced to attend. I seek to assist them in navigating an educational system that is often alienating and hostile.

Approximately 75 percent of my students are people of color and almost 70 percent participate in the free or reduced-price lunch program. Their education represents the only possibility for their further opportunity, yet the statistics are not stacked in their favor. This is very unlike my own privileged situation. My parents were both physicians. After earning her medical degree in Denmark, Mother emigrated to the United States. She met my father, a Pole, at Harvard Medical School. While the war in Vietnam raged, my parents lived in Germany, where I was born. Proficient in German and equipped with academic credentials, my father served in the U.S. Army hospitals. We ultimately moved to Portland, Oregon, where I graduated from high school. I was admitted to Stanford University with sophomore standing, due to the educational opportunities that prepared me for advanced placement examinations.

My parents never taught me German or Danish as a child because they felt there was little reason. Today, my mother finds it aggravating that I am learning Spanish. How can I explain to her what I can only partially explain to myself. I live four blocks from the high school where I have taught for the last seven years. The Mexican border town of Tijuana is visible from the football field. "Why do you have to live down there in that Navy town with the sewage problems?" my mother asks. "Why don't you live up by UCSD [University of California, San Diego] or someplace where people have academic discussions?" I want to remind her that she was able to attend medical school in a socialist country, simply because she had the right and preparation—she didn't require over $100,000! I say nothing; but I can't help but think about what future there will be for the young people who live on my block, my students at Mar Vista High School.

High school is often regarded as the "last stop" for students attending public schools; graduation is, more often than not, the "end of the line" for most working-class students. Public education is touted as designed to prepare all students for college, yet the vast majority of students from subordinated populations never make the move to the university. At Mar Vista, only about 15 percent of the graduating class of 1998 went on to a four-year college or university. The other 85 percent went out to find minimum-wage jobs, and a few enrolled in community college or vocational programs. Of those who enter community college, only 5 percent ever transfer to a four-year institution. And of those few who manage to enter a four-year university, over 50 percent drop out by the second year. These numbers clearly indicate that the power linked to higher education remains concentrated in the hands of those who have always held it.

Paulo Freire (1994) wrote that "provided with the proper tools for [dialogical] encounter, the individual can gradually perceive their personal and social reality, as well as the contradictions in it, to become conscious of his or her perceptions of that reality and deal critically with it" (14). I believe that one of my major responsibilities as a teacher is to provide my students with this kind of experience. Freire also suggested that students could "undertake a systematic study of their findings" (100), if they were provided the opportunity to do so. Within my interdisciplinary approach to teaching a combination of mathematics, English, and social sciences, students are encouraged and guided toward making connections between what for many seems like unconnected subject matter. Yet I have found that the less my teaching is fragmented into compartmentalized subjects, the more students are able to make sense of the material and its impact on their lives.

The Critical Interdisciplinary Classroom

For the past few years, I have had the opportunity to teach in an interdisciplinary classroom, where I teach English, mathematics, and social sciences to the same "team" of forty ninth-grade students. This means I work with each subject for three hours a day. Though this would be unremarkable in an elementary school, it is highly unusual at the secondary level, where academic periods are limited to fifty minutes. Teaching several subjects at once allows me to get to know my students more personally. This allows me to determine more accurately "the starting point at which people visualize the 'given' and to verify whether or not during the process of investigation any transformation has occurred in their way of perceiving reality" (Freire 1994, 88). What I have found over time is that dialogue is what truly connects the three subject areas. Extended periods of time allow for more flexible inquiry and the expression of "genera-

tive themes" as described by Freire. There is no question that establishing meaningful teaching and learning relationships with our students takes time—yet time is curtailed within the traditional structure of secondary education.

I teach both freshmen and senior students. Many of the students
who are now in my Advanced Placement English class were students
in my ninth-grade team when they first arrived at Mar Vista. The
title of the course may suggest an elite group of students from privileged backgrounds, but in fact, the advanced placement program at
Mar Vista serves a community where fewer than 10 percent of all
residents have taken any college-level courses. Most students in the
class are the first in their family even to consider applying to college
or university, which is an issue that we engage actively in our work
together. We spend as much time discussing issues related to access
and power as to Elizabethan poetry.

Freire's work, and critical pedagogy in particular, is often criticized for being too theoretical and abstract. For many, the practice
seems lost in complex theoretical language and ideological foundation. Certainly, a difficult text can take much time and concentration, but I truly have learned that my work as a teacher results from
the interaction of my theoretical perspective, reflection upon my
practice, and the actions and decisions I make within the classroom—Freire's definition of praxis, as opposed to practice alone. For
example, the course during the first six weeks of my ninth-grade team
is designed to help me to discover who my students are and to reinforce that the questions they ask and study can produce results that
can change the course of their lives. During the summer, I seek out
timely articles in major newspapers and magazines that deal with
teenagers or popular culture that include the results of a survey or
poll. I use these articles for teaching Language Arts with students, to
assist them in learning how to complete double-entry journal notes
that focus on the assumptions the author is making about teenagers
or other populations. Together we investigate the author's biases, as
well as the group or agency that funded the survey or poll. Then we
discuss mathematical sampling methods and explore ways proportions can be used to make generalizations about a population in a
sample. The social studies aspect of the unit includes a discussion of

norms, values, and mores. This discussion also assists students in contrasting the demographics of the population in the article to those of their school and community.

This study unit also has English and math components. While working critically with these surveys, students concurrently read Sandra Cisneros's *House on Mango Street*. They learn to use graphing calculators to generate random numbers for use in their own research into areas that are relevant to their lives. They work individually, in pairs, and in small groups. Together they select and develop their hypotheses, which they then test using an original research design. Their hypotheses are based on assumptions they have identified in the article(s) read during the beginning of the semester and the purpose of the group research projects is to test their own ideas using mathematically sound research methods. Examples of hypotheses tested by students last year include "Teenagers are more susceptible to advertising today than ten years ago" and "Most teenagers are mentally absent from school." My students develop survey instruments, administer the survey, and create spreadsheets for use in data analysis, using Excel. They learn to sum their results and create graphs and charts that aid them in developing conclusions. They deliver formal presentations to their classmates in seminar format and report their research in the form of a formal paper. The paper includes an abstract, methodology, results, conclusions, recommendations, and sources cited. The students accomplish all of this, even though they are only in ninth grade!

Unfortunately, most of my colleagues in the math department see little value in what I am teaching my students. Even with the best of intentions, they claim they do not have the time to spend on topics like sampling, analysis of survey distortions, research design, or the principles of valid and invalid arguments. Like most traditional math teachers, they prefer to remain within the more familiar world of linear equations, while they attempt to lead students to $y = mx + b$ with the very detached aura of expertise and abstraction that ultimately functions to alienate most students.

While reading Freire's *Pedagogy of the Oppressed* (1994), I came to recognize that my students' survey project challenged me to step back from the stage occupied by most high school teachers. "Just as educators may not elaborate a program to present to the people, neither may the investigator elaborate 'itineraries' for researching the thematic universe, starting from points he [or she] has predetermined" (89). Hence, I came to see that if I wanted my students to acquire critical-inquiry skills and the ability to challenge accepted views, I had to learn that this was only possible by ceding my absolute control over their learning process. The fervor for "content standards" currently gripping public education, which is accompanied by "accountability measures" that promote standardized testing, threatens the work of critical educators who strive to find a balance between teacher authority and student freedom in their classrooms. Yet there is no question in my mind that working with my students on investigation projects truly enabled me to become a more responsive teacher and to rapidly guide my students toward greater academic progress.

The Power of a Teacher

Freire often reminded us, for example in *Pedagogy of the Oppressed* (1994), that "those who authentically commit themselves to the people must re-examine themselves constantly" (42). This is not always easy. Because my students and I established a close relationship, we often talked about issues that were important or troubling to them. On some days this required making hard choices as a teacher—do I stay with the day's predetermined math lesson or do we move into the pressing dialogue and spend more time on math tomorrow? A teacher's ability to make such a decision well illustrates an important arena of power a teacher wields in the classroom: the power to choose the day's activities and subject matter.

An example of this occurred the day one of my students proclaimed that "AIDS was God's way of punishing gays." Was I supposed to sweep the comment under the rug and proceed with the math lesson on systems of equation? I knew, given their past experiences in the class, that my students would openly protest such a decision. And since the comment coincided with the brutal death of Matthew Shepard, most of the students held strong opinions. So I decided to turn our attention to this issue. Remembering that the *San Diego Union-Tribune* was sponsoring an editorial contest, I encourage students to enter into dialogue with each other and with me and then to write an editorial to submit to the paper. The students wrote editorials that engaged with issues of racism, intolerance, and ignorance in society. One student, Melissa, wrote about what she has heard in church about homosexuality; Shelli, another student who attended the same church, asked whether God could truly intend for us to learn to hate one another.

At that time some students had founded a new club to provide a forum for honest discussion about racism, prejudice, and stereotypes. The principal admonished me, the club's adviser, for permitting the word "homosexuality" to appear on the club's flyer. "Use another word," she said. At a subsequent meeting in her office, she explained to the club's president that a father had angrily inquired if there was a club on campus for gay students. "I definitely won't send my daughter to a school that would allow such a thing!" Jessica, the president of the club, looked the principal in the eye and said, "Well, we certainly wouldn't want that girl to grow up as ignorant as her father, would we?" I could hardly contain my admiration for the student, which won me no favors with a boss known to hold grudges.

This episode reminds us that we as teachers ultimately make pedagogical decisions related to the political vision of the world we hold—do we use our power to support the voices and intellectual development of our students or attitudes within schools that fail to challenge social inequities?

One particularly difficult day early in my teaching experience, I recall arrogantly berating a sixth-period math class. "Sometimes I wonder if you people ever learn anything I'm trying to teach you!" Suddenly, from the back of the room I heard a student yell back, "You teachers just don't know anything, do you? We learn something from everything you do, whether you want us to learn it or not!" On that day, I truly began to realize the tremendous power teachers hold within the classroom. I recognized how teacher attitudes and thoughtless comments can impact our students and, most important, that "dialogue cannot exist without humility" (Freire 1970, 71).

Teaching for the Future
One of the reasons I appreciate the contribution that Paulo Freire's work has made to my teaching is that my students often return to visit me. I hear echoes of our classroom dialogues as students talk to

me about their new lives. Freire believed that dialogue could not exist without hope and faith in our students. This is so true! For me teaching is filled with challenges, but also with hope and joy. My joy is often nourished by stories of my former students such as Samantha. She graduated from Mar Vista in 1998. The Chinese-Mexican daughter of parents who had never attended college, she was admitted to both University of California at San Diego and UC Berkeley and decided to attend Berkeley. I recall helping her find a map on the Internet, so she could figure out how to take the bus up to Berkeley for an orientation meeting in June.

When Samantha came to visit me in November of her first year in college, I asked her to speak with my ninth-graders about her high school experience. She spoke to my students with confidence and pride in what she had accomplished. When asked whether she missed her family, she simply responded "Yes." She talked about her classes at Berkeley and the books she was reading. When the class was over, she expressed her appreciation to me for everything she had learned and for how it had prepared her and her classmates to handle the university.

As we walked together, she shared her experiences. Her dark eyes shone with anger as she described the commercially sponsored televisions in every classroom and the low-expectations of teachers at Oakland Tech High School, where she was doing an internship. One year later, Samantha returned to see me again. She had decided to do a double major in business and education. She wanted to teach because she felt that she knew "what's going on from the inside." For me it was joy to hear her passion and a privilege to have shared in the formation of her future.

REINVENTING TEACHER EDUCATION:
TEACHING AND SOCIAL JUSTICE

MARTA P. BALTODANO, TEACHER EDUCATOR

I was born and raised in Nicaragua. My working-class parents labored very hard to provide their six children with the education their own parents had not been able to afford for them. Being the eldest of a large family had many disadvantages, but at the same time it gave me the opportunity to be the first one in my family to realize my parents' hopes and expectations that their children would earn college degrees.

For me, the process of becoming aware began in my senior year in high school. I had as philosophy teachers some of the most progressive thinkers in the country. Many were priests who were part of the liberation theology movement and later became ministers of the new revolutionary government in Nicaragua. It was through them that I first learned about Paulo Freire and his widely acclaimed book *Pedagogy of the Oppressed*, which was first published in 1970. Despite our young age, my classmates and I related Freire's concepts to the reality of our oppressed nation.

I received my college degree just when the Somoza dictatorship was falling apart. I became involved in human rights issues, probably forced by the reality of a country where it was a crime to be a teenager. I became a human rights advocate and worked—as did everyone else in Nicaragua—to bring down one of the most repressive regimes of Latin America. I want to emphasize that this was not an exceptional situation; my entire family was involved in this political struggle. My parents, brothers, and sisters, at different moments and in different ways, anticipating the actualization of a truly emancipatory political project, supported the new revolutionary Sandinista government.

Unfortunately, the time came when I could not continue to support the revolutionary government. My human rights advocacy made me acutely aware of the persistence of human rights abuses and the emergence of highly contradictory patterns of intolerance and violence against those who publicly questioned the direction of the revolution. During this time I struggled to find out how to position myself. Given Nicaragua's circumstances, there seemed to be little room for participating in a substantive process of social critique. Finally, I decided that I had to remain faithful to my work with victims of human rights violations, whatever the political cost. This decision was painful because my questioning caused some to see me as being in opposition to the Sandinista government instead of supporting it.

The National Literacy Campaign

One of the most fascinating projects of the revolutionary government was the national literacy campaign. Nicaragua had one of the
lowest literacy rates in Latin America, and the government announced the nationwide implementation of Paulo Freire's pedagogy
in an effort to teach basic skills while raising the political consciousness of hundreds of thousands of Nicaraguans. This was one of the
major ideological enterprises of the Sandinista administration.

During the initial stages of the campaign, Paulo Freire came to
Nicaragua and was welcomed as a hero. I recall seeing him on television surrounded by most of the members of the government, including commanders, priests, professors, and teachers. He looked some-
what astonished, but pleased, to be in Nicaragua, learning firsthand
of the early accomplishments of the literacy crusade. At that moment I wondered whether he understood the complexity of the
Nicaraguan situation and whether he learned about the contradictions within that project.

Despite the accomplishments of the national literacy campaign,
people were questioning the implementation and strategies used in
this effort. Basically, the complaints centered on an absence of a humanizing pedagogy—one that could authentically empower participants through a growing awareness that the oppressor could live in
any of us. Freire's pedagogy had been reduced to a mechanical
process of rote instruction.

Leaders in Nicaragua seemed to miss or ignore Freire's major
contribution. His pedagogy was not a technique, strategy, or lesson
plan, but a way of living, loving, and interpreting the world. The
revolutionary officials, even with the best intention, could not
comprehend or accept that Freire's concepts transcended the existence of a particular revolution or a political system—that in reality, a true revolution is nurtured with the authentic transformation
produced by an emancipatory pedagogy, and not vice versa. My fellow Nicaraguans fell into the trap of reifying Freire's pedagogy; they
could not understand that a profound transformative process had to
be initiated at the domestic level in order to advance to the public

realm. People in Nicaragua learned to read the word but not the world.

Discouraged with what I saw happening in my country, I came to the United States in 1991 ready to start my life over again as a graduate student. I was profoundly disillusioned with the notion that wide-scale social transformation was possible. It seemed as if I had experienced everything from violence and dictatorship to revolution and false consciousness. I was confused, and I decided that I needed to step outside of what had constituted my world to look at that reality from the outside. Needless to say, I felt hopeless and sought a new vision that could restore my faith in humankind.

Later, in Freire's *Pedagogy of Hope* (1995), I found words that best described my dilemma at that time: "Without a minimum of hope, we cannot so much as start the struggle. But without the struggle, hope, as an ontological need, dissipates, loses its bearings, and turns into hopelessness. . . . Hence the need for a kind of education in hope" (9).

After spending thirteen years as a community activist and practitioner in Nicaragua, I came to study in the United States, looking for some ideological and theoretical framework that could help me to understand where we in Nicaragua had gone wrong. I rediscovered Freire in graduate school, learning how his pedagogy had become a cutting-edge theory in North America and Europe. At that time, I remained very skeptical about Freire's relevance to First World societies. I could not understand how Freire could be revived and transposed to a context very dissociated from the reality of Third World societies.[1]

But there was another problem, too. My greater difficulty with all this was related to witnessing the continued appropriation of Freire's work for personal and academic purposes, totally unrelated to the daily reality of teaching in schools and the personal transformation required to be coherent with his philosophy. I spent the next two years struggling with this issue: Why do educators who claim to be grounded on Freirean pedagogy fall into a deep incoherence between what they preach, their teaching practices, and their personal lives? They do not seem to understand that from the moment they dichotomize Freire's pedagogy—reducing it to a political discourse or a method—they have decapitated the very essence of his philosophy. Anyway, I was ambivalent about the possibility of truly practicing and implementing critical pedagogy, particularly after being exposed to its concepts in such varied and contradictory contexts.

It was later in my life, when I began my doctoral studies in education in 1992, that I began to make peace with Freire. For the very first time I found a mentor who understood the incredible complexity of Paulo's pedagogy and taught Freire's principles by practicing his philosophy in the interaction with her own students, and the connections they made with their children in the classroom. It was at that point that I realized that for most of my life I had been exposed to people who had fallen into a permanent stage of false verbalism—talking with little action—and who, as consequence, failed to honor one fundamental principle of Freire's work—the union of theory, practice, word, and action—namely, praxis. This was the beginning of my awakening process. I began seeing how Freire's principles could become alive, could transcend the novel, chic theory to become practices that were embedded in a profound transformation of ourselves as human beings in our work with others.

During the last five years, I have been challenged to question more deeply my emotional, ideological, and social location. Through this at times painful process, I have had to unlearn some of the values that I acquired during my own schooling process that both distorted my identity and caused me to work in the interest of other people's ideological and academic agendas. Moreover, I became aware that I was both a product and a victim of cultural domination; and, further, that I was pursuing a degree that positioned me to be part of a privileged intellectual elite—a group that traditionally has legitimized the discourse of hegemonic groups. Freire's philosophy helped me to better understand and contend with this dialectical and contradictory social location.

Teacher Education

My work as a teacher educator and researcher of teacher preparation programs not only has given me the opportunity to deepen my knowledge about Freire's pedagogy, but also has restored my faith in social transformation. I have discovered that education, as both a subversive force and a political calling, can take place in teacher education, despite this discipline's alienating structures.

When I began working in teacher education, I become more aware of how the cycle of discrimination and oppression is reproduced in schools through one of the key actors of the educational process—the teacher. I have become conscious of my implication in the process of training teachers as ideological agents of the establishment, and the fact that, unless there is a deliberate effort to reconceptualize the formation of teachers, I too would be equally responsible for the transmission of institutional injustices.

The more I worked with teachers, the more I questioned our program. What is our program doing to prepare teachers to work with children who look like me? Are my intern teachers aware of their power in the classroom and their role in the transmission of stereotypes about culturally diverse and working-class students? What is my participation in the reproduction of injustices? And, in the long run, what can I do in my role as a teacher educator to prevent culturally diverse children from internalizing feelings of shame, deficiency, and failure? I suddenly realized the immense responsibility I had before me, and I felt moved to challenge the program and, particularly, my students to understand their role in the transmission of dehumanizing practices and values.

The teacher preparation program where I work is founded on a strong progressive agenda. Issues of sexism, racism, classism, and other forms of oppression are explicitly embedded in the entire curriculum. More than 50 percent of the students in the program are of color, and I wanted to test the coherence of the philosophy of the department with the actual practices and beliefs of its teachers.

With the support of the director of the program and some colleagues, I worked to deconstruct the process through which student teachers learn to teach. I researched the values that teachers were taught and the ideology embedded in their learning process. In so doing, I became aware that the dominant ideology, in addition to being reproduced in different aspects of the program (e.g., administrative practices, the decision-making process, faculty hiring policy, student admissions, and so forth), was reproduced throughout the entire curriculum. This is particularly the case in the educational foundation courses, methods classes, student-teaching supervision, and even in the internship advising process, where we are supposed to seek to educate critical educators and transformative intellectuals, rather than to train the ideological agents of the ruling class.

It was in conjunction with this dawning awareness that Freire's pedagogy began making sense to me. The notion that education can be both alienating and emancipatory became manifest in the context of the reality of teacher education. With the support of the leadership of my program, we decided to give life to the concept of education as a political calling and a subversive force—as proclaimed by Freire—by deepening the transformation of the curriculum and practices embedded in the education of teachers. We believed that by reconceptualizing the nature of teacher education, we could begin to break the hegemonic cycle of domination carried out by our faculty and teachers.

Our overall goal has centered on challenging the practices of teacher education programs that produce legions of unprepared, uncritical teachers, by seeking to critically prepare competent teachers who also identify with their role as community activists and cultural workers.

One of the greatest challenges to the program has been the resistance of teachers and faculty to confront the implications of the "banking" concept of education—the idea that students are receptacles of the teachers' knowledge, which they deposit in the students—which has been so thoroughly ingrained throughout the entire educational system. In spite of our strong commitment to democratize the student-teacher relationship, our students often resent the fact that they are not given successful recipes for teaching or methods that can contribute to the subjugation of unruly students. The fear of expressing dissident ideas and the possible implications of carrying them out in their own classroom cause many teachers to resist critical pedagogy in anticipation of unpleasant consequences.

In the same way, the faculty has felt uncomfortable transcending the problem-solving discourse and incorporating a problem-posing methodology when they themselves have not experienced that process. Very often in the name of maintaining the intellectual rigor of courses, the faculty and intern teachers—self-identified as progressive educators—focus on the simple transmission of *legitimate*, traditional values, without engaging in practices that can be democratic and generative of knowledge.

We constantly strive to democratize the interaction and relationship with our students to create conditions for dialogue that support and enhance both personal and social empowerment. We go beyond therapeutic or feel-good "get-together" sessions by challenging our assumptions and our participation in the success of an economic system that makes imperative the violence and discrimination of marginalized groups. This process assumes a willingness on our part to take risks, to admit our vulnerability in front of our students, and at the same time to experience our authority to facilitate critical dialogue.

It is essential to trust our students, as well as to anticipate and understand their reactions. The process of unlearning the values that have given shape to their lives is very painful, particularly, when that process is perceived as a rejection of their own familial or religious upbringing. Our readiness to deal with the multiplicity of reactions from our student teachers—a sense of dissonance, resistance, fragmentation, and anger—is perhaps one the most complex and difficult tasks of this process.

The anxiety that this new way of interacting with students generates requires a strong commitment to social transformation and a profound faith in their ability to change. Very often I am assaulted by the same questions. How do I share knowledge without depositing it? How do I support the development of political consciousness in my students, without silencing their voices? How do I remain critically conscious of my own power and deal with the contradiction of a reality that socializes students to more readily accept coercion than dialogue? How do I survive in a world where the notion of excellence is translated in a controlling, managerial, authoritarian model of teaching? How do I keep hope alive in spite of the permanent co-optation and demise of emancipatory projects? Only through a process of intensive self-critique of and reflection on our actions can we honor the authenticity of Freire's principles and begin to address these questions. Entering consistently into this process of critical inquiry is perhaps one of the most arduous tasks of my work as a critical educator, yet it is a most essential commitment.

An ongoing discussion about the role of teacher education in the reproduction of social inequalities is closely tied to the philosophy of our program. Now, we officially proclaim that there is no neutral education and that the education of a teacher is not an innocent enterprise. We assist our teachers in becoming more aware of their own biases and recognizing how classroom practices are mediated by gender, language, class privilege, sexual orientation, ethnicity, religion, and personal experiences.

Despite the strong multicultural emphasis of the program, there is a realization that the concept of multiculturalism has been gradually reified and appropriated, becoming another sanitized policy, with lots of rhetoric but little change in the asymmetrical relations of power at work in classrooms. As a consequence, the program has reconceptualized the multicultural framework so as to include a broader vision of diversity. This entails the implementation of an antibias, antiracist pedagogy that reclaims the original intent of multicultural practice. We challenge our teachers to recognize the multiple facets of oppression (Young 1990), not only in terms of race and gender, but also in terms of class privilege. In the introductory courses on public schools, we talk about schools as public spheres, so the program clearly states its expectation that the mission of teachers is to form critical students and reclaim the true meaning of democracy.

By means of support groups and mentorship initiatives for nontraditional students and by encouraging discussion among faculty members, we are constantly questioning the traditional assumptions that schools are egalitarian, democratic institutions. This is belied by the fact that economically disadvantaged groups are overrepresented among high school dropouts, those requiring remedial courses, prison populations, teenagers who get pregnant, and special-education students. The program encourages teachers to become conscious of how those facts are unequivocal signs of the limited individual mobility that education in its traditional format offers to members of subordinate groups.

It is significant that this sort of discussion generates ambivalent feelings among the faculty. Some of them believe that teacher educators have a historic responsibility to transform the teaching profession; others believe it is irresponsible to talk about education as a political act if we do not offer concrete paths to create political changes. Implicit in those reactions is the fear of freedom. As Freire wrote in his book *Teachers as Cultural Workers* (1998b), we should not let fear of what is difficult paralyze us.

Teachers as Researchers

One of the major academic assignments of the program is the completion of the master's thesis, or teacher-research project. The purpose of this task is to challenge our students to bridge their academic self with their teaching practices and connect their knowledge with the lives of their students. Teacher-interns conduct ethnographic research on the lives of some of their students and theorize on the basis of their findings to finally reflect on the implications of their discoveries for teaching. During one entire semester, teachers reflect on their own socialization process, the expectations defined by their upbringing, and the internalization of stereotypes about their students. We ask teachers to recognize their own biases and the way they define their expectations. We ask them to visualize how those preconceived assumptions about their students are the smaller pieces of a larger process that is later translated in structural injustices that keep particular social groups subordinated.

Through several courses dealing with society and school, we engage student teachers in a process of critical reflection on the asymmetrical relations of power in society and schools and the dangers of cultural tokenism. We encourage student teachers to practice and live an authentic multiculturalism, one that is not only a lesson plan, a celebration of heroes, food and holidays, but a radical transformation of attitudes, beliefs, and values.

Classroom Environment

As part of a deliberate effort to transform the traditional "banking model" of education, we question authoritarian disciplinary models. We ask student teachers to discuss and negotiate with their students the class rules and to use their authority in a wise but effective manner. As Freire stated in a letter to North American teachers (Shor 1987):

> It is contradictory to proclaim progressive politics and then to practice authoritarianism or opportunism in the classroom. A progressive position requires democratic practice where authority never becomes authoritarianism, and where authority is never so reduced that it disappears in a climate of irresponsibility and license (212).

However, the balance required to form a critical mind demands of teachers an effective use of their authority. In *Teachers as Cultural Workers: Letters to Those Who Dare to Teach*, Freire (1998) brought up an example in his sixth letter:

> One of the worst things in all this is the breakdown of the relationship between educators and learners. And what can be said of the teachers who never assume authority in the classroom, who constantly show weakness, doubt, and insecurity in their relationship with the learners? . . . I remember from my adolescence the image of [a] weak, defenseless, pale man who carried with him the fear of the boys who made his weakness a plaything, together with the fear of losing his job, in the fear generated by those kids. While I witnessed the destruction of his authority, I, who dreamed of becoming a teacher, promised myself that I would never allow myself to be subjected to such a denial of my being, neither by the all-powerful authoritarian, the arrogant teacher who always has the last word, nor by the insecurity and complete lack of presence and power exhibited by the teacher (56).

It is not unusual for first-year teachers to succumb to some of those extremes, particularly when they realize that the entire school culture assigns them the role of guardians. Shocked by this reality, novice teachers usually resort to the complacent attitudes that produce chaotic classrooms, wasting precious opportunities to help students to succeed. Long periods of frustration ensue, which often end with teachers adopting behaviorally oriented rewards and punishments in their classrooms. This reward-and-punishment system alienates students and subjects them to a "culture of silence" that impairs their development of critical knowledge.

In contrast, we believe that children need to learn self-control and respect for others as an ongoing part of the school curriculum (Charney 1991). Therefore, we encourage teachers to devote a significant amount of time in their daily schedule to issues of student behavior and classroom life. Only through deep and consistent discussions of these issues can teachers assist students to develop strong identities, critical awareness, and a capacity for reflection. In similar ways, the program encourages teachers to become aware of the political implications of tracking and ability grouping and the economic and social entanglements of meritocracy (Darder 1991).

Curriculum and Assessment

The teaching task is above all a professional task that requires constant intellectual rigor and the stimulation of epistemological curiosity, of the capacity to love, of creativity, [and] of scientific competence and the rejection of scientific reductionism. The teaching task also requires the capacity to fight for freedom, without which the teaching task becomes meaningless (Freire 1998, 4).

We work to incorporate Freire's ideas by encouraging teacher-interns to problematize the curriculum with their students and incorporate children's experiences as vital components of the learning process. We ask our teachers to resist the fascination with prepackaged curricula that often serve only to ease the first-year teacher's fears of incompetence or failure, while it reinforces their passivity. Instead, we believe that teacher preparation programs must infuse the curriculum with rigorous scholarship and challenge the idea that teachers only benefit from pragmatic theory or knowledge. A major challenge in my work with teachers is to overcome their apathy, fear of theory, and dismissal of intellectual practices that they believe are not related to their survival as school bureaucrats. Our program constantly struggles with this issue as it becomes more and more difficult (because of time constrains) to demand that teachers read more, problematize their practices, do research, and theorize about the process of schooling.

We are still working to develop consensus among the faculty regarding the role of intern teachers in their classrooms. What we seek is for teachers to be seen as intellectuals and researchers, rather than managers of prepackaged curricula. In an effort to make this shift in perception, we have begun to address this issue not only as a vital component of an organized classroom, but as essential to the creative and expressive competency and ongoing development necessary for teaching children. As Freire clearly argues in *Teachers as Cultural Workers* (1998), teachers "should not venture into teaching without the necessary competency to do it. [Being a teacher] does not give persons a license to teach what they do not know. Teachers' political, ethical, and professional responsibility puts them under an obligation to prepare and enable themselves before engaging in their teaching practice. Teaching requires constant preparation and development on the part of teachers. . . . Such development [should be] based on a critical analysis of their practice" (17–18).

Controversy surrounding the politics of teaching reading in California has escalated to bizarre proportions. In the midst of this controversy, our program is working to implement Freire's vision of literacy. We advocate literacy not as a mastery of pedagogical techniques and vertical transmission of skills but as a way of reading the world. The current political debate and the imposition of a new standardized test to measure teachers' ability to teach literacy has forced the program to use creative ways to incorporate a balanced literacy program in its curriculum. However, teacher-interns resist this process in varied ways as they are constantly pressured by their districts and schools to focus on drills, phonics, spelling tests, and psychometric instruments that are said to scientifically measure their students' reading skills. Freire proposes a pedagogy of reading that uses the "learner's reality as the starting point, in beginning with what they already know, from the pragmatic value of the things and the facts of their daily lives, their existential situations" (Macedo and Araujo 1998, xii). Freire's philosophy "rejects mere narrow-minded and mind-narrowing repetition of phrases, words, and syllables as it proposes that the learners 'read the world' and 'read the word,' which are inseparable actions" (xiii). We encourage our teachers to comprehend that the decoding of the written word has the most meaning in the context of students' experiences.

Early in the program, teachers become aware that assessment is often used to prevent the social mobility of nonmainstream students. Teachers learn how, through grading, tracking, ability grouping, and exclusive reliance on standardized tests, they initiate the process of ranking students from a young age. They learn how that process is later translated into determining the economic location that those students will have as adults in the larger society. By exposing the problematic nature of testing and meritocracy, the program challenges teachers to examine how their decisions indirectly define students' fate and their participation as workers or leaders within the political economy.

As part of that concern, the program officially adopted the California Learning Record in the preparation of our teachers. The Learning Record is a comprehensive system of student assessment that involves the teacher, student, and parent(s) in observing and documenting a student's academic progress. We consider this to be one of the few inclusive methods of assessment, for it examines students' learning in a holistic manner. We extend the discussion of assessment to an examination of the academic and socioeconomic dimensions of homework, particularly the implications for working-class and immigrant parents. The Learning Record's participatory assessment principle requires that teachers, students, and parents all be fundamentally involved in the process of determining students' strengths and learning needs.

Final Thoughts

The challenge of sustaining our ongoing efforts must not be underestimated. The contradictions that teacher-interns feel are immense; it must be remembered that the concepts of critical pedagogy call into question the very nature of the traditional schooling system and how it envisions the role of teachers. Critical education concepts contradict the culture of schools and can cause new teachers to experience a sense of isolation and discouragement, despite their commitment to making changes. So it is not surprising that first-year teachers very often resist these concepts. Faculty and staff also experience dissonance and conflict as they struggle to unlearn previous practices and integrate more authentically a critical approach.

Furthermore, the administration of the teacher education program must struggle with its responsibility to demand a coherent implementation of the philosophy of the program and the challenge of democratizing the decision-making process, while contending with the pressures of an underfunded, understaffed department. Despite these difficulties, our program represents a concrete example of how Paulo Freire's pedagogy can be applied to the daily reality of teacher education. Critical pedagogy's detractors charge Freire and his followers with being obscure, incomprehensible theorists. In the case of people who appropriate Freirean concepts in superficial ways, undoubtedly some of those accusations are true. Very often, however, I wonder whether these accusations are not in fact expressions of a strong fear of theory and fear of freedom, expressions of internalized subordination, or possibly the inevitable result of our antidialogical socialization process.

There is an ongoing struggle between the temptation to remain at a theoretical level and the temptation to jump into unreflective or blind activism. I become ever more convinced that negotiating these dialectical forces requires a daily cross-examination of our own beliefs and practices, and the continuing development of our humility and profound love for people and the world—qualities Paulo Freire espoused in his work and in his life.

TEACHING FREIRE'S PEDAGOGY

EVELYN MARINO WEISMAN, TEACHER EDUCATOR

For the past four years I have worked in the field of teacher education at two public universities. My work has involved supervising student teachers as well as teaching courses to students who are enrolled in the Multiple Subject Credential Program, which prepares them to teach more than one subject. The majority of my students have been white and have had limited contact with people of color. For the most part, they are largely unaware of the conflicts and social inequities that exist for members of subordinate groups. Yet in the surrounding school districts in Southern California where most of these teacher candidates will eventually work, the ethnic and racial diversity of the student population continues to increase. Further, many teacher candidates who are people of color have experienced such intense societal pressure to assimilate into the mainstream that they have moved away from identifying with their primary cultural group and the struggles they face. Consequently, there is a tremendous need in teacher education to bring about an understanding of the ways existing power structures work to marginalize students who are not members of the dominant group. More often than not, this is done by devaluing their cultural and linguistic identities and instilling an uncritical acceptance of the social and political order. Promoting a consciousness of the political dimensions of schooling among teacher candidates requires incorporating into teacher education programs the principles of a critical, transformative pedagogy, exemplified in the work of Paulo Freire.

Prior to working in higher education I spent over twenty years in the California public school system as a teacher, bilingual program coordinator, and administrator. Most of that time was devoted to work in the field of bilingual education, to which I became strongly committed. I worked very hard and believed I was doing all that I could to promote academic success for children of diverse cultural and linguistic backgrounds. After beginning my graduate studies at the Claremont Graduate University and becoming familiar with Paulo Freire's work, I began to realize how I had in fact participated in perpetuating many established practices in the schools which served to alienate bicultural students and almost guarantee their failure. My efforts to improve schooling conditions had focused on using the native language of the students for instruction and had largely ignored the many ways in which the norms of the dominant culture constrict their cultural identities and chances for academic success. Examples of just a few of these practices include placing a greater emphasis on English language acquisition than on learning in the primary language, incorporating elements of the students' culture in the curriculum only in superficial ways, and failing to collaborate with parents as genuine partners in the educational process.

My work in teacher education at the university level has included teaching courses in the Cross-Cultural Language and Academic Development (CLAD) and Bilingual CLAD credential programs, which are designed to prepare teachers to work effectively with a culturally diverse student population. State guidelines for these courses focus on developing an understanding of learning theory, instructional methodology, culture, and cultural diversity. Although such understandings are important, if teacher preparation programs are to be truly responsive to the needs of culturally diverse students they must also incorporate discussion of racism, language domination, and the existing power structures that shape the educational experiences of these students. Unless teachers are aware of the sociohistorical and political conditions that inform the lives of their students, they will be unable to counter the discriminatory practices that contribute to patterns of academic underachievement among subordinate groups. Only by moving beyond a narrow focus on teaching methods and toward a more humane pedagogy that validates multiple perspectives and promotes students' critical engagement with their world can we hope to improve the quality of education for all students (Bartolomé 1994).

When I teach courses that focus on the theoretical foundations of bilingual education, multicultural education, and curriculum and instruction for diverse student populations, one of my major goals is for students to critically examine their own attitudes about cultural diversity and the societal conditions that contribute to the formation of their beliefs. Once these aspiring teachers become critically conscious of the political context in which they work, they can begin to consider how their actions in schools can serve either to support the status quo or to challenge it. My goal reflects Freire's (1994) idea that "to surmount the situation of oppression, people must first critically examine its causes, so that through transforming action they can create a new situation" (29).

Dialogue and Making Connections

Freire emphasized that dialogue is essential to the development of critical consciousness. In my classes I promote dialogue centering around topics raised in reading assignments. The articles that I select for students to read offer critiques of the inequities within school structures and the wider society. Students meet first in small groups to engage in dialogue about ideas or issues raised by the readings that may challenge their existing beliefs about educational equity and societal meritocracy. I provide them with questions to guide their discussion and encourage them to relate the concepts to their own experiences. This is followed by a large group discussion that incorporates the responses expressed within the small groups. One of the major goals is to have students become conscious of their own biases. By reading and participating in thoughtful dialogue about other perspectives, students can begin to understand many of the social conditions faced by students from subordinate groups. This becomes particularly important in light of the fact that the majority of my students are white. Discussion of white privilege and racism provides students with a different perspective of the world. For many students this is the first time that they have engaged critically with these issues.

Since many of the students are usually employed as teachers or teaching assistants in public schools, I encourage them to relate the readings to what they have observed in their school settings. For example, students begin to link the concept of racism in the schools to explicit examples of teacher comments about the academic potential of certain children and the need to overcome perceived deficiencies in their cultures. Often students with little experience working in public school settings will claim that these incidents are not—indeed, cannot—be representative of most schools. Students with more experience and awareness are able to provide many examples of oppressive practices. Through dialogue these experiences are analyzed and critiqued, deepening student teachers' understanding and consciousness about the realities of oppressive classroom conditions that function to perpetuate inequality.

At this point, I must point out that it is imperative that we create the conditions for open dialogue in our classrooms—dialogue that fosters honest appraisal and critique of ideas. To accomplish this it is important to establish an atmosphere of trust in which students feel comfortable speaking their minds. I particularly stress this point because in the first class sessions it is not uncommon for mainstream students to express ethnocentric views and ignorance about the struggles of marginalized communities. When this occurs it is difficult to refrain from responding with impatience or becoming judgmental. However, to do so only silences students and denies them the opportunity to explore their attitudes and views with greater depth. I have found it helpful to remain respectful but to also use probing questions to uncover the underlying assumptions and misconceptions that guide their thinking. Of particular importance is to convey to all students that I do not possess "the answer" and that along with them I am also a learner. This concept presents a dramatic shift in paradigm for most students, who are accustomed to viewing the professor as the source of knowledge. In contrast to the authoritarian role that teachers play in traditional educational settings, a critical classroom incorporates the teacher as both academic guide and facilitator of reflection, critique, and action in the learning process of students.

I have frequently noticed that initially, white middle-class students have the most confidence of all groups in expressing their views, while students of color remain relatively quiet. This is not surprising given the fact that these students are products of an educational system that promotes conformity to the values of·the dominant group and restricts the voices of subordinate groups. But though students of color may at first be hesitant about sharing personal views or painful experiences, gradually they become very open about the ways their lives have been shaped by sociopolitical conditions. A Laotian woman describes her harrowing escape from Laos during the war and her experiences with racism in this country. A Puerto Rican man speaks of a childhood experience with racism directed against his family when they lived in an all-white apartment complex. He explains that although they knew it was the actions of just a few people, none of the other families ever challenged it and thus condoned the racism by their silence. He challenges us to consider how many times we had heard a racist remark and remained silent, afraid to speak out.

Student responses during these types of discussions vary depending upon their life experiences and their willingness to uncover their own biases. Students of color may often be prompted to reveal their own struggles with adapting to the demands of societal norms, but some are reluctant or even resistant to acknowledging the ways in which they have contributed to their own oppression by their uncritical acceptance of the social order. Gradually these students gain insights and reexamine how they have accepted the ideology of the dominant group and learned to devalue their cultural identities. When students are asked to write critical reflections in journals their comments often reflect this developing awareness:

> As a child I was embarrassed by my native language and culture. I grew up with few Vietnamese peers. When I finally did meet other Vietnamese I felt really uncomfortable because I felt I had nothing in common with them. I guess I didn't want people to associate me with them.

> I grew up in a predominantly Anglo area. All my friends were white. I think that subconsciously I thought that being black was a bad thing and that in order for me to be successful I had to disassociate myself from the stereotypes that go along with being black.

For white students, dialogues about cultural differences and racism in particular can be extremely uncomfortable. Though some white students are open and willing to explore their biases, most feel threatened. Discussions centering on the existence of institutional racism, white privilege, and differential power relations challenge deeply ingrained beliefs about the innate fairness of the system and society. In one discussion about the existence of white privilege, several white students rejected this concept and maintained that differential treatment based on class was no different than that tied to race. They insisted that poor white students and families suffer the same discrimination as poor black families. When these students are challenged to consider the privilege that they hold as members of the dominant group—even if they are poor—they can become defensive and steadfastly cling to the idea that racial discrimination is an individual phenomenon, not the result of systemic forces. These discussions are stressful for everyone, including me, and nothing seems to get really resolved. Afterward I always question my ability to manage the conflict and to successfully guide students in adopting a more critical perspective about their world. At times I am tempted to discontinue these intense dialogues. I begin to wonder whether students, especially white students, are gaining any insights at all. But then when I read students' written reflections I see a developing consciousness beginning to surface in some of their writings. One white student wrote:

> I have always considered myself to be fair and free of racial prejudice. However, I am now aware that I have benefited from racism. I was struck by the realization that I tend to consider "white as normal" as described by Enid Lee. I was initially distressed by this, but now I think it is a positive indicator of my increasing self-awareness in this respect.

However, some students may continue to question their participation in the oppression of subordinate groups by contrasting their own experiences of gender or class discrimination. One student wrote:

> As a white single mom I have been treated with the same lack of respect described by other races, but it doesn't seem to matter because I am white.

Although the disrespect experienced by this young woman is real and important and does matter, the concern here is with a common tendency of some students to become defensive and resistant to entering more deeply into dialogues where racism is the central topic of discussion. These students often attempt to shift the dialogue to the superficial conclusion that "we are all as oppressed," while other students refuse to speak and others simply elect to drop the course. Frequently students will express the opinion that the discomfort created by the intense dialogue is counterproductive and unnecessary to their development as educators. In his journal one white student declared:

I see people as individuals not as members of a certain group. I do not know at this point how ethnic distinctions could help me professionally as a teacher.

Although it is difficult to cope with the recognition that not all students are ready and willing to confront oppressive structures related to racism, class, gender, and other forms of exclusion, I have found that many students are able to make significant shifts in their thinking. Through dialogue and reflection, students deepen their understanding of the issues and become more aware of how they have unconsciously internalized social values and norms that support inequality. This recognition is a crucial first step in beginning the process of constructing a new ideology that can serve as the foundation for a very different kind of teaching.

From an awakening consciousness students are moved to consider initial actions that they might begin to take to reshape their classroom environments. Toward this end I have my students read and discuss articles written by classroom teachers who support the cultural and linguistic identities of their students while also preparing them to critique their world. They provide specific examples of elementary school classroom practices that exemplify a vision of schooling in which all children can thrive and become critical subjects in their world. Examples of learning activities for elementary school children introduced in my courses include role playing to develop children's understanding of the European conquest of Native American lands; language activities that support the development of English proficiency without devaluing the students' home languages; and the use of books and actual photos of people from diverse backgrounds to counter stereotypical images.

With time, students begin to generate their own creative ideas and activities for shaping classroom settings that promote social justice and equality. They propose developing units of study around the cultural differences within their schools, inviting community members into classrooms as guest speakers, and seeking out parents as valuable resources in their students' learning. Through dialogue, critique, and reflection my students begin to see the connection between their classrooms and the social conditions around them. Further, they become increasingly conscious of the ways in which their teaching is directly linked to the broader effort of creating a more just society.

Students Conduct Critical Research Projects

Engaging students in problem-posing research has also been a powerful tool for facilitating a more critical understanding of issues related to cultural and linguistic diversity. In this assignment, students become involved in a semester-long project in which they must investigate an issue or problem within their own classrooms or school communities that is personally meaningful to them. As a starting point, students develop the questions they wish to examine and then conduct interviews and/or classroom observations to explore their questions in depth and to generate solutions to the problems they find. Students are thus able to construct their own knowledge through firsthand experience. The goal is not only for them to increase their level of awareness about attitudes, school practices, and policies that perpetuate inequality but also for them to consider how they can apply this consciousness to their work to become agents of change. Some of the topics selected have included bilingual education, parent involvement, racism in schools, and patterns of teacher-student interaction. These research reports often demonstrate impressive development of insight and growth in their theoretical understanding.

Generally, when I first tell students about the research project, they frequently express anxiety and claim they have no idea what to do. However, after several weeks of engaging in dialogue about a variety of issues and linking these to our life experiences, most students are able to identify a topic. I meet individually with the students who might still need help and guide them to consider issues that impact their lives in meaningful ways. I have found that this support is crucial and when it is not provided students may flounder and become frustrated with their work. On the other hand, with support most students become very enthusiastic about their projects, since it is often the first time they have had an opportunity to explore a topic or problem that has deep personal meaning for them.

One student was concerned about the lack of parent participation at her school and decided to examine this issue from the perspective of the community, as well as the school. By interviewing parents and teachers she found that the ignorance and negative attitudes of school personnel had prevented any kind of meaningful parent involvement. This student has begun to work with the school staff regarding the views and resources within the community. For another student, classroom observations resulted in a recognition of the pervasiveness of low teacher expectations for children of color and his own responsibility to bring about change. In his project paper he commented:

> As a result of this research project I can see and understand more clearly the issue of racism in the schools. I have learned that it is my responsibility to address racism and even if necessary to scathe the conscience of those who are indifferent.

For other students, a more critical examination of teacher-student interactions in the classroom results in an increased awareness of the power they wield as teachers. A future bilingual teacher came to the realization that her ability to speak with Latino students in Spanish did not by itself automatically guarantee their academic success. Moreover, her classroom observations revealed that teachers who value the cultural identities of their students do make a crucial difference. This student wrote:

> A child's success in school seems to hinge on the attitudes of the adults around him. This study has taught me that there are things I can do to make a difference. I can do all that I can to involve parents and to strengthen the student's identity. This project has opened my eyes to how important having a positive identity really is in a student's success at school.

Often students' studies reveal the persistence of demeaning comments that teachers make to and about children from subordinate groups. Students reported observing teachers who praised children for speaking English but ignored accomplishments made in the native language. They also noted that referring to children as "slow learners" and "at risk" was a common practice. One student reported that she overheard a teacher say, "I don't let them speak their language in class; they can do that outside." As they reflect on their findings, students are often surprised at the extent to which discriminatory practices exist in the schools.

In the final class sessions, students share their projects, what they have learned from their work, and their ideas for taking action that might promote critical change. Other class members are encouraged to ask questions and make suggestions. I draw on my own experiences and encourage others to do the same as we consider various strategies for coping with some of the problems the projects uncover. This is a critically important aspect of the class because there is a tendency to become depressed and overwhelmed by the enormity of the problems that exist. Thus, the ability of my students to identify the multitude of prejudicial attitudes within schools and society must be accompanied by a consideration of their own power as teachers to change the system.

Struggles and Successes

When I first began my journey as a critical educator, I had only a vague idea of the challenges I might face. There have been many, beginning with having to overcome not only my students' but my own years of conditioning by traditional educational practices. As a consequence, I must consistently keep in mind that the majority of my students come to my class having experienced a pattern of schooling that is teacher-directed and that encourages the passive acceptance of fragmented knowledge created and transmitted by others. They come expecting to be lectured to, told what to learn, and evaluated on the basis of narrowly defined standards. Accustomed to a teacher-directed system, students tend to be overly concerned about the expected length, format, and grading system for journal entries and papers that call for critical reflection. It takes time for them to imagine an approach to education that views everyone in the classroom as teachers and learners. To demonstrate that I am a learner along with them I will often disclose my own struggles with learning to recognize and transform my biases. This is helpful in decreasing the distance between the students and me and fosters an environment of trust in which students are willing to take risks and speak openly. As their teacher, I provide guidance but I do not behave as though I have all the answers. I believe this helps them to understand that adopting a critical approach to education is a continuous learning process and not without struggle.

It is significant that my students generally lack any familiarity with the process of critique. It is a challenge to move my students to recognize the power of their own voices and to question the social structures that shape their lives. They have been socialized to passively accept and perpetuate classroom practices such as tracking, standardized testing and assessment, and prefabricated curricula without questioning the negative consequences of these practices on students from subordinate groups.

However, these students often hold or develop through their work as teachers strong beliefs about the necessity for equal educational opportunities for all students. A factor that has been significant in promoting the critique of existing social structures is the presence of at least several working-class students of color in the class. When these students share their experiences and perspectives it enables other students to understand societal conditions more profoundly in a new light. Listening to the real-life struggles of their classmates forces students to examine alternative perspectives much more seriously than if they were just reading about it in a book.

A more difficult challenge has been confronting attitudes of denial and resistance to a different worldview. I always have to remind myself that such views stem from years of socialization and adaptation to the dominant culture and are not easily changed. The fact that there are always some students who demonstrate minimal growth is a source of frustration for me since I have such a strong desire to be able to inspire every one of these teacher candidates to create empowering conditions for their own students. But as a colleague recently mentioned to me, we need to accept the fact that people may be at different points in their journey toward a transformative pedagogy and each step that they do take is an important one.

Despite the frustrations, there have also been many moments that have made it all worth the effort. Although there are individual differences in the extent of growth that students make, at some point in the semester most students begin to exhibit a greater willingness to explore alternative perspectives, and there is evidence in their journals and in dialogue sessions of a developing consciousness. Student evaluations and comments revealed that for many of the students the class has served as a powerful learning experience. Most students mention how much they learned through the collaboration with their fellow students. One white student described how she felt fortunate to have had the opportunity to engage in such meaningful discussions with people of color, providing her with a new view of the world. A Mexican American student stated that the class process had given her confidence and hope to change the lives of her students. Most important, for students of color the act of giving voice to their experiences with racism and other forms of oppression affirms their reality and provides them with an opportunity to critique these issues and consider their own role in the transformation of their lives and their world.

Final Thoughts

My first steps toward adopting a critical approach in my teaching have not been easy. I recognize that my students leave my program feeling a lot of uncertainty; there is no teacher's guide, no blueprint to tell them how to proceed, since by its very nature a critical pedagogy must be responsive to the specific educational context. As such it is a continually evolving process of inquiry that makes enormous intellectual and emotional demands on teachers. It is an exhausting enterprise, and feeling unsure of exactly how to proceed at a specific point in the class can create anxiety, particularly since most of us have been taught to follow an orderly path to attain learning goals. I am still learning how to cope with and accept the uncertainties, ambiguities, and inevitable discomfort that are inherent in critical dialogue. But the more I delve into a critical teaching practice, the more insight I gain into the possibilities for making substantive changes in the debilitating conditions that plague our schools.

That semester was an extremely difficult one for me as I was faced with serious resistance and hostility from a number of students. These students refused to engage in critical dialogue and frequently expressed hostile comments, and one even refused to complete some assignments. I had never been confronted with such tremendous resistance. Added pressure came from the knowledge that my university required me to teach specific content and evaluation of my performance was linked to standards that largely reflect a traditional model of educational practice. This caused me to ask myself some hard questions: Was all this constant tension really worth it? Am I willing to continue taking the risks necessary to create an educational context in which students can acquire the necessary consciousness to transform their own educational practice?

I spent the year reflecting on these questions, the difficulties I encountered, and the connections between power relations in the society and educational institutions that subsequently impact teaching practice in the classroom. This period of reflection was important and helped me to return to my work with a renewed strength. I came to understand in a very personal way that there are many obstacles along the path to creating conditions for social justice. When obstacles are encountered it may be necessary to take time for reflection, but then it is important to continue to move forward with our work.

In light of recent legislative efforts in California to limit educational opportunities for subordinate groups, the need for critically conscious and politically active educators becomes increasingly urgent. During the past year, I was particularly distressed by what seemed like the passive acceptance by many bilingual teachers of the elimination of bilingual instruction, as a consequence of the passage of Proposition 227 in June 1998. The requirement of the exclusive use of English in what were formerly bilingual classrooms has functioned to erode the confidence of many bilingual teachers to be able to make a positive difference in the lives of their students. Their own educational experiences have denied these teachers the opportunity to develop their critical capacities and the ability to effectively challenge the oppressive conditions in which they must work. This disturbing observation has renewed my commitment to prepare teachers who understand the relationship between power and knowledge and who are willing to take the necessary steps to recreate our schools.

Ultimately, we must ask ourselves what kind of a society we wish to live in and what we are going to do to make our vision a reality. Paulo Freire spoke to a pedagogy that viewed education in the interest of transforming the structures of domination and exploitation in schools and society. Pursuing such a vision entails our willingness as educators to embrace the challenges of teaching in a manner that creates the place for students to find the courage and power to question and to act in the interest of a more democratic and just world.

TO NAME, TO REFLECT, TO ACT: TEACHING CRITICAL LITERACY

EVANGELINA BUSTAMANTE JONES, TEACHER EDUCATOR

I have been a teacher for almost thirty years. My students have been primarily Latinos, and/or members of poor communities; many have been marginalized by labels like "dropout," "remedial," or "limited English proficient." I have seen and felt the effects of inequitable schooling on many of my students. For the past eight years I have brought these experiences to my work as a teacher educator. I teach "student teaching" seminars, as well as language arts and reading methods in both bilingual and nonbilingual elementary and secondary credential programs. In my courses I want future teachers to learn about Paulo Freire's contribution to our understanding of learning and teaching because I am convinced it is fundamental to any vision of democratic schooling.

Credential students in my courses recognize that the current educational system has historically failed to value the knowledge or meet the academic needs of culturally and linguistically nonmainstream students. Yet most of them have not had an opportunity to consider how and why this happens. Given the differences in their understanding of the structural inequities embedded in our schools, my initial task is to establish a foundation for critical theory. We begin by acknowledging that the majority of institutions of schooling in this country are founded on an ideology of education called "banking" education—an ideology that perpetuates the status of students as passive objects (Freire 1970); this in turn causes the *disabling socialization* of learners (Shor 1987). In contrast, as Freire (1970) proposed, when people reflect upon their experiences and position in the world, they become *subjects* who are able to critically think and act upon the resulting perceptions that emerge from such reflection. A passage written by Hector, one of my seminar students, speaks to this issue:

> Throughout my education I simply learned something because I was told to do so; I never stopped to question if what I was learning was valid or truly of importance to me. I went through my education allowing others to shape me in the image they wanted and not giving me the opportunity to wonder about what kind of image I wanted. I was told this is how I needed to be and I believed it. Now I have come to realize I have the power to create myself in any way I see fit. The only thing I lacked was the knowledge of my strength. This is critical pedagogy: becoming aware of who you are, your past and how you can change what is happening to you and your surroundings.
>
> .

Although the students are struck by the power of Freire's ideas, they also resist the ambiguity that arises as they begin to recreate their roles as learners, or to deconstruct their previous visions of themselves as teachers. They continue to want me, their professor, to equip them with an array of models and formats for the work I assign and to supply prescribed solutions to situations they will encounter in their classrooms. After all, my students have been successful enough to reach graduate-level status in our system of schooling and are quite competent in their role of passive objects—this is their comfort zone and they do not wish to leave it. It is not easy to counteract sixteen years of exposure and socialization to the methods and practices of status quo schooling. It seems equally difficult for these student teachers to trust their own insights into the lives of their students, even when they seem to understand that it is this form of critical consciousness that must be integrated into their daily practice in schools.

In fact, I must confess that I am at times tempted to go ahead and give them what they want because it would be so much easier, neater, and more simple to do so. Instead, I struggle to provide learning contexts in which students can begin to recognize that they already possess the personal strengths, creativity, and resources needed to work as critical teachers. I want my students to learn that they can assess their own development; that their own histories as learners forms the basis upon which they shape their teaching; and that they can gain insights and critical awareness by examining the lived experiences that students bring into the classroom. They are encouraged to reach into themselves and back into their histories; and often they come to the same conclusion as Hector did above— "This is critical pedagogy: becoming aware of who you are, your past and how you can change what is happening to you and your surroundings."

Introducing Freire's Principles of Critical Literacy
In my elementary literacy methods courses I use reflective and problem-posing processes so that students begin to see their teaching role as cultural mediators. This approach engages the different ways that bicultural teachers, who are conscious of the power wielded by the dominant society and its influence on the language and culture of bicultural students, use their lived experiences to create biculturally affirming learning contexts (Jones 1998). This critical approach is firmly anchored in Freire's notions of culture, power, language, and schooling. The following represents a brief example of my efforts to introduce this approach to student teachers.

During their two eight-week student-teaching assignments, preservice teachers apply literacy theories and strategies learned through both coursework and classroom observations. At the end of the academic year they write a paper on their personal philosophy of literacy. These are placed in their professional portfolios, which are comprehensive, well-organized representations of what they have learned and achieved during the program. Unlike most research papers, however, this one evolves through several stages of writing. During the first semester, students write a series of short reflections about their literacy experiences. These form the foundation for a position paper on literacy written at the end of the first semester. In the second semester, they rethink and revise this essay to more closely reflect their increased depth of knowledge. Thus, the final paper represents a year-long exploration of lived experiences, theoretical frameworks, direct observation, and firsthand teaching experiences. Through this practice they begin to appreciate the historical dimension of their own knowledge development.

Reflective writing leads many of my students to delve into memories of themselves as immigrants in a confusing, often hostile, school environment, or as students whose teachers' middle-class perspectives on social class, language, or cultural values resulted in limited expectations. They juxtapose these recollections with critical and constructivist literacy theories and strategies endorsed through our program of study.[2] Our department's conviction is that constructivist and critical approaches, centered on learners' making their own meaning from texts through the use of their own prior knowledge and experience, should form the basis of literacy development for all children. Too often, students whose language and social class are different from those of the mainstream group are denied the opportunities to use their experiences and thoughts because they do not reflect the middle-class perspectives of mainstream society.

The focus of each reflection shifts so students gradually widen their scope to view all of the literacy events in their lives as meaningful. For example, at the start of the first semester, they write about their earliest recollections of being read to, or of being told stories by their parents, grandparents, other family members, or caregivers. In class, we discuss the connection between hearing stories told by people who loved them and the resulting motivation that they felt to retell their stories. Another reflection deals with the roles played by family members in literacy events, and the ways in which literacy was used in the home.

School literacy reflections deal with their first day of school and first experiences in an English-language classroom. A number of our students emigrated from Mexico or other Latin American countries, arriving at different ages and with varying degrees of Spanish literacy. Other students, also Latinos, entered school already bilingual. They write about experiences related to the differences they encountered at school regarding the language status of Spanish compared to English, and about the roles they played as language brokers for non-English-speakers. Still others are English speakers who have mastered Spanish through high school, college, and study abroad. They also write about their academic and cultural immersion experiences as second language learners, although these accounts usually differ from American immigrant experiences. Their recollections, while also fraught with anxiety, confusion, and frustrations, describe additive processes brought about through individual choice rather than subtractive processes linked to language domination and cultural invasion.

Continuing the exploration of school literacy experiences, students analyze the ways their teachers taught—both good and bad examples—and are asked to recall the quality of their teacher-student relationships and those of their classmates in regard to their status and treatment. For many students, the school literacy reflections are difficult to write. At first, a few of them tell me that because some of these recollections are quite painful, they don't really want to reexperience them in writing. Although I respond with empathy, I ask them to share as much as they can. Often, over a period of several weeks, most students shift their focus from the pain they felt to the reasons they think these events were so difficult.

Other students say they don't remember much at all about their earliest school memories; some even tell me they kept falling asleep in class and recall only one or two art activities. The initial papers these particular students write are vague, general, and unfocused. Although I respond to all papers with my reactions, comments, and additional questions, I return vague papers with more pointed, more specific questions based on what they did write. For example, if a student says, "My teacher was nice to me, but I don't remember her ever talking to me," I will respond with, "Was this the case for all the students? Were there some students to whom the teacher did pay more personal attention? Where did you sit in reference to the teacher or the students she talked to the most? Who *did* talk to you? Who helped you, and how?" In other words, I encourage problem-posing through my responses to what they write.

At this point, some students remember classroom aides. I ask them questions like "How much time did the aide spend with you compared to the teacher? What kind of work did you do with the aide?" Several students remark that at the time, they felt confusion because on the one hand, they had concluded that they must not have been smart enough, or good enough, to be taught by the teacher, but on the other hand, they enjoyed being with the aide. Others remember feeling fortunate because the aide showed them real caring; for these students, the aide eventually became the more important adult in the classroom. Many recall classroom aides who nurtured them and held high expectations for them. It is important to remember such relationships, to remember how certain individuals make a difference in the development of academic identities.

Each time a reflection paper is assigned, there is dialogue, in written or oral form. Through such continued engagement among students, and teacher and student, memories are jogged through peer response read-arounds, leading other students to recount similar incidents or feelings. Students begin to ask each other and themselves even deeper questions. Students gradually take the lead during whole group and small group discussions as they engage the problem-posing process. As time goes on, students include greater detail in their essays, revealing more and more insights about what the remembered incidents might have meant. They also begin to show greater connections to what they are seeing, hearing, and learning in class and through their student teaching practice.

By the end of the academic year, most of the final essays display a thoroughness and depth of understanding about literacy development that is grounded in both theory and practice. One paper in particular has stood out for me. Like many others, it described a culturally relevant classroom where children's ideas will be listened to and validated, where biliteracy is valued and parents welcomed. In recalling this student's essays throughout the year, I knew she had experienced quite the opposite as a second-language learner. She concluded her essay by saying, "I want to be the teacher of literacy that I didn't have, and needed, when I was a child." In this one poignant sentence, this young Chicana demonstrated her ability to examine her own lived experience as a bicultural student in order to inform her practice as a biculturally conscious literacy teacher. When I encounter such a level of awareness in beginning teachers, I am inspired to dream about what future teachers like her will surely achieve.

Lived Experience As a Teaching Tool

Not only can reflection and dialogue about one's own experiences result in the development of an articulate and critical teaching practice, but this process can also be used to examine other people's experiences as well. Most of us start our teaching careers with a great deal of caring—we want to provide students with access to full participation in society by teaching them the skills, attitudes, and knowledge they'll need to shape their own futures. In the day-to-day hustle of work, we often operate on the notion that our caring will somehow supersede the oppressive conditions in school and serve as a sort of protective talisman that allows us to critique or confront inequitable situations without facing serious consequences. But new teachers must come to realize that they bear responsibility for self-protection and survival in a system that does not brook questioning or independent thinking. Self-protection is part of consciousness; it is based on critical awareness of how one's work is situated within much larger and more powerful systems.

Caring and committed teachers who do not examine the political context that surrounds their work in school or weigh the consequences of engaging in controversies can jeopardize their future in teaching. It is important to note that I am not advising my students to be silent when they see inequities, but I want to emphasize the importance of understanding and being prepared for the possible effects that acts of resistance based on their ideology can have on their opportunities to teach. And most important, I want students to begin to grasp the role resistance plays in the context of critical pedagogy.

Paulo Freire once said, "A radical educator has to know the forms and ways in which people resist, not to hide the reasons for resistance, but to explicate at the theoretical level the nature of this resistance . . . to provide pedagogical structures that will enable students to emancipate themselves" (Frederickson 1998, 14). As people examine lived experiences in the context of the subject under study, they engage in *problematizing* what they are studying. This consists of looking underneath the surface in order to understand how a body of knowledge originated, how it is structured, who participated in its structuring, and the consequences of this knowledge (Shor 1987). Problematizing is approached as problem-posing, or the asking of questions that strive to focus critical analysis upon previously unquestioned events.

In student teacher seminars, for example, we read and discuss articles about teachers who go against the grain, and I share with them my stories. I believe that my strength as a teacher educator emerges from the stories I share about my own teaching and learning, and from my practice of eliciting students' experiences for the purpose of critical reflection. I do not believe in using my experiences or those of my students as merely entertaining vignettes. Instead, we use them to seriously engage ourselves in the process that will help us be critically literate leaders in our school communities. I relate a story about my first teaching job as an example of caring and courage that were not grounded in consciousness.

Personal History As a Teaching Tool

The year was 1969, and I was a twenty-three-year-old English and social studies junior high school teacher, recruited by a school superintendent during a job fair on my college campus in the final semester of my master's program. Although I had done student teaching and a master's project, both of which involved working in a school of mostly Latino and African American students, I had not yet held a paying teaching position. In college I had been active in a Mexican American student organization that brought campuswide attention to social and labor issues in the surrounding community, and had participated in anti-Vietnam War events.

When I started my job hunting, I quickly realized that I was a sought-after candidate because I was a "minority," I was bilingual (although there were virtually no bilingual programs in place at this time), and I had a master's degree in English education. I was attracted to the junior high position by three factors: the job itself, which was teaching English to English speakers, teaching English as a second language (ESL), and teaching social studies in Spanish to Mexicano immigrant students; the physical and cultural setting, an agricultural community in San Diego County with a balanced population of Latino and white citizens; and the superintendent's vision of, and support for, progressive change. I wanted the chance to teach English and social studies in a school with a significant number of Mexicano and Mexican American students, because I felt I could provide a bridge toward full participation and success through my personal experiences as a second-language student. When I accepted the job, however, I did not consider how national and community-level sociopolitical conditions would affect my work, as naïve as that may sound. Nor did I foresee how these conditions, power relations, and school events would lead to my getting fired.

To begin with, I did not understand how deeply most of the district's administrators and teachers resented the new "interloper" superintendent and his ideas. For most of them, his hiring of several first-year teachers from outside the area represented unwanted changes to their standard way of doing things. When I encouraged students to write, read, and talk about topics they cared about in order to contextualize the prescribed grammar curriculum, the principal demanded that I use worksheets. Most of the teachers and the principal reacted with even more aloofness when they saw how positively students responded to my classes.

Second, I did not realize that up until just a few years before I took the job, this ethnically balanced community's history had included blatant segregation in its schools and housing, school segregation that had been dismantled to comply with state and federal mandates. At the same time, a rapid increase in the number of non-English-speaking Mexicano students had forced the schools to provide instruction comprehensible to them. I had been excited about the prospect of teaching social studies in Spanish to ESL students. However, there were no Spanish language texts to teach from, and none were purchased even after I asked for them. I ended up buying all the *National Geographic* magazines that I could find in thrift stores throughout the county so that my students could make their own books. It wasn't surprising that when I was evaluated by the principal, it was only done in the classes I taught to the "average" or "above average" English speakers. I was never observed when teaching the "nonreaders" and the ESL students.

The Mexicano immigrants and most Mexican Americans worked in the avocado and citrus groves or other low-level jobs, while the white population were primarily the growers, crew supervisors, or shop owners of the town's businesses. The town's power structure did not include Latinos. Teachers at the junior high reflected the town's attitudes about keeping Mexicans and whites separate, although they now had to teach in integrated classrooms. It was no surprise that most of these teachers did not embrace diversity in their students; instead, they resisted it, claiming that they had to lower their standards because of the Mexican and Mexican American students. Likewise, white parents believed that their children were not getting as good an education because of integration, even though only the English-speaking Mexican and Mexican American students were placed in the mixed classes.

Third, I did not realize how the political beliefs my husband and I held would affect my relations with other teachers and parents, and the kinds of teaching evaluations the principal gave me. In 1969, many Latino, African American, and poor men were being drafted to fight in the Vietnam War. Because my husband conducted draft counseling sessions in a neighboring town, a group of townspeople labeled us Communists, and demanded that the school board fire me immediately two months after school had started. Of course, that could not be done, but from then on I was targeted by the principal, who called me into his office on a weekly basis to criticize my work. An unending stream of parents came to observe my classes, worried that I was teaching radical notions, and ready to pull their children out of class. Only two parents actually did ask that their students be moved. The superintendent, quite friendly before the school board incident, refused to see or talk to me after that board meeting. He was afraid for his own job.

Finally, I did not understand that the rights and privileges of Americans to free speech were not in operation for junior high students. In anticipation of a national moratorium on the Vietnam War, a small group of students asked the principal if an assembly could be held to observe the event. These were white middle-class students, most of them members of my classes, whose parents were more liberal than the general population. The principal used a variety of strategies to dissuade them. He told them they could not request to hold a school event without being a bona fide organization, and for that they needed a sponsor, a charter, and a list of prospective members. They complied with everything, and were turned down by a couple of teachers before they asked me to sponsor them. With about two weeks to go, the students made their request, but the principal delayed his decision until two days before the moratorium, then still refused to allow an assembly or even individual talks conducted during home-room period. Finally, on the eve of the moratorium, the students asked him if they could at least wear and distribute black armbands to show their views nonverbally (nationally, armbands were being commonly used to show an antiwar stance), and reluctantly he said that would be permissible, as long as school was not disrupted. The students pooled their own money to buy black material, and I agreed to buy it for them because the fabric store was beyond the students' biking distance. That night I also cut it into armband-size strips.

The next morning, careful to arrive long before it was time to punch the time clock, I handed the bag of armbands to the student group outside the school grounds, and went to my classroom. The group was besieged by other students for armbands, and wore them to their first class. Though school itself was not disrupted, the reactions of most teachers ranged from anger to irritation to discomfort as they conducted classes that day. By lunchtime, word had gotten out to the community, and many more parents were upset when they saw the armbands their children brought home at the end of the day.

This was the last straw for the community and for the principal. Within a short amount of time, the principal warned me to resign or I would be fired; he advised me to voluntarily resign so that my work record would not be marred by a termination. However, I refused to do so because I did not think my performance in the classroom was weak, especially not for a first-year teacher, and I did not think I could be terminated for my political beliefs or for my sponsorship of students who wanted to voice their own political beliefs. In spite of the weekly sessions with the principal at which he delivered criticism of my work, my formal evaluations indicated adequate ratings, but the principal showed me notes detailing observations containing a number of fabricated classroom incidents he claimed to have seen while passing in the hall (some notes even had dates of Saturdays and Sundays). It was ironic to me that although one of the reasons for my choosing this job over others had been the opportunity to work with Mexicano and Mexican American students, my professional struggles took most of my time and energy. Only my work with primarily white students and my potential influence upon them was criticized. It was clear that people who participated in the power structure were interested solely on the effects my work might have on their own children.

Most of the parents of the students who had distributed armbands, several Mexican American and white community members, and two school board members stood by me, but the teachers union did not give me the support normally given to members. The American Civil Liberties Union heard about my situation and defended me in the hearing before the school board that I was granted, but I lost, and I was terminated. In less than a year, it appeared that my teaching career was over, because a termination usually meant nobody else would hire you. I was devastated to think that my life's goal of being a teacher was destroyed.

Even though I knew many unfair practices had been perpetrated against me, for many years I blamed myself for getting fired. I kept thinking that if I had just been a better teacher, I could have prevented all of it, until I finally realized that I could have been the finest teacher and still have ended up with the same results because the entire situation was driven by politics, power struggles, and issues of control. And even now, almost thirty years later, I choke up when I tell this story to my students. The emotions—fear, humiliation, anger, hopelessness—return as if it were only yesterday.

It is difficult to lay bare my naïveté and lack of consciousness when I relate my story, but I am willing to share my own vulnerability because I think such stories reveal how crucial it is for teachers to possess a political and social consciousness in addition to competency in their content area, teaching skills, and caring hearts. This story allows my students to problematize the whole dynamic of teaching within a well-established system that disempowers students, teachers, and parts of the community. I ask my students to think about and discuss all the elements in the story that are driven by sociopolitical issues. I ask them what I could have done differently without having to give up my principles and beliefs. I ask them to consider what issues teachers now face that are different from the ones in my history, and which ones are still with us—and why that is. I ask them to list which current sociopolitical conditions and events might create a similar context of activism in their students and how they as teachers might shape their own leadership roles accordingly. I warn them never to walk into a job without having researched the sociopolitical conditions, the history of the community, the power relations between teachers and administrators, and the level of support and protection available to them as new teachers. And most important, I emphasize the power of personal history as an effective teaching tool—a tool that helps us examine, critique, and transform the inequities we find in the daily process of schooling.

Transformation Must Begin with Oneself

I have described in some detail two of the pedagogical practices I have found that make the most significant difference to my students as they reexamine the institution of education. I construct learning contexts that invite them to create (or recreate) themselves as teachers and learners. Over time, critical pedagogy becomes central to many, but not all, my students. Some of them persist in their beliefs that the system of schooling we have here needs reform, not transformation. Even those who say they want to be critical educators find it difficult to maintain a critical practice, and that is usually because the hardest part of critical teaching is to allow *oneself* to be transformed. Yet, for Paulo Freire our "capacity to begin anew" constitutes one of the most essential qualities for fostering the transformation of teaching and learning in our practice as cultural workers. Herein lies the secret in living our practice.

NOTES

1. Donaldo Macedo and Ana Maria Araujo Freire explain in the foreword to *Teachers as Cultural Workers: Letters to Those Who Dare to Teach* (1998) that "we are experiencing a rapid *Third-Worldization* of North

America, where inner cities more and more come to resemble the shanty-towns of the Third World, with high levels of poverty, violence, illiteracy, human exploitation, homelessness, and human misery. The abandonment of our inner cities and the insidious decay of their infrastructures, including their schools, makes it very difficult to maintain the artificial division between the First World and the Third World. It is just as easy to find First World opulence in the oligarchies in El Salvador, Guatemala, and many other Third World nations" (ix).

2. Jeannie Oaks and Martin Lipton (1999) define constructivism as a pedagogical approach that seeks to "build on problems and experiences that require students to construct, understand, and use knowledge that is important, challenging, complex, related to real life, and rich in meaning" (110).

A LEGACY OF
HOPE AND STRUGGLE

BY PETER McLAREN

P aulo Freire died on May 2, 1997.
Born Paulo Reglus Neves Freire on September 19, 1921, in Recife, in the northeast of Brazil, he became a legendary figure in the field of education. A courageous scholar, social activist, and cultural worker admired for his integrity and humility, Freire became internationally renowned for developing an anti-imperialist and anticapitalist literacy praxis used by progressive educators throughout the field.

In his early twenties Freire joined the Law Faculty at the University of Recife. His work at the Social Service for Industry (SESI), and his participation in the Movement for Popular Culture of Recife helped to motivate him to devote his energies to the area of adult literacy. He abandoned his work as a lawyer shortly after his first case in order to study the relationships among pupils, teachers, and parents in working-class communities in the northeast of Brazil. Freire finished his doctoral dissertation in 1959, and in 1961 the mayor of Recife appointed him director of the extension service of the University of Recife and asked him to develop a literacy program for that city. Freire soon began to develop new methods in the teaching of adult literacy.

Freire's approach to literacy was greatly influenced by his activities in the Catholic Action Movement, by Catholic collectivism, by the Basic Church Communities (Communidades Eclesiales de Base) and by his close association with the bishop of Recife, Dom Helder Camara. In 1962, in the town of Angicos, in Rio Grande de Norte, Freire's approach to literacy was used to help three hundred rural farmworkers learn to read and write in forty-five days. By living communally with groups or peasants and workers, a literacy worker was able to identify generative words according to their phonetic value, syllabic length, and social meaning and relevance to the workers. Such words represented the lived reality of the workers. Each word was associated with issues related to existential questions about life and the social factors that determined the economic conditions of everyday existence—words such as "wages" or "government." Themes were generated from these words, and these were then codified and decodified by groups of workers and teachers known as "cultural circles." Reading and writing thus became grounded in the lived experiences of peasants and workers and resulted in a process of ideological struggle and revolutionary praxis known as *conscientização*. Workers and peasants were able to transform their "culture of silence" and become collective agents of social and political change. The success of this work, which was supported by the United States Agency for International Development, marked the beginning of what was to become a legendary approach in education.

In 1963, Freire was invited by President João Goulart and the minister of education, Paul de Tarso Santos, to rethink adult literacy programs on a national scale and to work with the national literacy program, the Movement for Basic Education. By 1964, 20,000 cultural circles had been planned to assist 2 million illiterate workers learn to read. However, all of that was interrupted when a right-wing military coup overthrew Goulart's democratically elected government that year.

Despite Freire's internationally celebrated work with the poor, which had begun in the late 1940s and continued unabated until 1964, Freire was accused of preaching communism and was arrested. He was imprisoned by the military government for seventy days; was ejected from his post as director of the national literacy campaign; and eventually was forced to leave Brazil. According to Freire's leading biographer, Moacir Gadotti, the Brazilian military considered Freire to be "an international subversive, a traitor to Christ and the Brazilian people" and accused him of developing a teaching method similar to that of Stalin, Hitler, Perón, and Mussolini. He was furthermore accused of trying to turn Brazil into a "Bolshevik country" (Gadotti, 1994). (Gadotti was one of the founding members of the Workers' Party [Partido dos Trabalhadores] and was Freire's superior in the administration of São Paulo's Municipal Secretariat of Education.)

Freire remained in exile for sixteen years, years that were tumultuous and productive. He stayed for five years in Chile as a UNESCO consultant with the Research and Training Institute for Agrarian Reform, then received an appointment in 1969 to Harvard University's Center of Educational and Developmental Studies associated with the Center for Studies in Development and Social Change. In 1970 he moved to Geneva to work as a consultant to the Office of Education of the World Council of Churches, where he developed literacy programs for Tanzania and Guinea-Bissau that focused on the re-Africanization of their countries. He was involved in the development of literacy programs in the former Portuguese colonies of Angola and Mozambique, where he was motivated by the work of the West Indian social philosopher Frantz Fanon, a reengagement with the works of Marx, and personal sympathy for Amilcar Cabral's Popular Movement for the Liberation of Angola (Movimento Popular Libertação de Angola), the Mozambique Liberation Front (Frente de Libertação de Moçambique), and the African Party for the Independence of Guinea-Bissau and Cabo Verde (Partido Africans para Independência da Guinea-Bissau e Cabo Verde).

In 1969 Freire assisted the governments of Peru and Nicaragua with their literacy campaigns; in 1971 he was back in Geneva, establishing the Institute of Cultural Action. He returned briefly to Chile after Salvador Allende was assassinated in 1973, provoking General Pinochet to declare him a subversive. From 1975 to 1978 he participated in literacy work in São Tomé and Principe.

In 1979 Freire made a brief visit to Brazil under a political amnesty; finally, in 1980, he returned to Brazil to teach at the Pontifical Catholic University of São Paulo (Pontifícia Universidade Católica de São Paulo) and the University of the Countryside (Universidade de Campinas) in São Paulo State. Freire would go on to undertake literacy work in Australia, Italy, Angola, the Fiji Islands, and numerous other countries throughout the world.

In São Paulo, Freire witnessed growing resistance to the military government: the 1978 and 1979 strikes by the metalworkers of São Bernardo, an industrial area of São Paulo, and he joined the Workers' Party, or PT (Partido dos Trabalhadores), which was formed 1980. When the Workers' Party won the 1989 municipal elections in São Paulo, the newly elected mayor, Luiza Erundina, appointed Freire municipal secretary of education for São Paulo, a position he held until 1991. During his tenure in this position, Freire continued his radical agenda of literacy reform for the people of that city. Under Freire's guidance, the Secretariat of Education set up a literacy program in the city of São Paulo, or MOVA-SP, which contributed to strengthening popular movements and creating alliances between civil society and the state. Freire also created the Movement to Reorient the Curriculum (Movimento de Reorientaçao Curricular), which attempted to create collective work through a decentralization of power and the fostering of school autonomy, and the reconstruction of the curriculum around critical community issues.

Freire's literacy programs for disempowered peasants are now employed in countries all over the world. They are based on a recognition of the cultural underpinnings of folk traditions and the importance of the collective construction of knowledge. By linking history, politics, economics, and class to the concepts of culture and power, Freire managed to develop both a language of critique and a language of hope that work dialectically and have succeeded in helping generations of disenfranchised peoples—*los marginados*, "marginalized ones"—to liberate themselves.

Freire's pedagogy of the oppressed is a clarion call to unhinge established structures of capitalist exploitation. With a liberating pedagogy such as Freire's, educators and cultural workers throughout the world, men and women from different ethnic backgrounds, have an opportunity to engage in a global struggle for transforming existing relations of power and privilege in the service of greater social justice and human freedom. Freire's pedagogy was influenced by the work of Lucien Febvre, the French *nouvelle pédagogie* of Celestin Freinet and Edouard Claparéde, and the writings of Lezek Kolakowski, Karen Kosik, Erich Fromm, Antonio Gramsci, Karl Mannheim, Teilhard de Chardin, Che Guevara, Frantz Fanon, Albert Memmi, Lev Vygotsky, Amilcar Cabral, and the Christian Personalism theory of Tristiande Atiade and Emanuel Mounier, not to mention the classic works of Hegel, Marx, Rousseau, and Dewey. Freire's pedagogy is anti-authoritarian, dialogical, and interactive, and puts power into the hands of students and workers. Most important, Freirean pedagogy puts the social and political analysis of everyday life at the center of the curriculum.

What is remarkable about Freire's work is that scholars in numerous disciplines—literary theory, composition, philosophy, ethnography, political science, sociology, teacher education, theology, etc.—continue to vigorously engage it. He has given the word "educator" new meaning, inflecting the term to embrace multiple perspectives: border intellectual, social activist, critical researcher, moral agent, radical philosopher, and political revolutionary. To a greater extent than any other educator of this century, Freire was able to develop a pedagogy of resistance to oppression. And he lived what he taught. His life is the story of courage, hardship, perseverance, and unyielding belief in the power of love.

One could convincingly argue that Freire's name functions emblematically to mark an epochal turning point in the way that educators have come to view the politics of knowledge. Just as Whitehead pronounced that all philosophy was a series of footnotes on Plato, some educators would doubtlessly claim that all subsequent critical endeavors in education are footnotes on Freire's work. Such claims are surely justified, but Freire would probably reject any notion of the epochal quality of his contribution to education, since to demarcate the period of his influence as *l'époque Freireane* would be to affirm a general history of education, a perspective that goes against the grain of Freire's own work.

Some have assigned to Freire's work the Archimedean conceit of the idealist, utopian view of the social order. Such a perspective risks overlooking the pragmatic dimensions of Freirean pedagogy, especially when one considers the success of many of his international literacy campaigns. Freire's work holds vital importance, not for its methodology of literacy but ultimately for creating a pedagogy of practical awareness that presages critical action.

Freire believed that the challenge of transforming schools should be directed at overcoming socioeconomic injustice linked to the political and economic structures of society. Any attempt at school reform that concerns itself only with social patterns of representation, interpretation, or communication and does not connect these patterns to redistributive measures and structures that reinforce such patterns exempts itself from the most important insights of Freire's work. Freire's approach stipulates a trenchant understanding of patterns of distribution and redistribution in order to transform the underlying economic structures that produce relations of exploitation.

Freire was also concerned with practicing a politics of diversity and self-affirmation—in short, a cultural politics—not as an end in itself but rather in relation to a larger politics of liberation and social justice. Consequently, a Freirean pedagogy of liberation is totalizing without being dominating in that it always attends dialectically to the specific or local "act of knowing" as a political process that takes place in the larger conflictual arena of capitalist relations of exploitation, an arena where large groups of people palpably and undeniably suffer needless privations and pain due to alienation and poverty. Thus, a pedagogy of the oppressed involves not only a redistribution of material resources but also a struggle over cultural meanings in relation to the multiple social locations of students and teachers and their position within the global division of labor.

Has Freire's name become a floating signifier to be attached adventitiously to any chosen referent within the multistranded terrain of progressive education? To a certain extent this has already happened. Liberal progressives are drawn to Freire's humanism; Marxists and neo-Marxists, to his revolutionary praxis and his history of working with revolutionary political regimes; left liberals, to his critical utopianism; and even conservatives begrudgingly respect his stress on ethics. No doubt his work will be domesticated by his followers in order to make a more comfortable fit with various conflicting political agendas. Indeed, selected aspects of his corpus are appropriated uncritically and decontextualized from his larger political project of struggling for the realization of a truly socialist democracy. Consequently, it is important to read Freire in the context of his entire corpus of works, from *Pedagogy of the Oppressed* to his recent reflection on this early work, which he called *Pedagogy of Hope.*

The modality of theoretical envisioning deployed by Freire is decidedly modernist, but, as I have argued elsewhere (McLaren, 1997), some trappings of poststructuralist discourses are immanent but barely registered in Freire's articulation of subjectivity and agency. The "globalization" of capital, the move toward post-Fordist economic arrangements of flexible specialization, and the consolidation of neo-liberal educational policies demands not only vigorous and ongoing engagement with Freire's work, but also a reinvention of Freire in the context of current debates over information technologies, global economic restructuring, and the struggle to develop new modes of revolutionary struggle.

Freire's pedagogy offers a powerful context from which to consider rebuilding democracy and living and struggling for a qualitatively better life for the oppressed, for the nonoppressed, and for generations to follow. His pedagogy poses the challenge of finding new ways of facing up to our own frailty and finitude as global citizens while at the same time searching for the strength of will and loyalty to hope that will enable us to continue dreaming utopia into reality.

As Freire's future hagiographers wrestle in the educational arena over what represents the "real" Freire and his legacy, Freire's work will continue to be felt in the lives of those who knew him and who loved him. Just as important, his work will continue to influence generations of educators, scholars, and activists around the world.

His pedagogy of the oppressed helped me as a young man to begin to unlearn my privilege as a white, Anglo male, and to "decolonize" my own perspective as an educator teaching in the industrialized West. I first began reading Freire after five years of teaching in an inner-city school in my hometown of Toronto. As I tried to analyze my inner-city teaching experiences once I had left the classroom to pursue graduate studies, Freire's work helped me both to recognize and to name my own complicity in the oppression that I was trying to help my students resist. In other words, Freire's writings helped me to unlearn the influences of my liberal heritage that positions so many white teachers as "missionaries" among the disenfranchised.

Further, Freire's work has helped me to recognize how the system of education is situated within a discourse and legacy of imperialism, patriarchy, and Eurocentrism. More important, Freire's work was able to help me develop counterhegemonic strategies and tactics of urban educational reform. This project is a difficult one, especially for many white male educators who want to make a difference in the metropolitan contexts of contemporary urban schooling. It is also a difficult lesson for teachers and prospective teachers who come from the ranks of the privileged. Of course, Freire acknowledged that de-colonization was a project that knows no endpoint, no final closure. It is a lifetime struggle that requires insight, honesty, compassion, and a willingness to brush one's personal history against the grain of "naïve consciousness" or commonsense understanding.

In 1996, I was honored to share the platform with Paulo Freire and Augusto Boal (who developed the "theater of the oppressed" on the basis of Freire's work) at the Rose Theater in Omaha, Nebraska. It was the first time the three of us had made a presentation to-gether. Freire was remarkable during our dialogue with the audience, fielding questions with great intellectual agility. What struck me most about Paulo Freire was his humility and kindness. His enthusi-asm for mentoring students did not diminish as he grew older. He spent a great deal of his time meeting with educators from a wide va-riety of public and private sectors who would routinely visit his home in São Paulo. His dozens of awards and honorary degrees were kept out of public view in the personal quarters of his home, and he rarely talked about his accomplishments but chose to emphasize what had yet to be done in the struggle for liberation. I remember his willingness to help translate a speech I gave at the Pontifical Catholic University of São Paulo—even though he was sick with the flu—when the official translator experienced difficulty.

The week after his unexpected death, Freire was scheduled to attend a ceremony in Cuba where Fidel Castro was to present him with a major award for his contribution to education. According to his friends, Freire looked forward to this as the most important award of his life.

Shortly before his death, Freire was reported to say something to the effect that he "could never think of education without love and that is why I think I am an educator, first of all because I feel love." Márcia Moraes, who teaches in Rio de Janeiro State University and who was a friend of Freire's, remarked to me recently: "Freire is not leaving the struggle, he has merely changed his location."

We will miss him.

Peter McLaren
University of California, Los Angeles

A LETTER TO HIM WHO
DARED TO TEACH

January 14, 1998

Querido Paulo,
*When we learned of your death, we were stunned. Perhaps we
envisioned you immortal. Our reactions were akin to having
someone unexpectedly throw a bucket of cold water on our
faces. We experienced so many emotions in a matter of minutes—disbelief, sadness, shock, disappointment, outrage. But
those of us who knew you were also consoled by the sheer joy
of having known you and the rich gifts of love that you be-
stowed upon our lives.*

*I regret that our relationship never quite recovered from that
conference in Boston. Too many things seemed to run against
our reconciliation—the distance, the language, the time, the
people. Perhaps, this is as it was meant to be. Yet, a friend told
me recently that she had mentioned to you how much I loved
you—to which you sighed deeply as you affirmed your love for
me. Through this experience, you taught me that the sense of*

"A Letter to Him Who Dared to Teach" first appeared in A. Darder, "Teaching
As an Act of Love" in A. Darder, ed., *Reclaiming Our Voices* (Los Angeles: California Association of Bilingual Education, 1998), pp. 25–44.

disconnection we often feel within our movement is based, more often than not, on our distortions and false readings of our humanity—for our hearts somehow continue to embrace one another, rooted in the solidarity of our shared political dream for justice. Moreover, beyond our words and physical interactions, there seems to exist a living historical connection among us—one that should help us engage suffering and injustice as a human phenomenon rather than the distinct experience of one particular group of people.

Dear friend and comrade, we have learned so much from you. For many of us, you will always remain "our father in the struggle . . . our political mentor." It was you who awakened our consciousness of liberation. It was you who humanized our political soul. Your words illuminated our steps, as we struggled to make our road to the now. Your life quickened our senses and revitalized our teaching with a revolutionary sense of ethics, discipline, coherence, and dignity. We are blessed to have known the love of your presence. And in the spirit of the hope you embodied, many of us recommit ourselves daily to struggle more seriously for that authentic democratic socialism of our dreams.

With an understanding that liberation is possibility—not fate nor destiny nor burden—we are filled with a vision of a world where human beings will strive consistently to live a revolutionary solidarity, fueled by the integrity of our minds, hearts, bodies, and spirits. It is a radical dream of many colors, many sounds, and many places. It is one where we undertake our ethical responsibility of creating and re-creating a just society—a society where the commitment to humanity supersedes the greed of economic profit.

Your message to us was not that we should make you an icon of teachers—being objectified was everything you fought against. Instead your wish was that we should reinvent your ideas, build on them, transform them, understand them as historical contributions of a particular moment in time, and lay foundations for the children of the future.

In keeping with your wish, we must now carry on. We must continue to struggle over meanings, make sense of capitalist relations of production, critique the devastating impact of "globalization," champion education within the larger political project of liberation, refuse apolitical theories that veil injustice, and uncompromisingly confront issues of economic restructuring, class and gender inequalities, and the racialization of populations around the globe. And all this we must do with as much scientific specificity as the quickening of our hearts.

Most important, we thank you for a life well lived! In all that we do and say, we will carry your legacy of love and hope, confident that you remain in our hearts and minds forever. ¡Presente!

With love and solidarity,
Antonia Darder

BIBLIOGRAPHY

Aboud, F. E. 1987. "The Development of Ethnic Self-identification and Attitudes." In M. J. Rotheram and J. S. Phinney, eds., *Children's Ethnic Socialization: Pluralism and Development*. Newbury Park, Calif.: Sage.

Alexander, R. 1984. *Primary Teaching*. London: Holt, Rinehart & Winston.

Anderson, J. 1997. *Che Guevara: A Revolutionary Life*. New York: Grove Press.

Apple, M. 1995. *Education and Power*. London: Routledge.

Araujo Freire, A. M., and D. Macedo. 1998. *The Paulo Freire Reader*. New York: Continuum.

Aronowitz, S. 1992. *The Politics of Identity: Class, Culture and Social Movements*. New York: Routledge.

Bartolomé, L. 1994. "Beyond the Methods Fetish: Toward a Humanizing Pedagogy." *Harvard Educational Review* 64(2):173–194.

Carnoy, M. 1983. "Education, Democracy, and Social Conflict." *Harvard Educational Review* 43:402.

Carnoy, M. 1997. Foreword, *Pedagogy of the Heart*, by Paulo Freire. New York: Continuum.

Cavanaugh, J. 1996. "Global Economic Apartheid." Speech aired on Pacifica Radio KPFK and distributed by Alternative Radio, Boulder, Colorado.

Charney, R. S. 1997. *Teaching Children to Care: Management in the Responsive Classroom*. Greenfield, Mass.: Northeast Foundation for Children.

Chyng Sun, 2001. Video. Northampton, MA.

Cisneros, H. 1993. *Interwoven Destinies: Cities and the Nation*. New York: Norton.

Clairmont, F. F. 1995. *The Rise and Fall of Economic Liberalism*. Mapusa, India: Other India Press/Third World Network.

Clark, B. K., and M. P. Clark. 1947. "Racial Identification and Preference in Negro Children." In T. M. Newcomb and E. L. Hartley, eds., *Readings in Social Psychology*. New York: Holt.

Collins, Chuck, et al., eds. 1999. *Shifting Fortunes: The Perils of the Growing American Wealth Gap*. United for a Fair Economy.

Cross, W. E. 1991. *Shades of Black: Diversity in African-American Identity*. Philadelphia: Temple University Press.

Darder, A. 1991. *Culture and Power in the Classroom: A Critical Foundation for Bicultural Education*. New York: Bergin & Garvey.

_____. 1995a. "Bicultural Identity and the Development of Voice." In J. Frederickson and A. Ada, eds., *Reclaiming Our Voices: Bilingual Education, Critical Pedagogy and Praxis*. Ontario, Calif.: California Association for Bilingual Education.

_____. 1995b. *Culture and Difference*. Westport, Conn.: Bergin & Garvey.

_____. 1998. "Teaching As an Act of Love." In A. Darder, *Reclaiming Our Voices*, pp. 25–44. Los Angeles: California Association for Bilingual Education.

Darder, A., and P. Torres. 1999. "Shattering the Race Lens: Toward a Critical Theory of Racism." In M. Kinyada and R. Tai, eds., *Critical Ethnicity: Countering the Way of Identity Politics*. New York: Roman & Littlefield.

Darder, A., and P. Torres. Forthcoming. *21st Century Racism*. New York: New York University Press.

Davis, M. 1990. *City of Quartz: Excavating the Future in Los Angeles*. New York: Vintage Books.

Derman-Sparks, L. 1989. *Anti-bias Curriculum: Tools for Empowering Young Children*. Washington, D.C.: National Association for the Education of Young Children.

Derman-Sparks, L., C. T. Higa, and B. Sparks. 1980. "Children, Race, and Racism: How Race Awareness Develops." *Interracial Books for Children Bulletin* 11:3–9.

Dowbor, L. 1997. Preface, *Pedagogy of the Heart*, by Paulo Freire. New York: Continuum.

Fine, M. 1990. *Framing Dropouts: Notes on the Politics of an Urban Public High School*. New York: State University of New York Press.

Frederickson, J., and A. Ada. 1995. *Reclaiming Our Voices: Bilingual Education, Critical Pedagogy and Praxis*. Ontario, Calif.: California Association for Bilingual Education.

Freire, P. 1970. *Pedagogy of the Oppressed*. New York: Seabury.

_____. 1973. *Education for Critical Consciousness*. New York: Continuum.

_____. 1985. *The Politics of Education*. South Hadley, Mass.: Bergin & Garvey.

_____. 1987. "Letters to North American Teachers." In Ira Shor, ed., *Freire in the Classroom*, pp. 211–214. Portsmouth, N.H.: Boyton/Cook.

_____. 1993. *Pedagogy of the City*. New York: Continuum.

_____. 1994. *Pedagogy of the Oppressed*. New York: Continuum.

_____. 1996. *Pedagogy of Hope*. New York: Continuum.

_____. 1997a. "A Response." In Paulo Freire, J. Fraser, D. Macedo, T. McKinnon, and W. Stokes, eds., *Mentoring the Mentor: A Critical Dialogue with Paulo Freire*, pp. 303–329. New York: Peter Lang.

_____. 1997b. *Pedagogy of the Heart*. New York: Continuum.

_____. 1998a. *Pedagogy of Freedom*. Boulder, Colo.: Rowman & Littlefield.

_____. 1998b. *Teachers as Cultural Workers: Letters to Those Who Dare to Teach*. Boulder, Colo.: Westview.

Freire, P., and F. Betto. 1985. *Essa Escola Chamada Vida*. São Paulo: Atica.

Freire, P., and A. Faundez. 1989. *Learning to Question: A Pedagogy of Liberation*. New York: Continuum.

Freire, P., and D. Macedo. 1987. Literacy: Reading the word and the world. New York: Bergin & Garvey.

Gadotti, M. 1994. *Reading Paulo Freire*. Albany, N.Y.: State University of New York Press.

Galeano, E. "In Defense of the Word." In R. Simonson and S. Walker, eds., *Multicultural Literacy*. Saint Paul, Minn.: Graywolf Press.

Giroux, H. 1983. *Theory and Resistance in Education: A Pedagogy for the Opposition*. South Hadley, Mass: Bergin & Garvey.

_____. 1988. *Teachers As Intellectuals: Toward a Critical Pedagogy of Learning*. New York: Bergin & Garvey.

_____. 1997. *Pedagogy and the Politics of Hope: Theory, Culture, and Schooling*. Boulder, Colo.: Westview.

_____. 1999. *The Mouse That Roared: Disney and the End of Innocence*. Lanham, Md.: Roman & Littlefield.

Glover, A. 1990. *Two-year-olds and Race: The Development of Racial Awareness and Racial Attitudes*. Pacific Oaks Occasional Paper. Pasadena, Calif.: Pacific Oaks College.

Golding, P. 1998. "Global Village or Cultural Pillage." In R. W. McChesney, E. M. Wood, and J. B. Foster, eds., *Capitalism and the Information Age*. New York: Monthly Review Press.

Goodman, M. E. 1964. *Race Awareness in Young Children*. Reading, Mass.: Addison-Wesley.

Gorostiaga, X. 1993. "Is the Answer in the South?" Report presented at the United Nations International Seminar on First World Ethic and Third World Economics, Sigtunn, Sweden.

Gramsci, A. 1971. *Selection from the Prison Notebooks.* New York: International Publishers.

Greider, W. 1997 *One World Ready or Not: The Manic Logic of Global Capitalism.* New York: Simon & Schuster.

Hatcher, B., and B. Troyna. 1993. "Racialization and Children." In C. McCarthy and W. Crichlow, eds., *Race Identity and Representation in Education.* New York: Routledge.

hooks, b. 1994. *Teaching to Transgress: Education for the Practice of Freedom.* New York: Routledge.

Huston, A. C. 1983. "Sex-typing." In P. H. Mussen and E. M. Hetherington, eds., *Handbook of Child Psychology.* Vol. 4: *Socialization, Personality, and Social Development.* New York: John Wiley.

Jones, E. B. 1998. "Mexican American Teachers as Cultural Mediators: Literacy and Literacy Contexts Through Bicultural Strengths." Ph.D. diss. Claremont Graduate University and San Diego State University, Claremont and San Diego, Calif.

Justice Policy Institute. 2000. *The Punishing Decade: Prison and Jail Estimates at the Millennium.* Report. Washington, D.C.: Justice Policy Institute; www.cjcj.org/punishingdecade/.

Katz, P. A. 1976. "The Acquisition of Racial Attitudes in Children. In P. A. Katz, ed., *Towards the Elimination of Racism.* New York: Pergamon.

———. 1987. "Developmental and Social Process in Ethnic Attitudes and Self-identification." In M. J. Rotheram and J. S. Phinney, eds., *Children's Ethnic Socialization: Pluralism and Development.* Newbury Park, Calif.: Sage.

Katz, P. A., and C. Seavy. 1973. "Labels and Children's Perceptions of Faces." *Child Development* 44:770–775.

Leistyna, P. 1999. *Presence of Mind.* Boulder, Colo.: Westview.

Lopez, E. F. 1998. "The Usual Suspects: Youth of Color, 'Deviance,' and the Culture of Violence." In A. Darder, ed., *Cultural Studies in Education: Schooling As a Contested Terrain.* Claremont, Calif.: Institute for Cultural Studies in Education.

Macedo, D. 1993. "Literacy for Stupidification: The Pedagogy of Big Lies." *Harvard Educational Review* 63. (2):183–206.

———. 1994. *Literacies of Power: What Americans Are Not Allowed to Know.* Boulder, Colo.: Westview.

Macedo, D., and A. M. Araujo Freire. 1998. Foreword, *Teachers as Cultural Workers*, by Paulo Freire. Boulder, Colo.: Westview.

McChesney, R. 1998. "The Political Economy of Global Communication." In R. W. McChesney, E. M. Wood, and J. B. Foster, eds., *Capitalism and the Information Age*. New York: Monthly Review Press.

McLaren, P. 1997a. "Paulo Freire's Legacy of Hope and Struggle." *Theory, Culture and Society*:147–153.

_____. 1997b. *Revolutionary Multiculturalism: Pedagogies of Dissent for the New Millennium*. Boulder, Colo.: Westview Press.

_____. 2000. *Che Guevara, Paulo Freire and the Pedagogy of Revolution*. New York: Rowman & Littlefield.

McLaren, P., and C. Lankshear. 1994. *Politics of Liberation: Paths from Freire*. New York and London: Routledge.

McLaren, P., and P. Leonard. 1993. *Paulo Freire: A Critical Encounter*. New York and London: Routledge.

Molner, A. 1996. *Giving Kids the Business*. Boulder, Colo.: Westview.

Naiman, J. 1996. "Left Feminism and the Return to Class." *Monthly Review* 48, no. 2 (June).

National Council on Crime and Delinquency. 2000. "Minority Youth and the Criminal Justice System." Report. N.C.C.D. Youth Law Center.

Oakes, J., and M. Lipton. 1999. *Teaching to Change the World*. New York: McGraw-Hill.

Ogbu, J. U. 1985. "A Cultural Ecology of Competence Among Inner-City Blacks. In M. B. Spencer, G. K. Brookings, and W. R. Allen, eds., *Beginnings: The Social and Affective Development of Black Children*. Hillsdale, N.J.: Earlbaum.

Ramsey, P. G. 1987. *Teaching and Learning in a Diverse World: Multicultural Education for Young Children*. New York: Teachers College Press.

San Miguel, G., and R. Valencia. 1998. "From the Treaty of Guadalupe Hidalgo to Hopwood: The Education, Plight, and Struggle of Mexican Americans in the Southwest." *Harvard Educational Review* 68, no. 3 (Fall):353–412.

Shor, I., ed. 1987. *Freire for the Classroom: A Sourcebook for Liberatory Teaching*. Portsmouth, N.H.: Heinemann.

Shor, I., and P. Freire. 1987. *A Pedagogy for Liberation*. South Hadley, Mass., Washington, D.C.: Bergin & Garvey.

Smith. J. N. 1995. "Making the Invisible Visible: Critical Pedagogy As a Viable Means of Educating Children." In J. Frederickson and A. Ada, eds., *Reclaiming Our Voices: Bilingual Education, Critical Pedagogy and Praxis*. Ontario, Calif.: California Association for Bilingual Education.

Spencer, M. B. 1985. "Cultural Cognition and Social Cognition as Identity Correlates of Black Children's Personal-Social Development. In M. B. Spencer, G. K. Brookings, and W. R. Allen, eds., *Beginnings: The Social and Affective Development of Black Children*. Hillsdale, N.J.: Earlbaum.

———. 1987. "Black Children's Ethnic Identity Formation: Risk and Resilience of Castelike Minorities." In J. S. Phinney and M. J. Rotheram, eds., *Children's Ethnic Socialization*. Newbury Park, Calif.: Sage.

Vigil, J. D. 1997. "Learning from Gangs: The Mexican American Experience." *ERIC Digest*, no. RC020943.

West, C. 1993 *Race Matters*. Boston: Beacon Press.

Wickens, E. 1993. "Penny's Question: I Will Have a Child in My Class with Two Moms—What Do You Know About This?" *Young Children* 48(3):25–28.

Wilson, W. J. 1997. *When Work Disappears: The World of the New Urban Poor*. New York: Vintage.

Wood, E. M. 1996. *Democracy Against Capitalism*. Cambridge, England: Cambridge University Press.

Wood, E. M. 1998. "Modernity, Postmodernity, or Capitalism?" In R. W. McChesney, E. M. Wood, and J. B. Foster, eds., *Capitalism and the Information Age*. New York: Monthly Review Press.

Young, I. M. 1990. *Justice and the Politics of Difference*. Princeton, N.J.: Princeton University Press.